# Learn to *Watercolor* in an Hour a Day

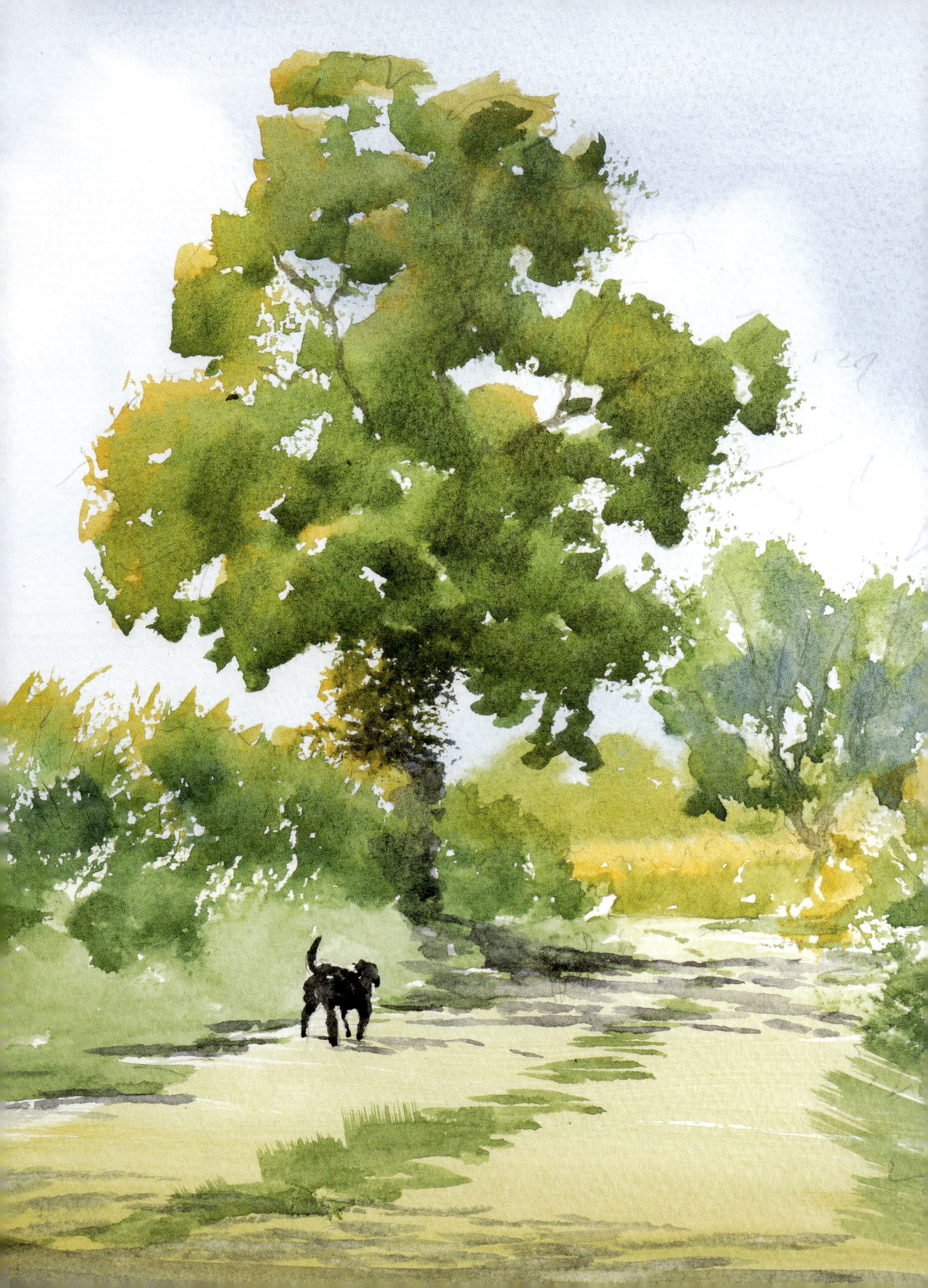

# Learn to *Watercolor* in an Hour a Day

**Techniques, Exercises and Practice Projects to Master the Art of Watercolor Painting**

**CHARLES EVANS**

DAVID & CHARLES
—PUBLISHING—

www.davidandcharles.com

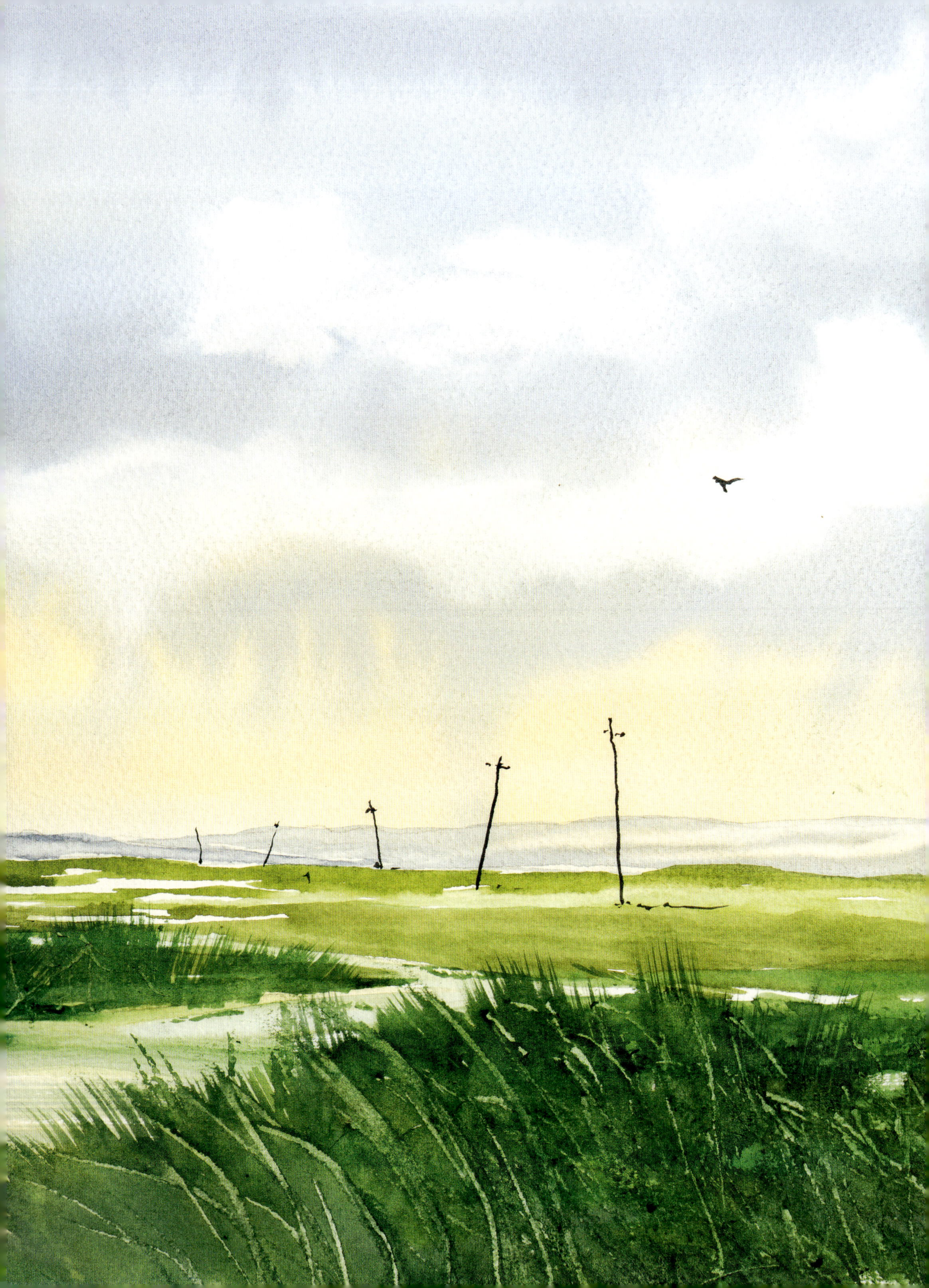

# Contents

# Introduction

**I wrote this book to dispel some of the mysteries – and to allay some of the fears that people have – about painting with watercolours. I always find it funny that watercolour has the reputation of being the most difficult medium to paint with and yet, when beginners start learning to paint, they invariably choose to paint in watercolour! Well, let's put some of those fears to rest.**

In this book you will learn how to put on various different washes, how to mix colours, how to achieve harmony in your painting and how to get pleasing results you can be proud of. You will also learn that you need very few brushes and colours to achieve all of this. If you read this book before going out to buy a huge number of unnecessary tools and materials, it will save you much confusion and stop you from making many mistakes.

I have also included a section on using watercolour pencils. These are very useful in their own right, especially when out sketching or working on smaller studies. Vignettes are lovely in watercolour pencils. You can add water at the time to turn your sketch into a painting or you can do it later, at your leisure. Some sketches look good as they are without adding water.

Through the exercises in this book, I have tried to cover a lot of the common subjects people have problems with – skies, foliage, reflections, waves and perspective. Some people prefer to paint figures, still lifes or flowers, and I have covered these subjects as well.

Most of the tuition is in the form of step-by-step illustrations so you can clearly see how each project develops.

I have spent many years demonstrating, entertaining and running workshops nationwide. Especially in the workshops, the buzz for me is the look on someone's face when they realize that they can do 'that thing', whatever that may be, that they thought they couldn't do. Hopefully, with the aid of this book, you too will get that look on your face by discovering that you also can do things you didn't expect!

C.M. Evans

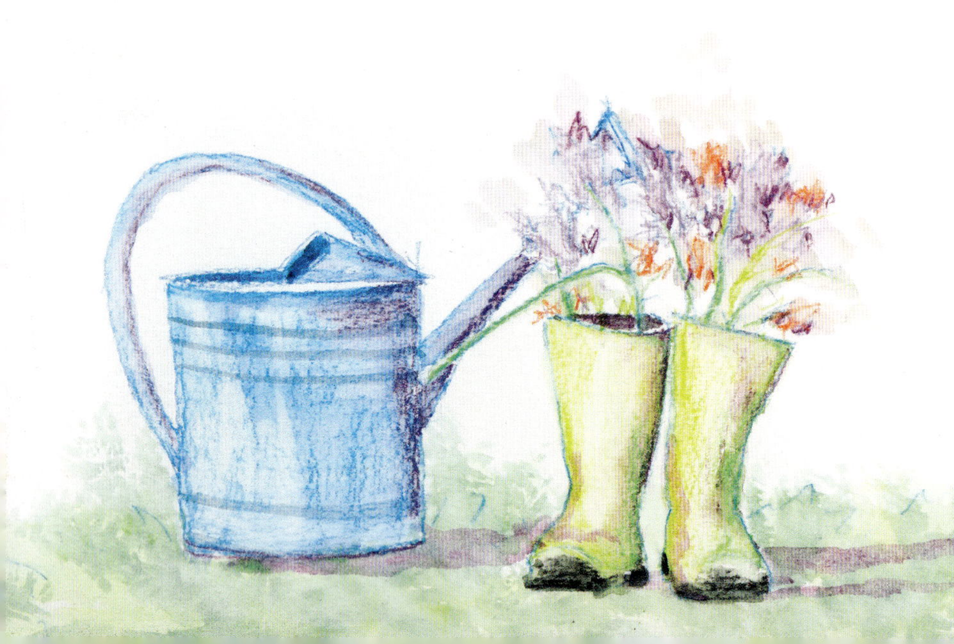

**DEDICATION**

This book is dedicated to Gail, who organizes everything including this book. She is my right-hand man (woman) (person!).

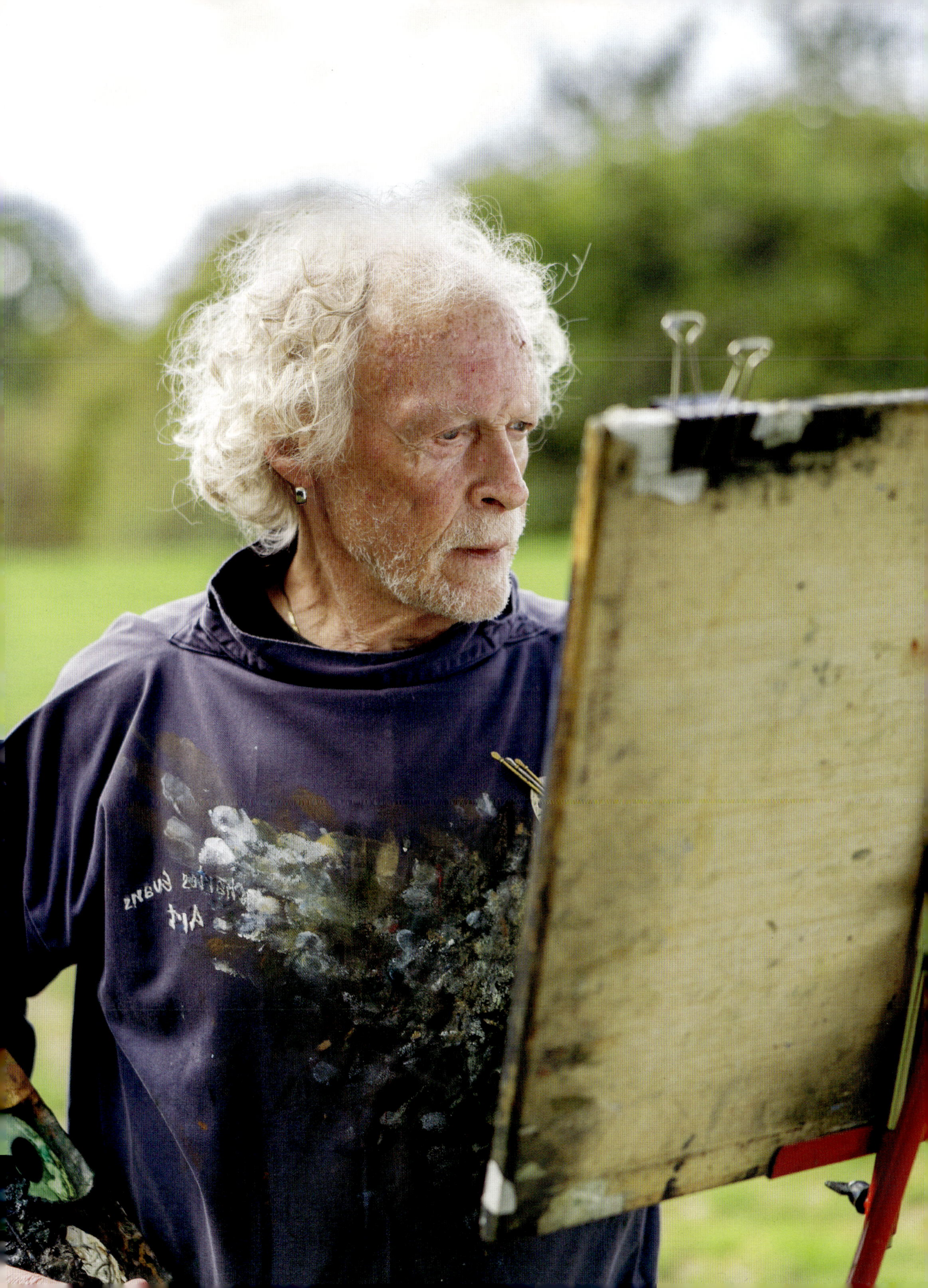

# How to use this book

**This book has been structured in such a way that it takes you from laying the first wash for a rural scene to painting seascapes, countryside and shaded city streets.**

As you work through the book you will notice that various exercises have timing suggestions ranging from 15 minutes to 60 minutes. First, you will find step-by-step exercises – sequences that allow you to practise basic techniques such as capturing light and shade, introducing recession and perspective and rendering texture. Then, several projects are designed to show you how your paintings can progress from simple landscapes to complex urban scenes. Each exercise or project is accompanied by a timer symbol like the ones below, indicating roughly how long an exercise or a project might take to complete, from a matter of minutes up to a full hour.

You may wish to copy the paintings as they appear on the following pages, or you may prefer to find scenes of your own and paint them from life.

Don't be too fazed by the title of the book because you don't have to stick too rigidly to the timing suggestions. No single exercise should take longer than one hour, but this does not include drying time, so you can afford to be quite leisurely with the projects. You will not be sitting a test or exam – so do not worry that you might be taking too long or that you have finished too early. These are all merely guidelines, so relax.

The book will take you through many of the common problems encountered in watercolour painting. Make sure you are comfortable in your surroundings, wherever you may paint,

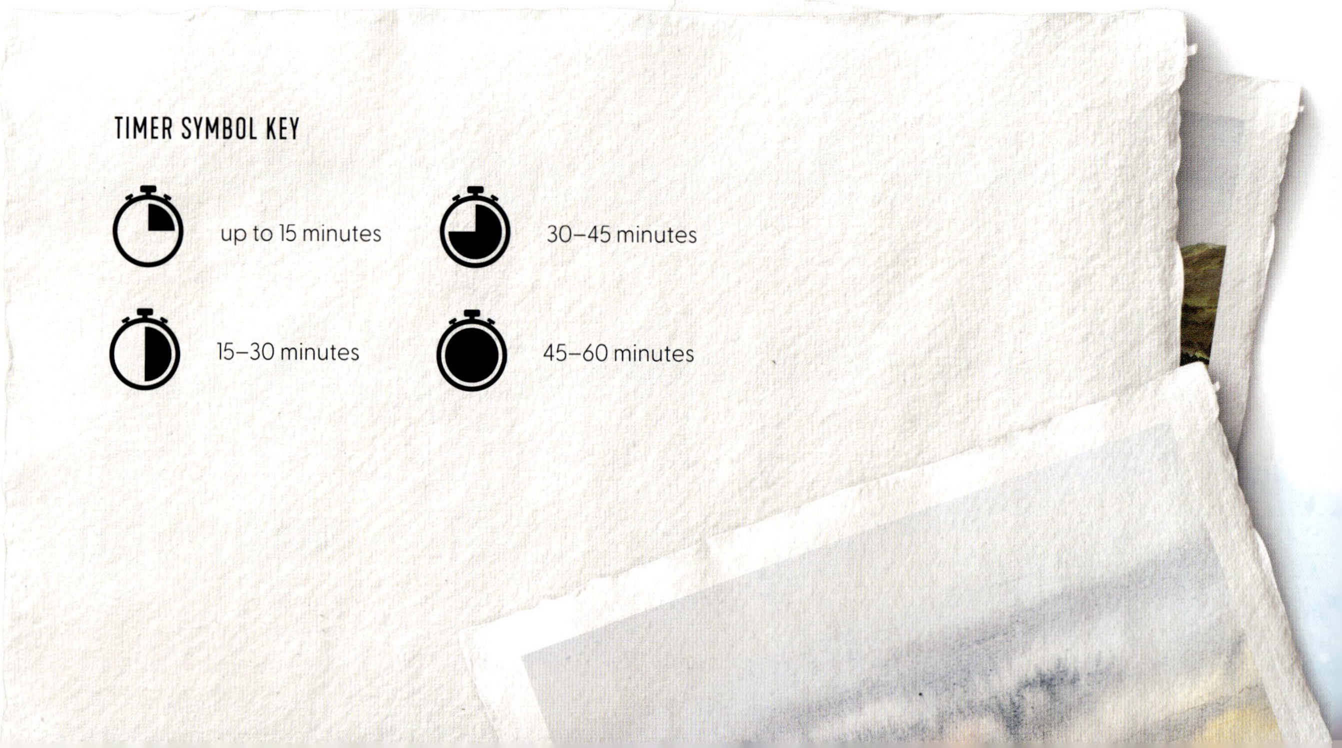

**TIMER SYMBOL KEY**

- up to 15 minutes
- 30–45 minutes
- 15–30 minutes
- 45–60 minutes

and work to whichever size you feel happy with. I normally paint quite large, but that is only because of the fact that everyone has to see what I am doing all of the time. This won't apply to you, so use a size of paper that suits you.

Everything is laid out in the book for you and all stage by stage from quick drawings through to completed paintings. You can use this way of painting in any scenario. As your confidence grows, and you venture outside to do your first on-location painting, think back to this book. Or, better still, take the book with you.

Finally, don't feel you have to complete the exercises all at once or that you have to copy every brush stroke. This book is for you to enjoy and to refer at your own pace to rather than feeling pressured.

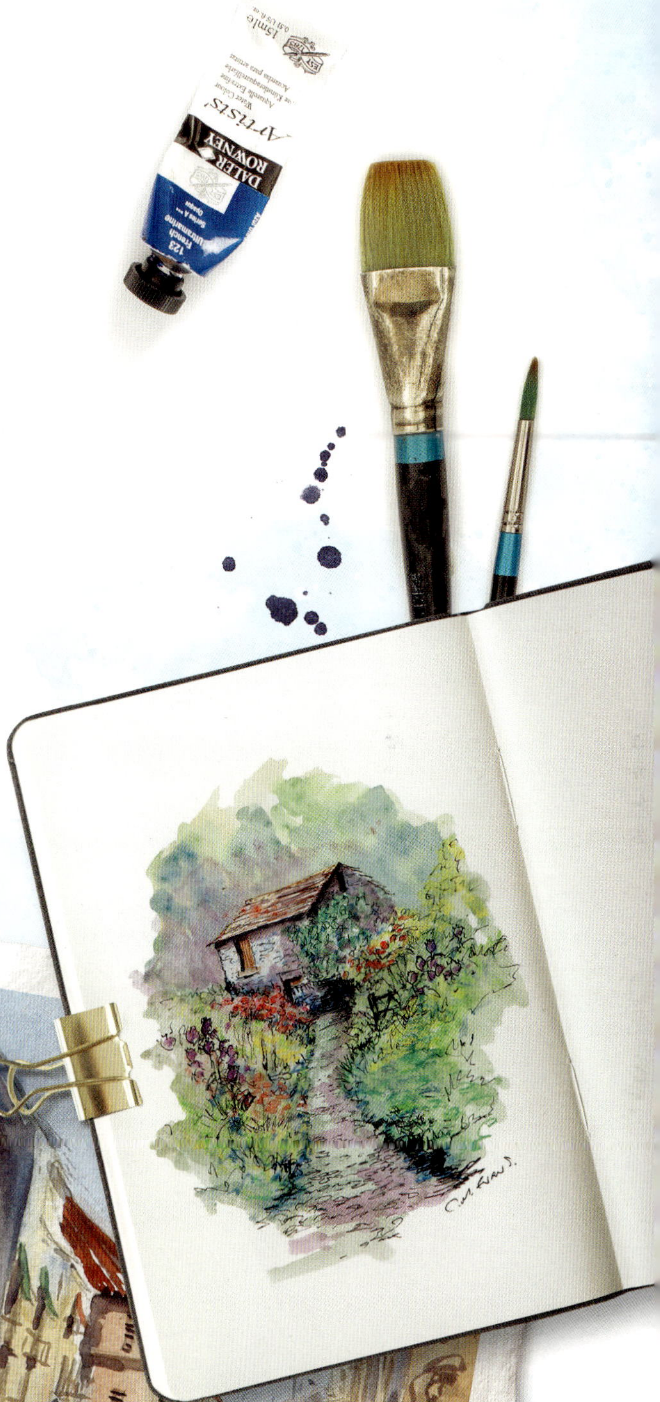

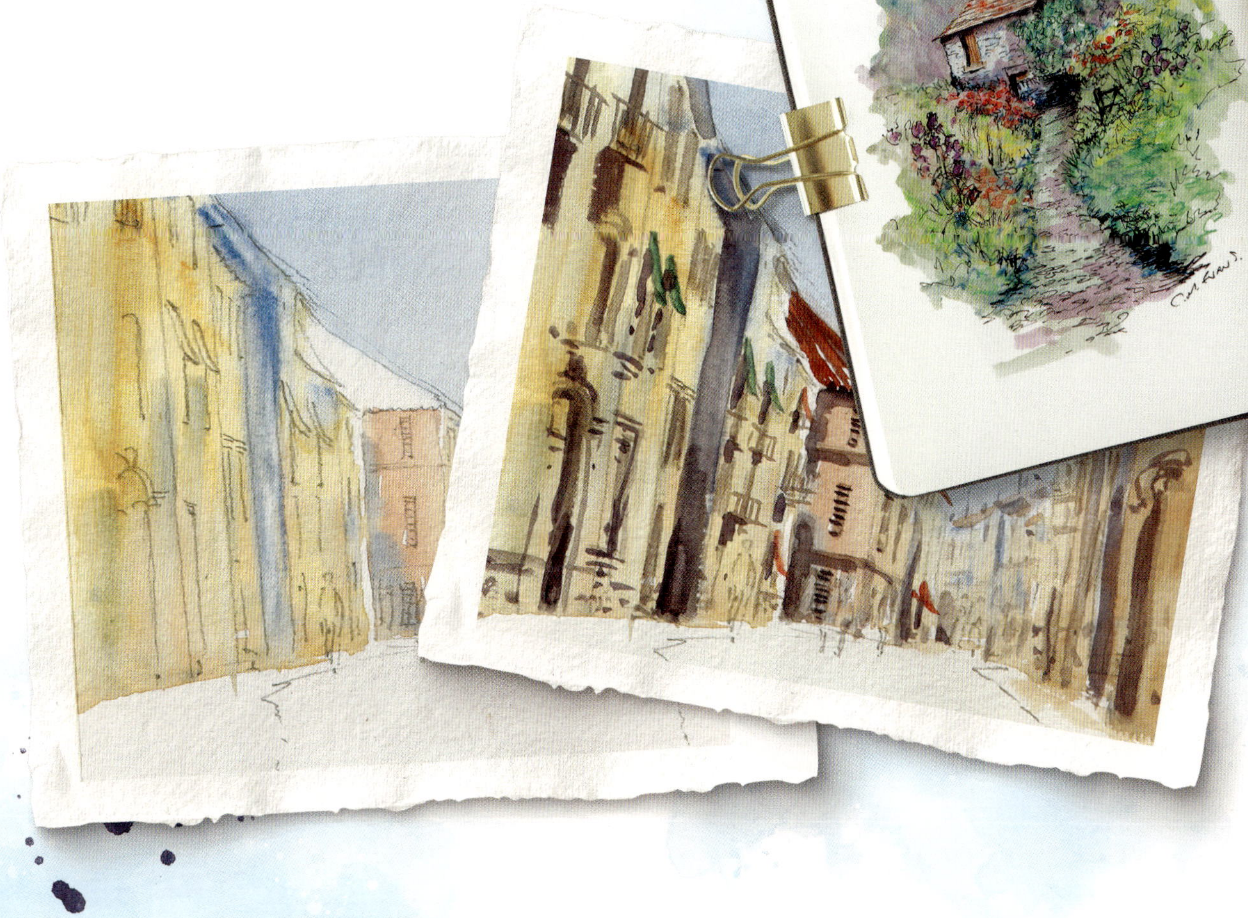

# Materials

All the materials used in this book are made by Daler-Rowney, and are easily available at art stores and via mail order. As you'll see in this section, I don't believe in burdening myself with stuff I'm never – or hardly ever – going to use. If you're just starting off, it makes sense to experiment with the basics shown here and buy additional materials only when you can't do without them.

## The workspace

On my travels around the world I've seen all sorts of workspaces: some people paint in their garden shed, some in an attic room with a skylight, some at the kitchen table and some in conservatories – and some even have the luxury of a purpose-built studio.

Possibly the most unusual 'studio' I've seen was a two-berth caravan with the roof cut off and a sheet of clear acrylic inserted: it certainly wasn't glamorous, but my word, what a fabulous workspace that was!

Wherever you paint, it's important that your workspace should be comfortable and relaxing, but above all it must be well lit. There is a great array of daylight simulation bulbs and lights available; these aim to replicate bright daylight in a north-facing room, and if you haven't tried working with them before, you'll find they really can make a difference to the colours in your paintings.

In my opinion, however, the best workspace of all is outdoors; it may take a sunny summer day to tempt you outside, but there really is no substitute for natural daylight.

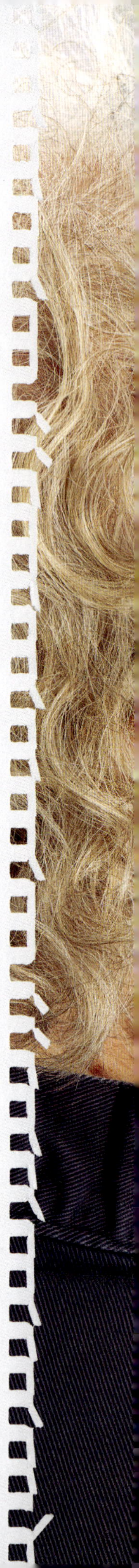

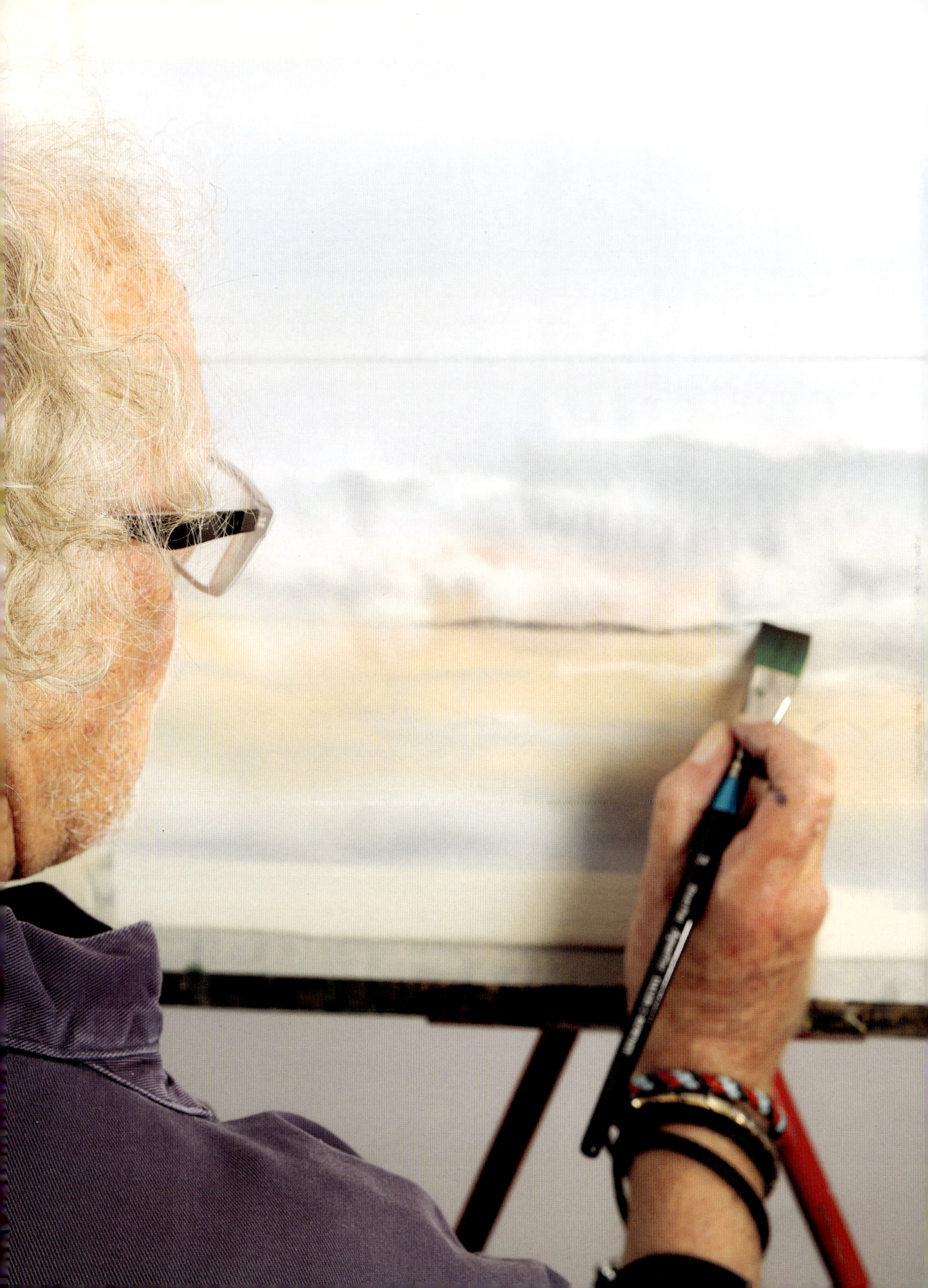

# Paints

Watercolour paints come in two types, with two grades in each type. You can buy paints in liquid form in tubes or dried in cakes called pans (small cakes are called half pans). I find tubes easier to use, as you can squeeze them out on to the palette and make up washes more quickly and in greater quantities than with pans; it's also simpler to mix colours from tubes and to keep each basic colour clean in the palette.

The grades available are artists' quality, which have a large proportion of pure pigment, and students' quality, which contain less pigment and more fillers. Although students' quality paints are a uniform, lower price, it's better to save up and buy the best paints you can get – for a start, you don't actually need that many, and second, there really is a difference in what you can achieve with them.

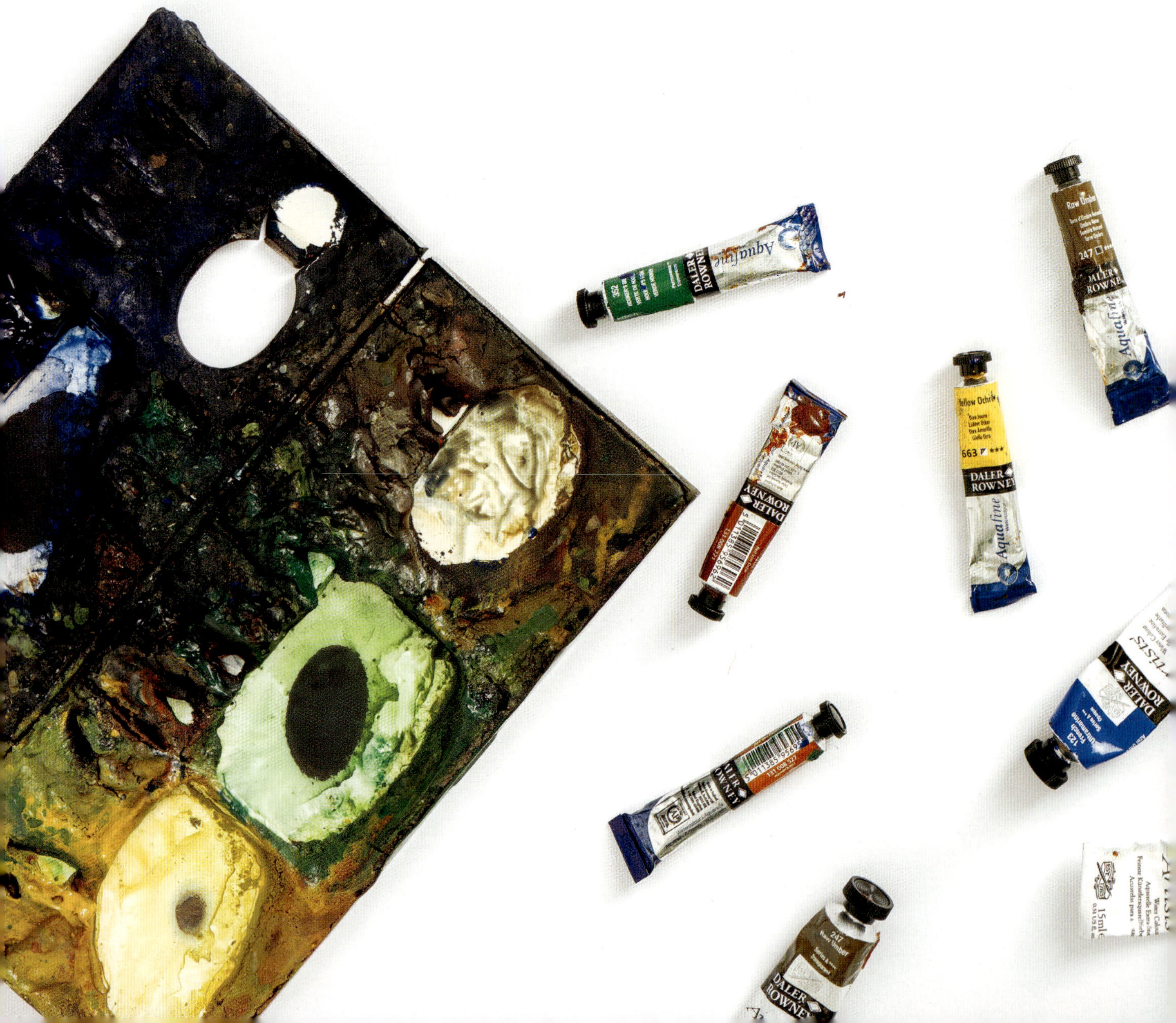

## BASIC COLOUR PALETTE

For the exercises and projects in this book I used my standard painting palette of artists' quality Daler-Rowney paints: yellow ochre, raw umber, burnt sienna, French ultramarine, alizarin crimson, light red, Hooker's green (dark) and cobalt blue. From these colours all the mixes used can be made up.

Each of these colours varies tremendously when it is brushed on to the paper, depending on the amount of water you add – and when I say 'a very watery wash' in the exercises and projects, I do mean a very watery wash. Take the time to familiarize yourself with each paint on its own before you start to mix colours. Some pigments are more transparent than others, and some react differently on a variety of papers. Finally, remember that watercolour paint dries some 50 per cent lighter than when it's applied in a watery wash, so learn how to make up washes to the strength you need. You can always go over a first weak wash – indeed, this can sometimes be just what you want – but if you can get it right first time, this saves waiting around, watching paint dry!

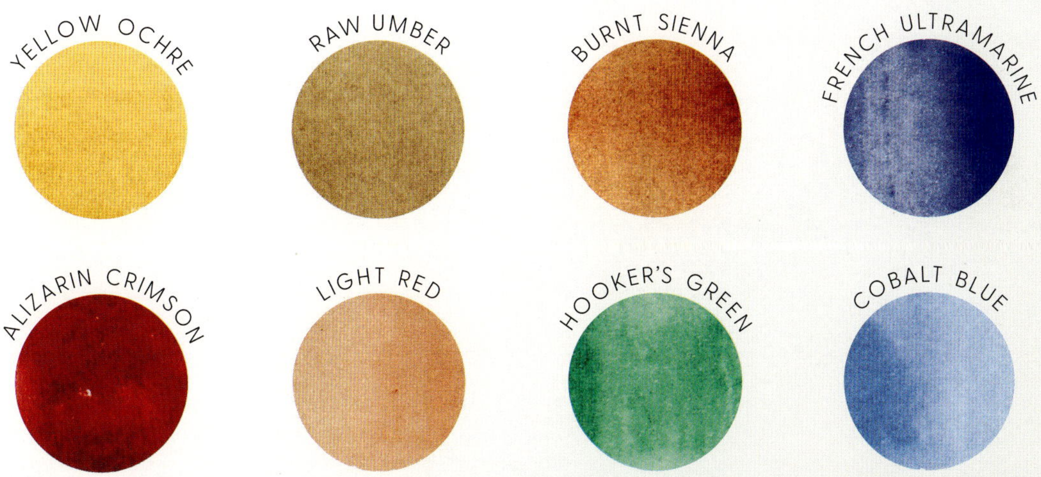


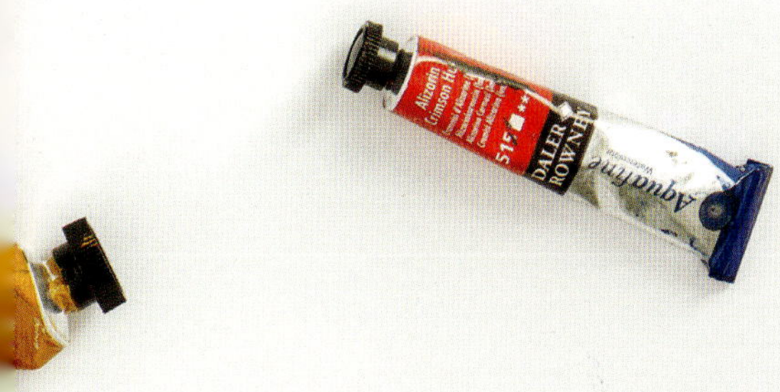

### NOTE

In addition to this standard painting palette, some of the exercises and projects also require cadmium red and cadmium yellow.

# Brushes and papers

**This may come as a bit of a surprise, but you really don't need great rafts of equipment that clutter up your workspace or weigh you down when you're out sketching.**

My attitude is that if I can't keep it in my painting bucket or hold it in my hand, it's surplus to requirements; and the fewer bits of stuff you have to think about – most of which you may never use – the more you can concentrate on what you really want to do: paint. Of course you don't have to use exactly the same brushes and paper that I do, but keep what you do choose to a minimum, and you'll be on the right lines.

## BRUSHES

Throughout this book I've used the same four brushes I use for all my painting. The largest is a 38mm (1½in) Dalon flat wash brush, which is totally synthetic, meaning that it can stand up to all sorts of hard work – I've used and abused mine for over 10 years and it won't win any beauty prizes, but it still does a really good job. This is the brush for covering the paper quickly, such as when stroking on clean water or making preliminary large washes for skies. The other three brushes – a 19mm (¾in) flat wash, a No. 8 round and a No. 4 rigger – are a blend of synthetic and sable from the Sapphire range. The sable gives great flexibility and pointing for the round brushes, and the synthetic bristles are tough and long-lasting. As you will see in the exercises and projects, I use the rigger for putting in final touches, the smaller flat wash for broader strokes, and the No. 8 for much of the work in between these.

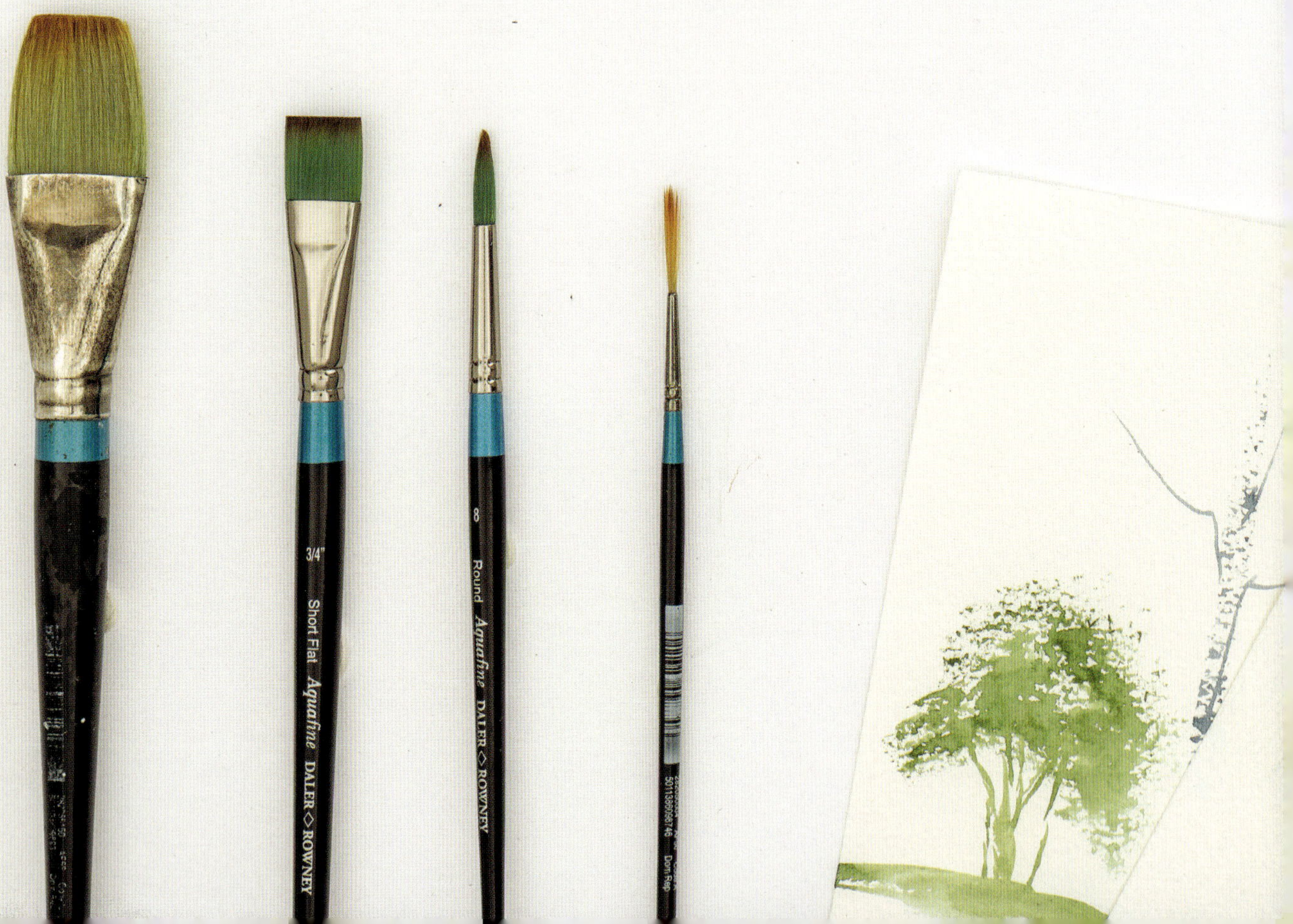

## PAPERS

Just as with all art equipment, there's a huge choice of papers, and you can spend too much time worrying about finding the perfect one. My choice for my own paintings, and for everything in this book, is 300gsm (140lb) Langton Rough, which has a couple of great advantages: it's identical on both sides (some papers have a right and a wrong side) so you can just start working, and you don't have to stretch it before painting – I just cut a large sheet in half and tape it to my board with masking tape.

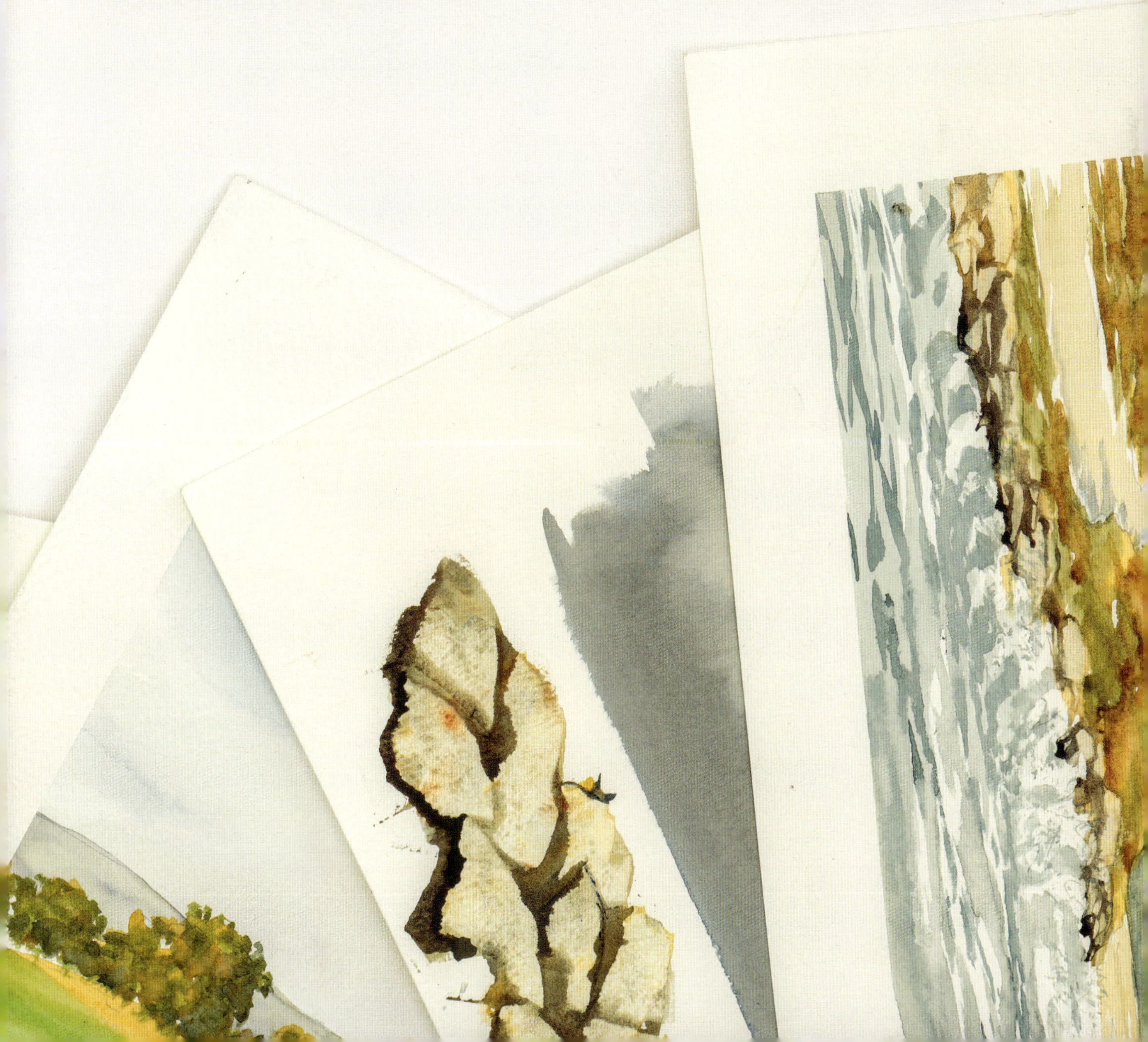

# Other equipment

**You'll have gathered by now that the aim of the game is to get painting, so you don't need to clutter up your workspace with bits and bobs that don't make life easier and only get in the way; all you need is a very few extra bits of equipment, and off you go.**

## PALETTE

The most useful rule for a palette is that the wells should be big enough to make up as much wash as you need – if not more – so you don't run out and have to make up new washes. Because I mostly use the same range of colours for all my paintings and mix from these, I can leave the paint to dry out in the palette and just clean out the wells at the end of the day.

## BOARDS AND TAPE

You need something stable and with a smooth surface for a board – a piece of MDF rounded at the edges is fine, but don't get anything too thick and heavy. Because I don't wet and stretch my paper before painting – which can just lead to another level of anxiety – I use ordinary masking tape to secure the paper to the board.

## PENCILS

This is easy: I use any old pencil I can lay my hands on, as I use a pencil only for simple outlines – no crosshatching, shading or toning. Pencil sharpeners tend to eat pencils, so it's best to use a sharp penknife for sharpening.

## WATERCOLOUR PENCILS

These are great for quick colour sketches on location, and you can use them dry or wet, as adding water makes the pigment behave like watercolour paint. A box of watercolour pencils isn't expensive, and it's nice to have a big range of colours, although I find that I use most of them only occasionally and stick to certain colours, just as with paints.

Another advantage is that if you're sketching outlines with watercolour pencils and you make a mistake with an outline – which every artist does – you don't need to erase the error: just stroke some water over the line and, hey presto! The mistake vanishes.

As with graphite pencils, use a penknife to sharpen watercolour pencils; this way, the points don't become brittle, and last longer.

For the watercolour pencil project in this book I've used Derwent watercolour pencils.

### TRY IT YOURSELF

You can 'wake up' your dried watercolours by adding water using a brush. Or you can do what I do, which is to add fresh paint on top.

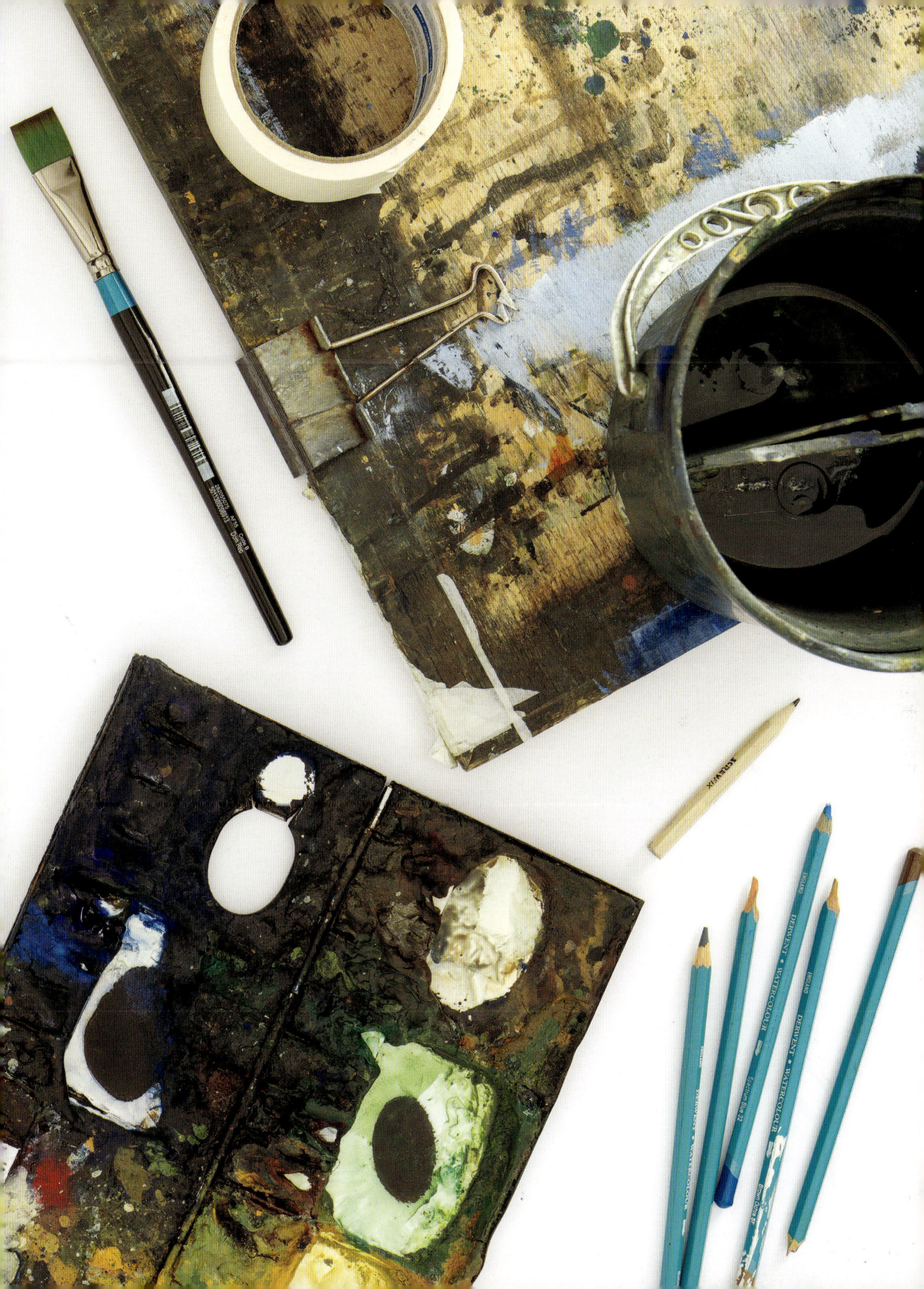

# Techniques

Because my approach to painting with watercolour uses so little equipment and few colours, there is very little to carry about. Start off painting outdoors with a simple scene so that it's a natural progression from what you have been doing indoors using the same techniques and materials.

## Painting outdoors

Most of the themes in this book are based on landscapes, and there is no substitute for getting out there. Painting outdoors means that you put down on paper only what you want to include, and cut out anything unnecessary – and taking a sketchbook and light materials is a great way to make a holiday even more enjoyable.

### SKETCHBOOKS

I use standard A4 sketchbooks with good-quality acid-free cartridge paper. This paper can sometimes buckle if you're putting on a lot of water in your washes, but it dries perfectly flat. The most important thing is to get a hardback, sewn-bound sketchbook: pages that are glued in tend to work loose and come out, while a sewn binding means that your sketches, studies and reference material will stay where they should be. And the usefulness of a hardback binding should be obvious – when you're popping the book in and out of a backpack, you need something that will protect your work.

### OTHER MATERIALS

A lightweight, sturdy easel is essential for painting on location; I use a Westminster metal easel and on windy days take the rubber feet off the ends of the legs and whack the legs hard into the ground. Watercolour pencils and graphite pencils are useful for sketching, and you'll need a penknife for sharpening. You can usually find a source of water near where you're working, from a stream, river, puddle or the sea, or you can take a small bottle of water with you.

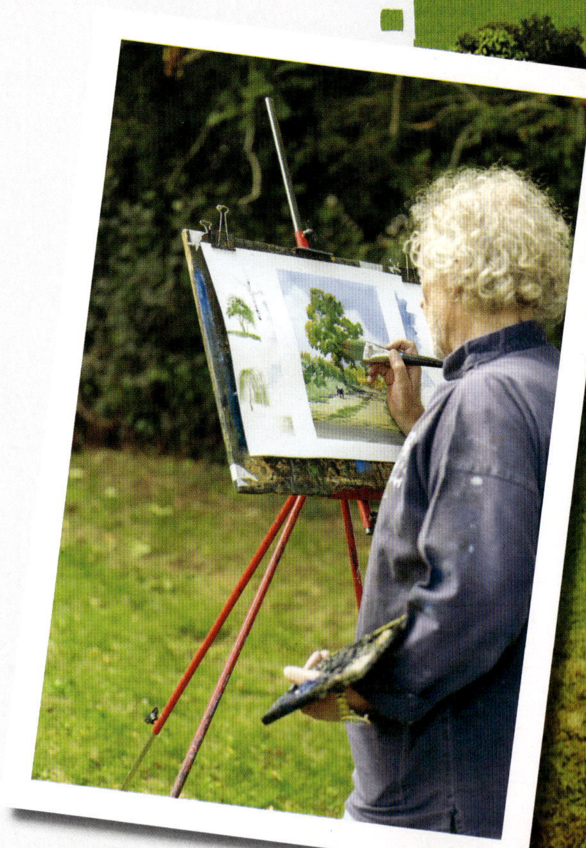

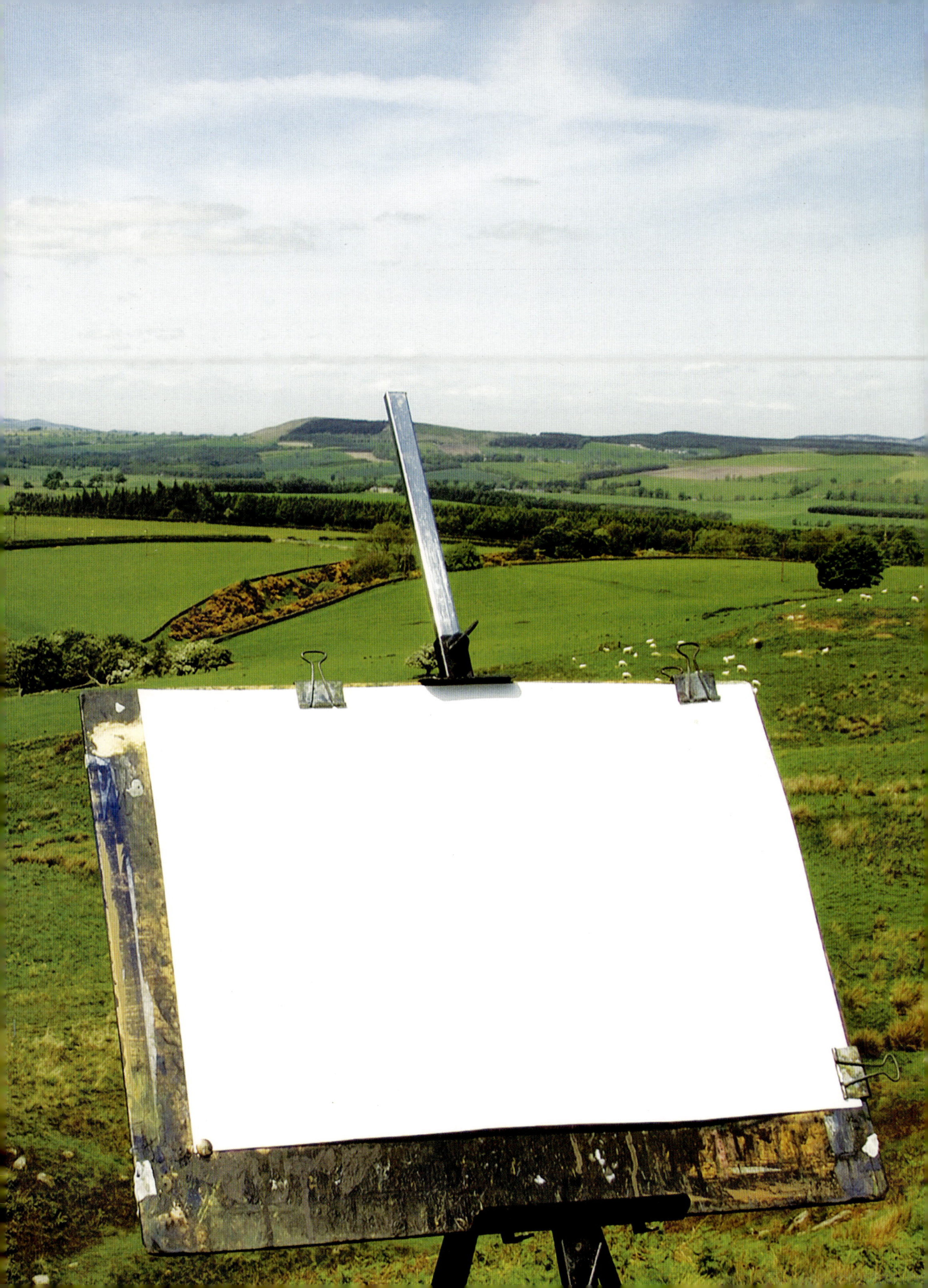

# Colour

**A large number of people confuse both themselves and their palettes by using too many colours. If there are 85 colours on offer in a colour range, as a beginner you may feel you need 84 of them immediately – but this means you have no chance of learning to mix fresh, vibrant colours, as you're almost certain to end up with flat, muddy mixes.**

The best thing is to limit your palette to a few workable and mixable colours – my selection, (see Materials: Paints), is a good start and has served me well for many years – and to play around with them; after all, isn't painting supposed to be fun? It's amazing what you can come up from a bit of experimenting with a few colours.

Another reason to keep the number of colours down is for when you go outdoors with a sketchbook and maybe an easel; the last thing you need is to carry a lot of gear, and popping eight small tubes in a pocket will see you through most scenes and situations. Mix, match and enjoy!

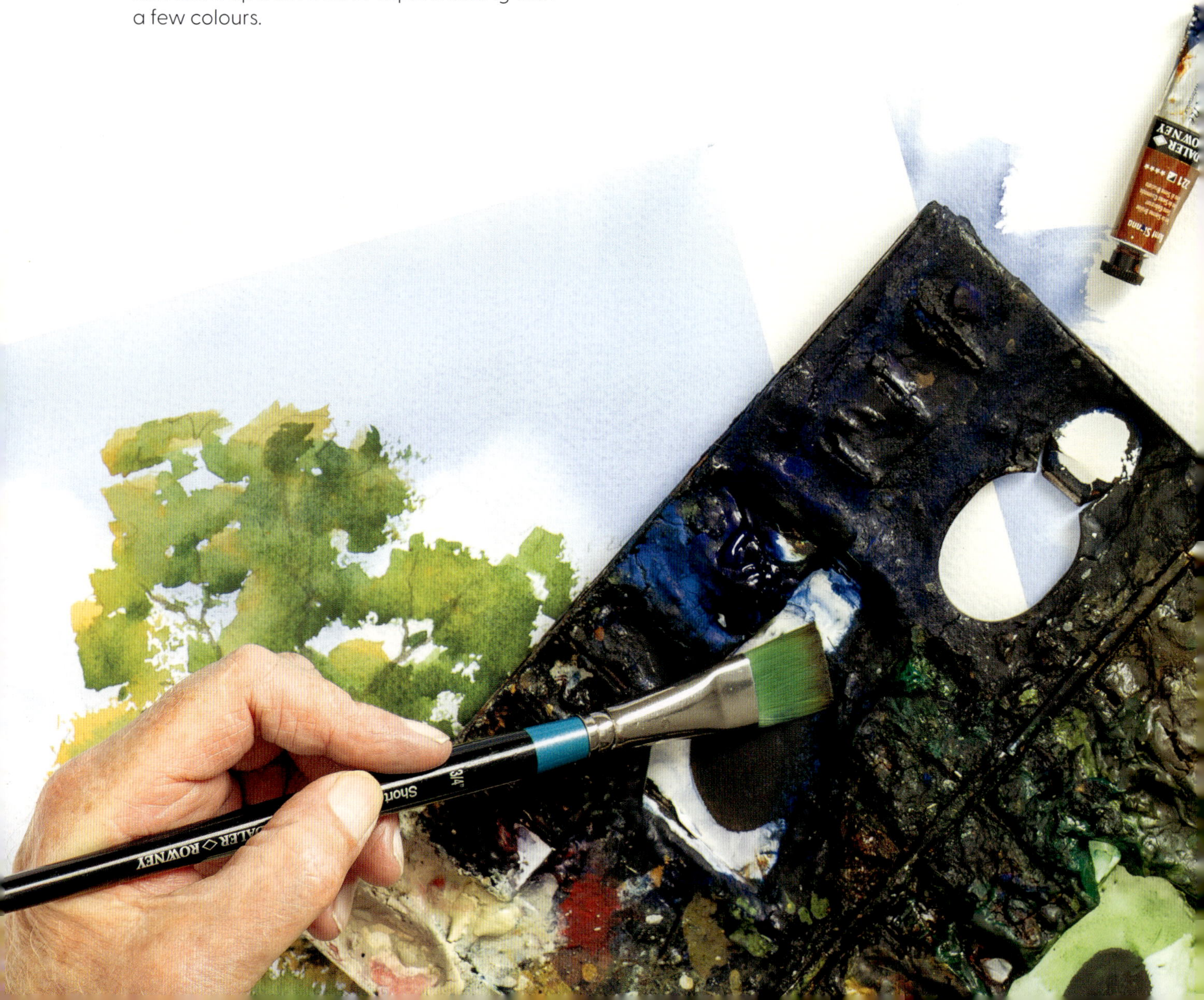

## SHADOW COLOURS

Rule 1 for shadows is that they are never just black. There is always a blend of the colour cast by the object and the colour of the surface on to which it is cast – even if the latter is white. In the projects I use a lot of shadows, particularly in the sky, where clouds cast shadows on to each other. The examples here show two of these; the two blues mixed with burnt sienna and alizarin crimson produce quite different shadows. To make lighter shadows just add more water to the two mixes. To make shadows darker, use less water in each mix. The blue used in the shadow is the same blue as used in the sky.

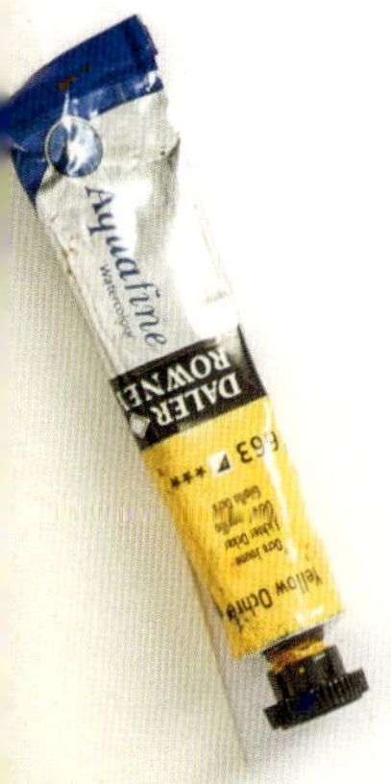

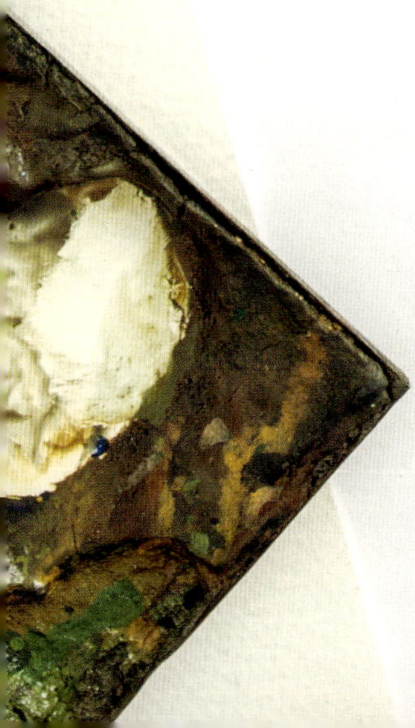

LIGHTER SHADOW

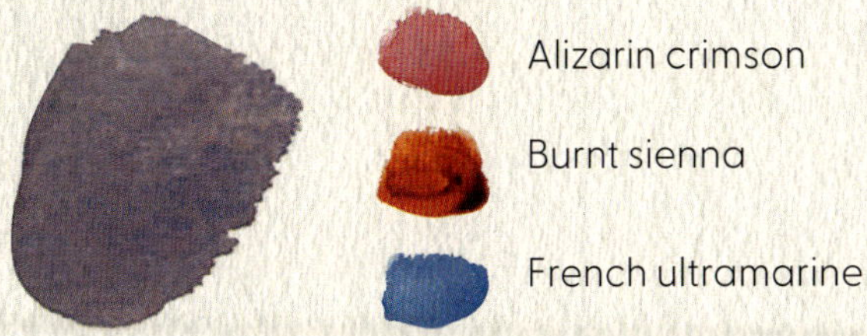


DARKER SHADOW

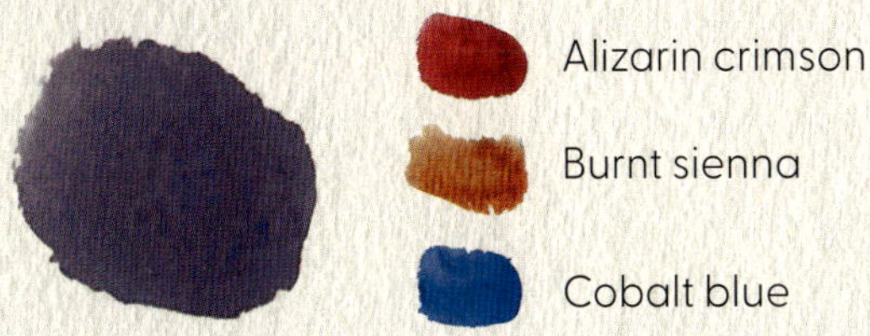

# MIXING GREENS

In my standard palette I use only one pre-made green, Hooker's green (dark). When used straight from the tube this is a pretty awful colour, but if I mix it with the other seven colours in the palette one at a time, this gives me seven different greens, some of which are shown here.

If that isn't enough I can then add a third colour to some of these mixes, giving me up to 12 greens. The danger with doing this is that you can end up mixing mud – inevitable in the landscape, but not in paintings – but if you vary the water in each element of the wash you should be able to avoid this and end up with a set of lovely clear greens. And you'll need these: look at any tree in leaf and you'll see not one, but a huge number of subtle greens.

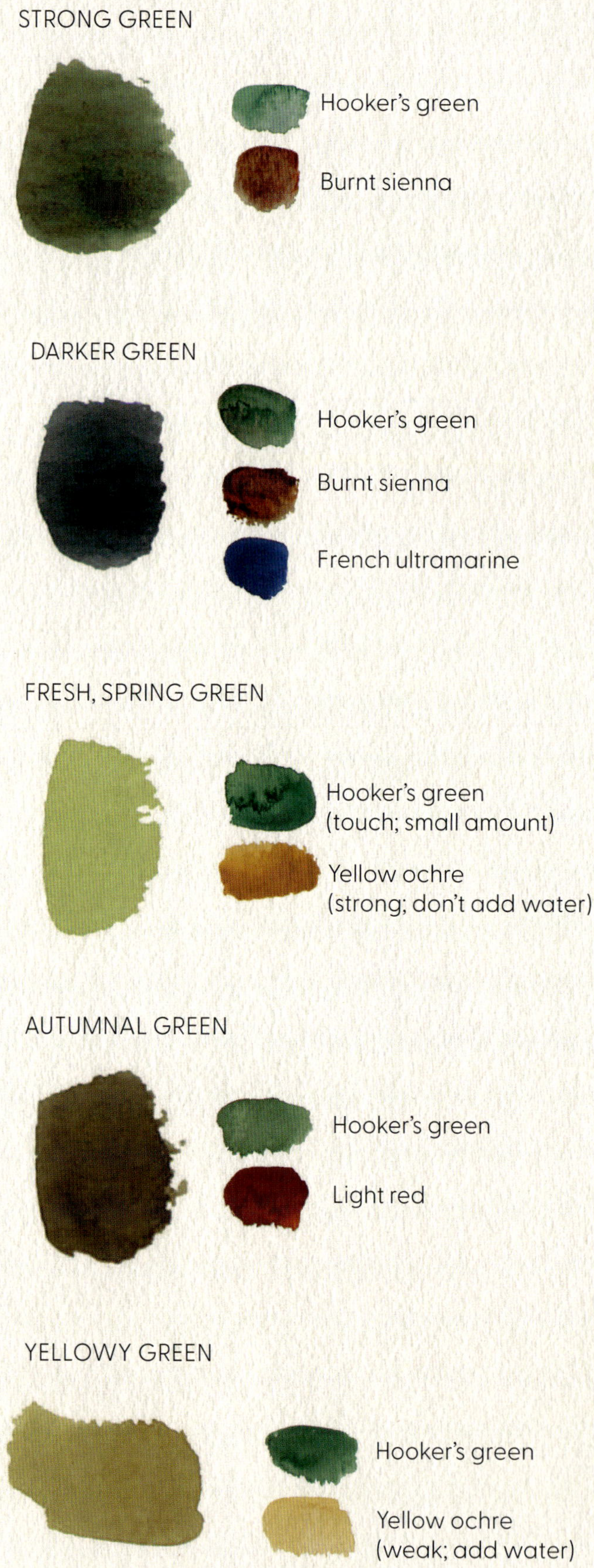

## SIENNA, OCHRE AND UMBER

A lot of people like to use raw sienna for their basic yellow shade, as opposed to yellow ochre, but I stick with ochre. True, it's a more opaque paint than raw sienna, but the answer is to stick loads more water into yellow ochre until it becomes transparent. This way you can avoid the potential problems of using raw sienna, which can become muddy very easily when mixed with certain other colours.

If you want to make the colour of raw sienna without having the paint ready made, mix a tiny bit of raw umber into yellow ochre, and there you have a great mix, which is useful for the colour of stonework on a building, for instance.

The examples here show the versatility of the 'brown' range of colours in my limited palette, and all are used in the projects in this book, for everything from tree trunks to human arms and legs.

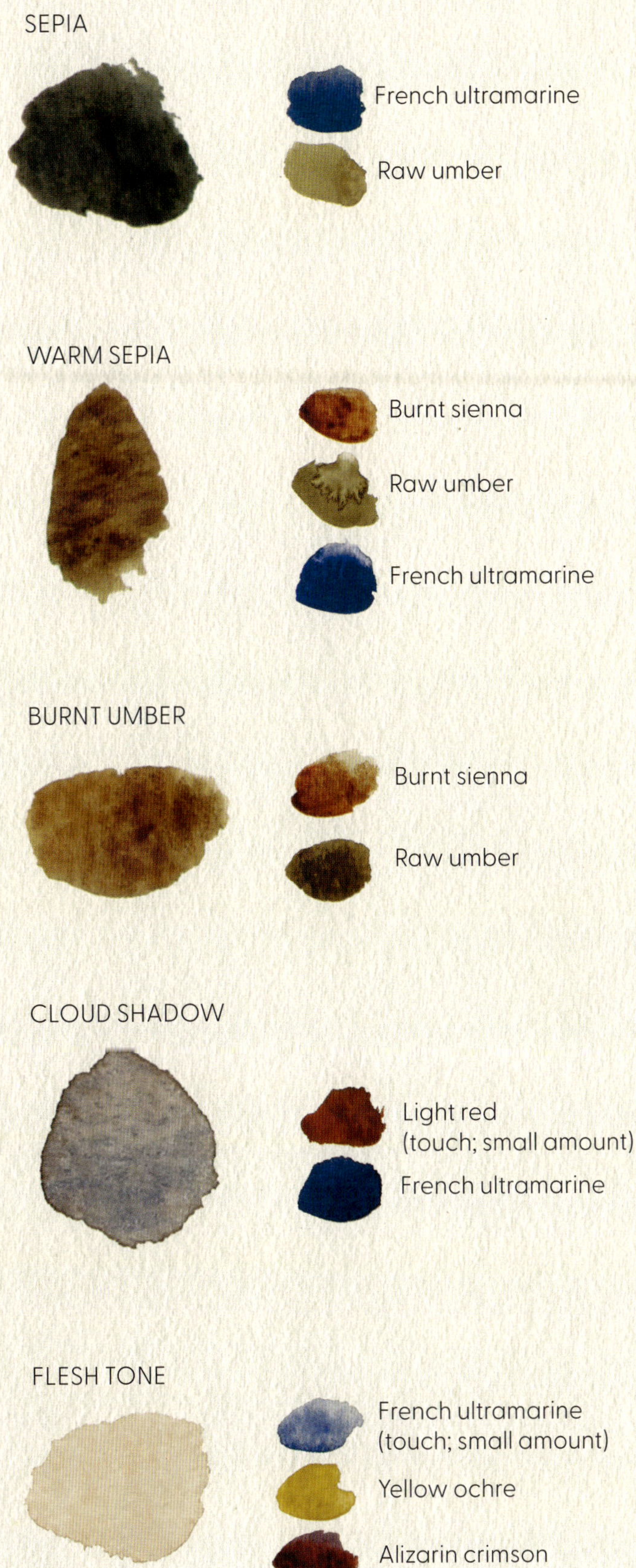

# The parts of a complex painting

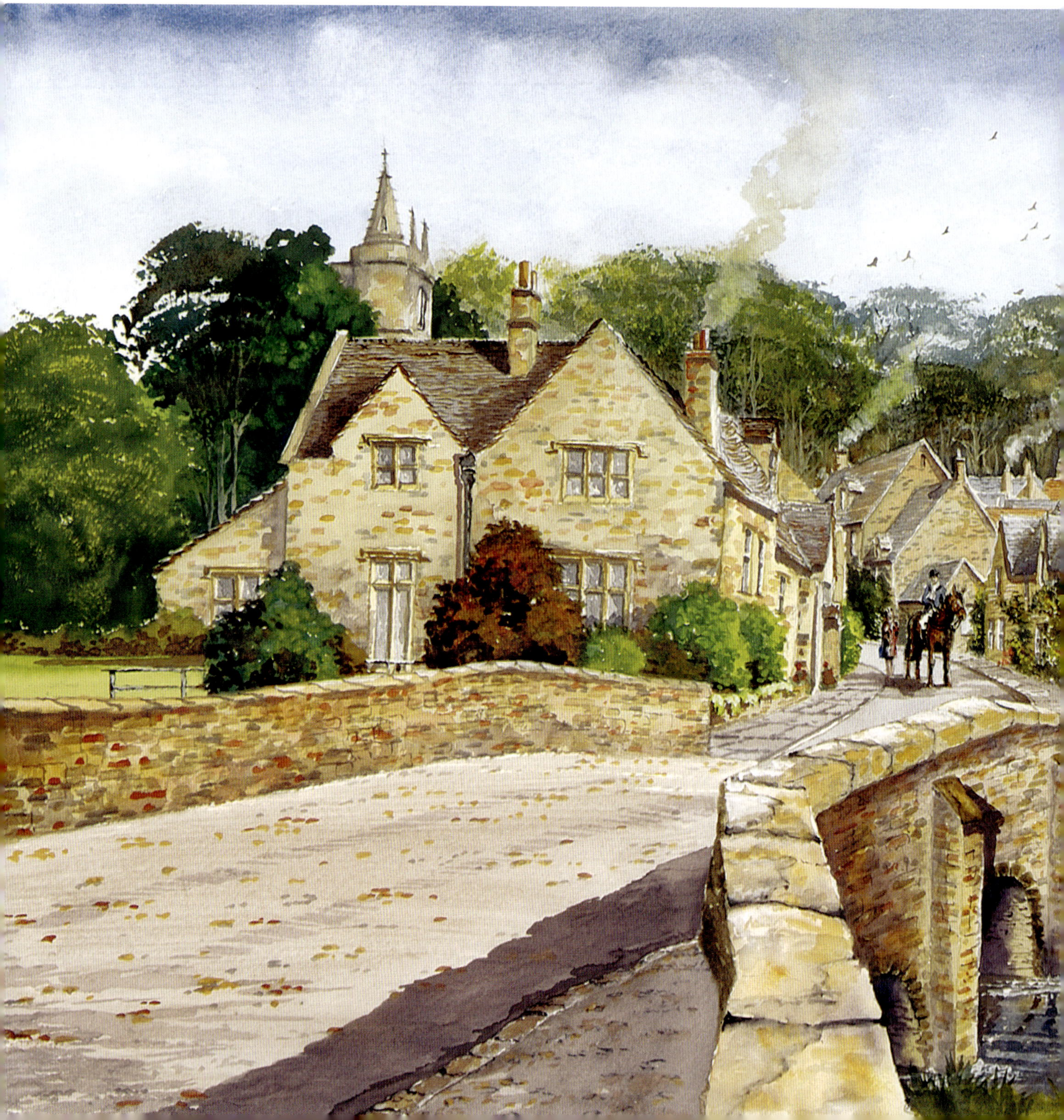

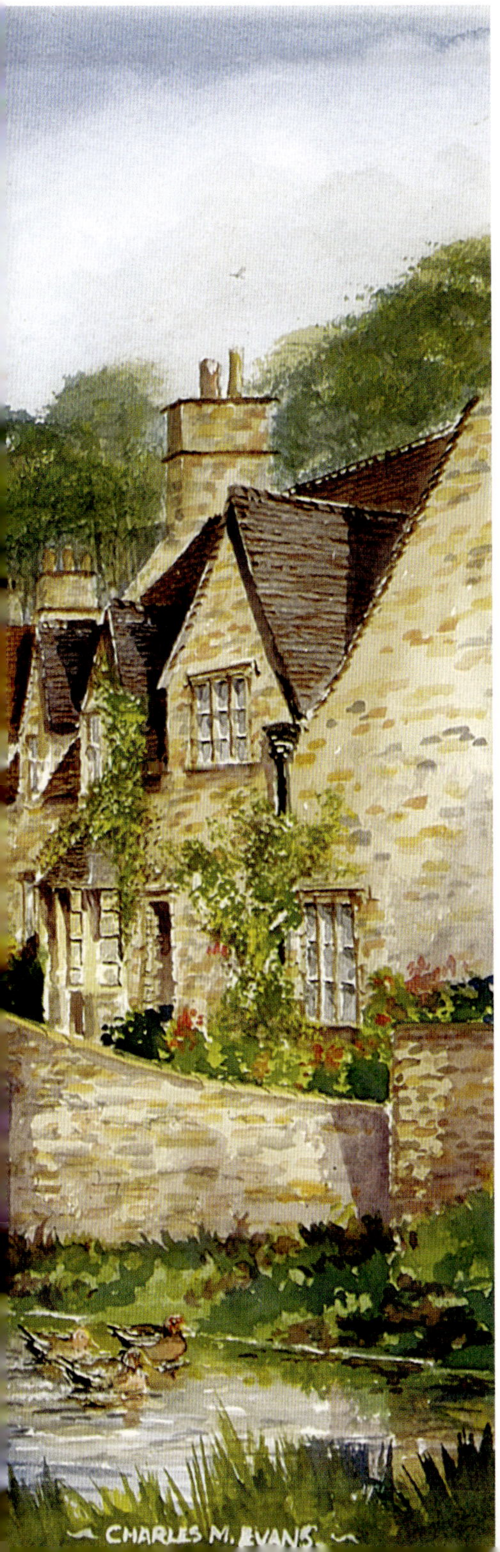


The many different elements in this village street – the river, the narrowing street, the masses of trees and foliage, the figures and the jumble of buildings – probably make this subject look pretty daunting at first sight. But now have a look at the areas I've picked out on the right and below, which all relate to the exercises and projects in this book, and you'll see that even a complex landscape can be broken down into its parts and then fitted together.

I don't use technical terms where simple, straightforward ones will do, so don't be daunted. Getting there takes practice – but isn't it worth the effort?

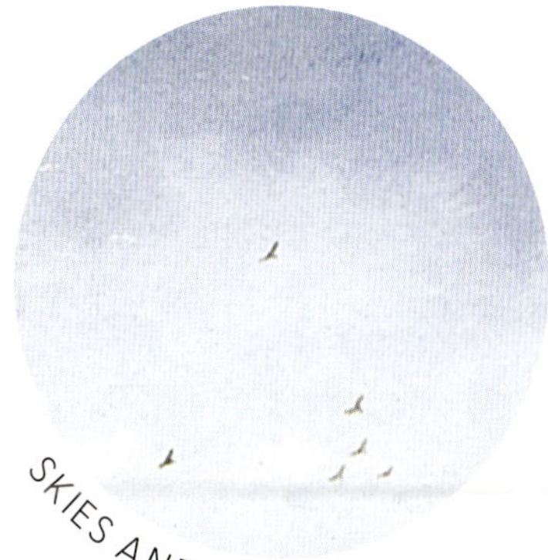

SKIES AND CLOUDS

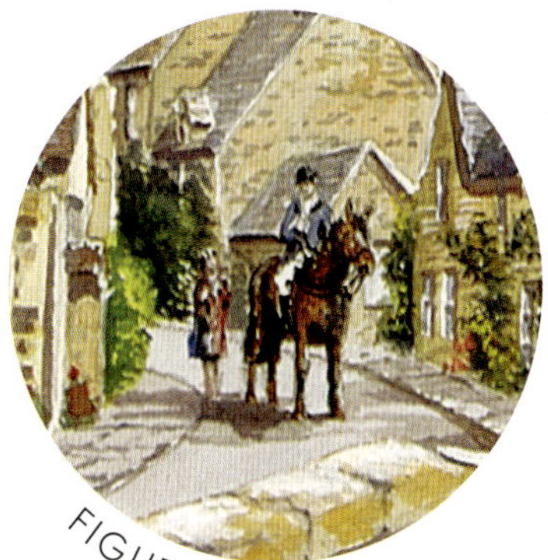

FIGURES

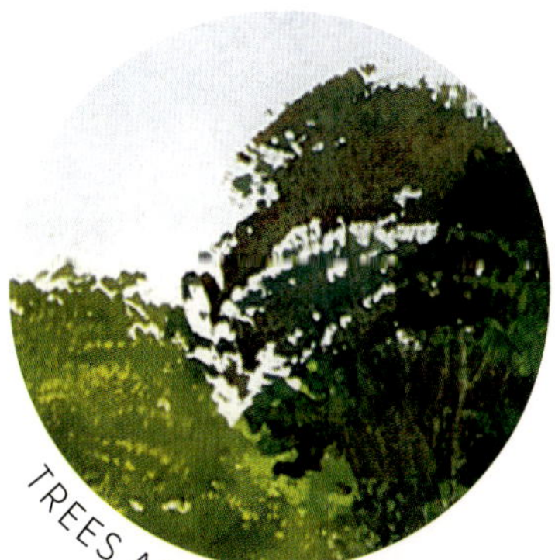

TREES AND FOLIAGE

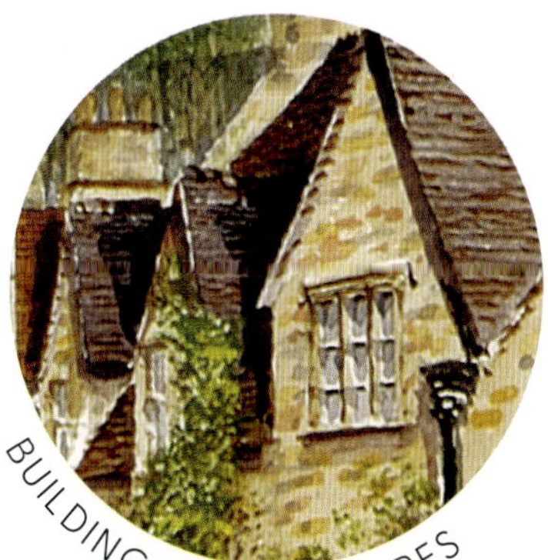

BUILDINGS AND TEXTURES

FLOWERS

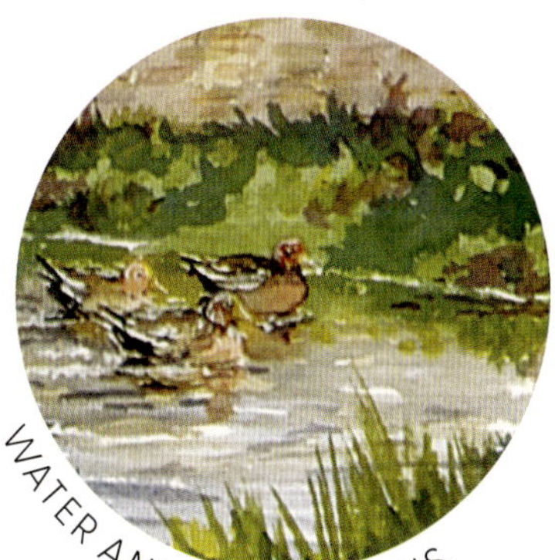

WATER AND REFLECTIONS

# Sky and land

Set the mood and the atmosphere in landscapes with the sky, adding more groundwork and details to match that sky. This first project shows a simple landscape, full of depth and atmosphere, with very few brush strokes.

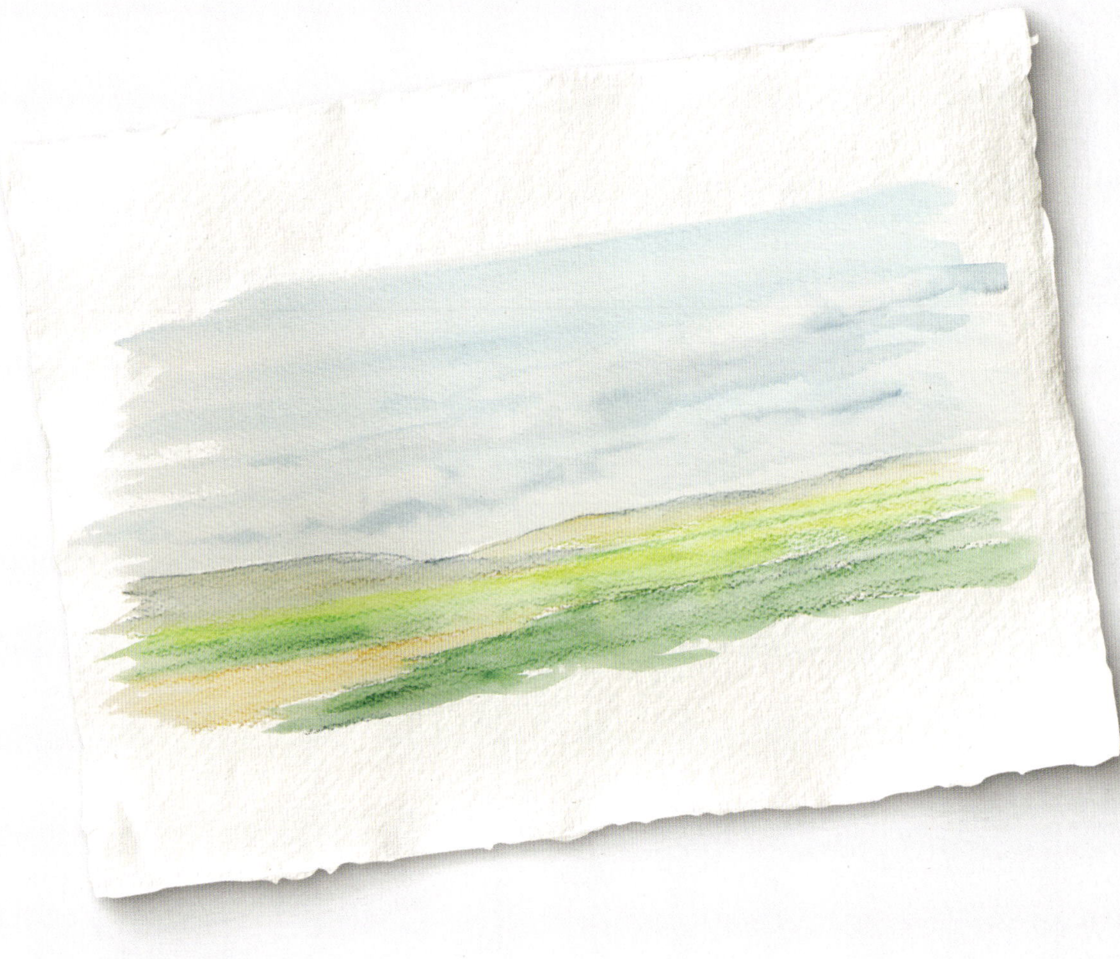

REFERENCE SKETCH

I used watercolour pencils to draw this quick little vignette, setting down the basic shapes and colours of the scene in front of me. It took 10 minutes.

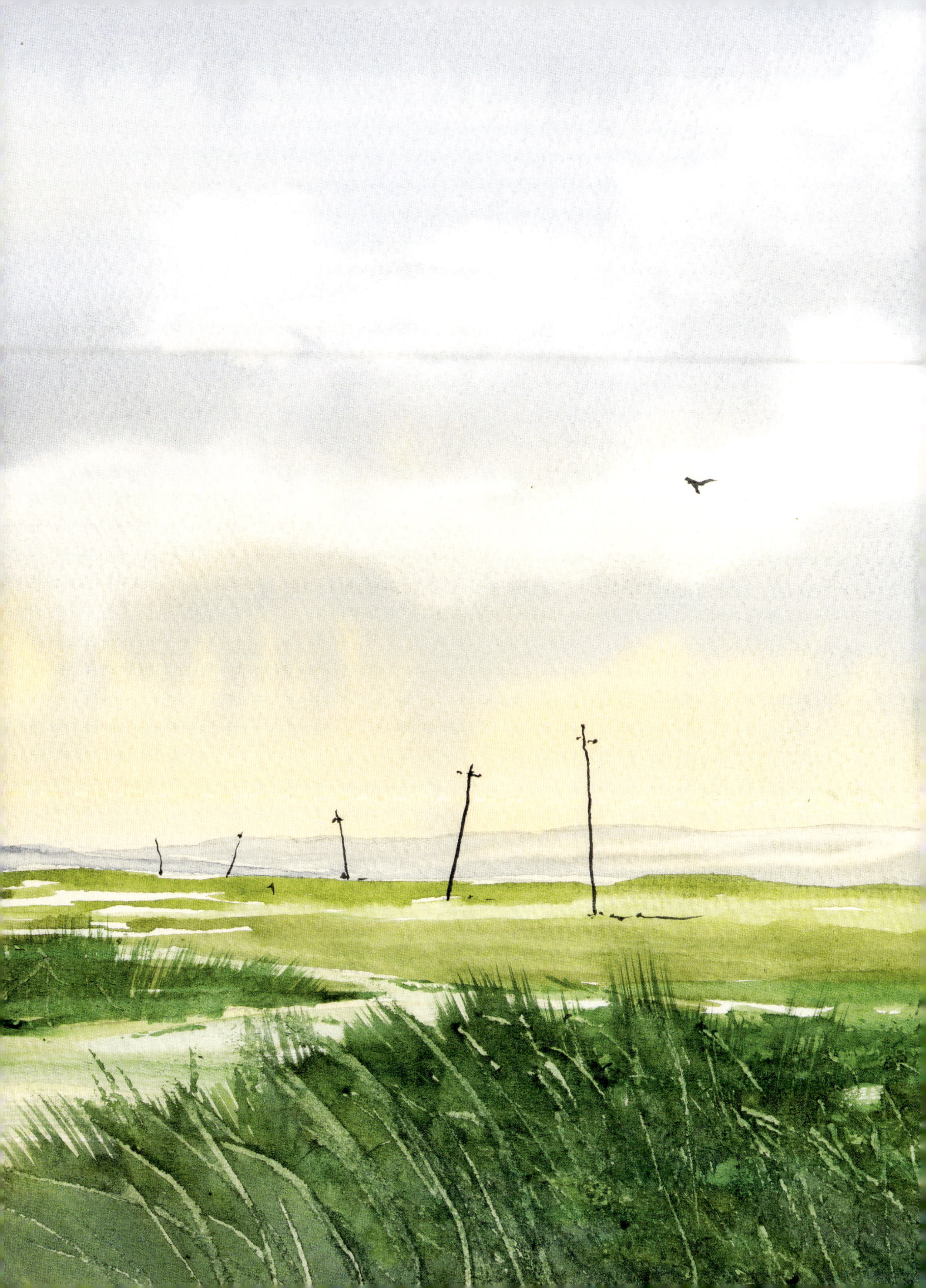

# EXERCISE: FLAT AND GRADED WASHES

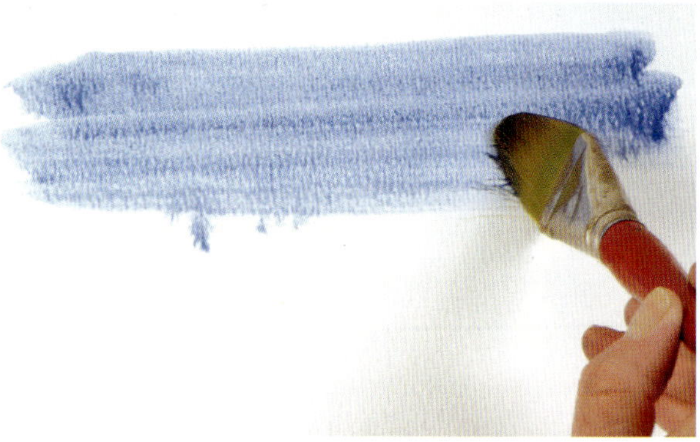

1. A flat wash is useful for large areas such as the sky or a background for the land, and is the basis of all watercolour painting. Make up a large amount of a watery wash of ultramarine. First use a 38mm (1½in) flat wash brush to wet the whole of the paper with clean water. Then load the brush with paint and stroke the colour on from side to side, working down the paper.

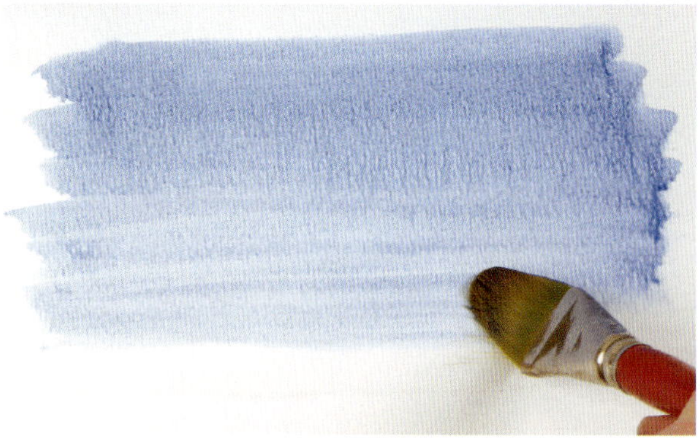

2. Continue to work down the wet paper, working quickly and reloading the brush as necessary to make sure the colour stays as much the same as possible from top to bottom.

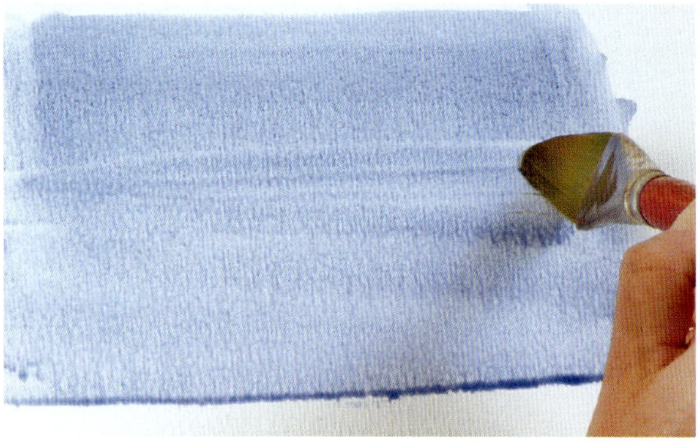

3. If you find that the coverage is uneven, you can add more paint where you've already been – but don't take any time over this: just whack on the paint while everything is still wet. It takes practice to achieve a flat wash, and different colours go on the paper in different ways, so be ready to use a lot of paint and paper.

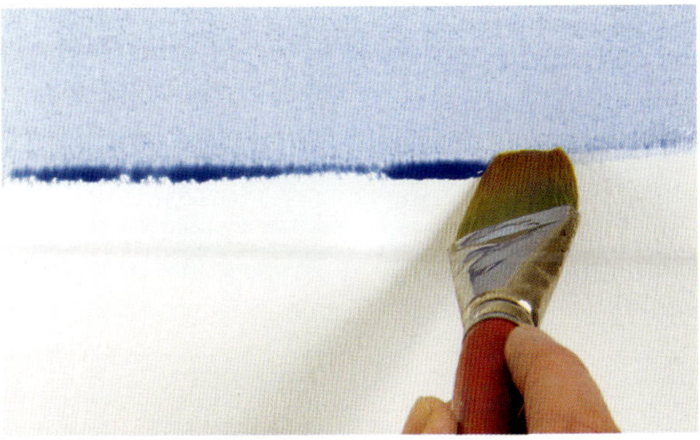

**4.** At the bottom of the wash you may find that you have a line or bead of watery paint – don't leave this as there's a chance it may seep up the wash as it dries, leading to the dreaded back-run or 'cauliflower' effect. Squeeze the bristles almost dry and go along the bead of paint with the brush edge, sucking water out of the paper.

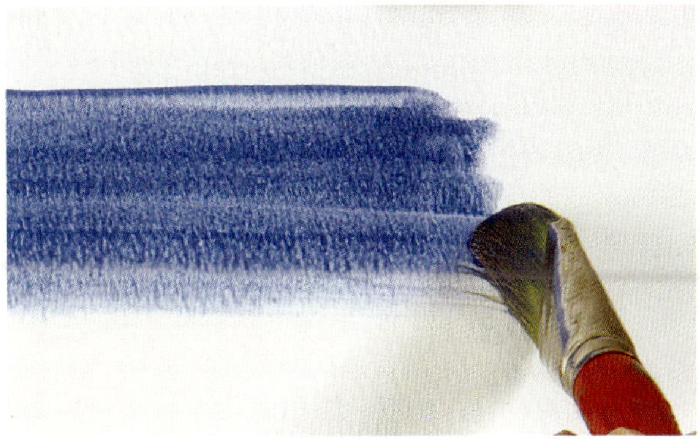

**5.** Graded washes are great for skies and for tinting paper before painting. Wet the paper with clean water as before, which avoids hard edges as the paint dries, then start as in step 1 opposite, working quickly from side to side.

**6.** As you go down the paper this time, don't refill or load the brush again, but continue to whack it on with gusto – as the paint runs out the wash gets weaker towards the bottom, and the result is a graded wash.

### TRY IT YOURSELF

Repeat the exercise with a different colour. Pop another colour in the middle while it is all wet and observe what happens.

# EXERCISE: VARIEGATED WASHES

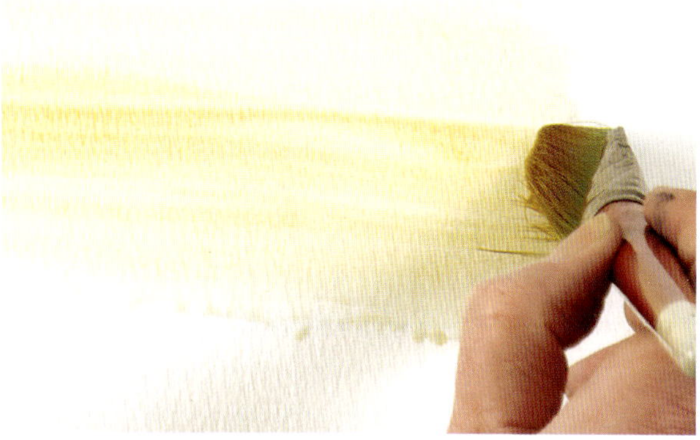

**1.** A variegated wash, in which you blend two colours, is a simple way to start a little landscape. Wet the paper as for the previous exercises and paint a flat wash of yellow ochre along the bottom third of the wet area.

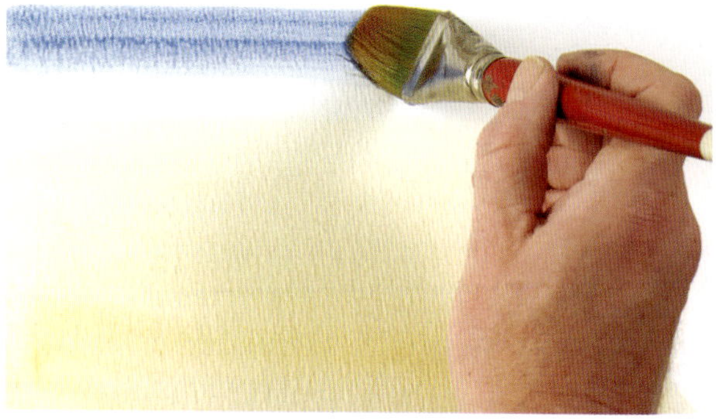

**2.** While this is still wet, rinse the brush and start a graded wash of cobalt blue from the top, using plenty of water and not recharging the brush as you go down the paper.

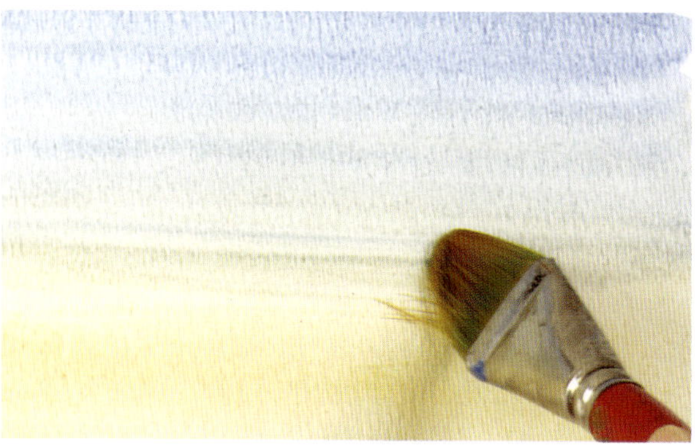

**3.** Bring the strokes of faint blue down over the top of the still-wet yellow wash, stopping a few strokes down. Don't go back over either wash, and allow everything to dry naturally and completely. And there's a variegated wash ready to develop.

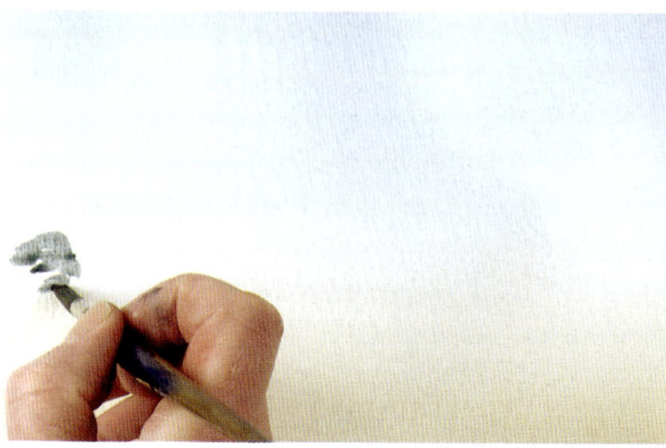

**4.** The horizon line is where the yellow land blends into the blue sky. Make a mix of Hooker's green and burnt sienna, and use a No. 8 round brush to drop some blobs for tree tops just above the horizon.

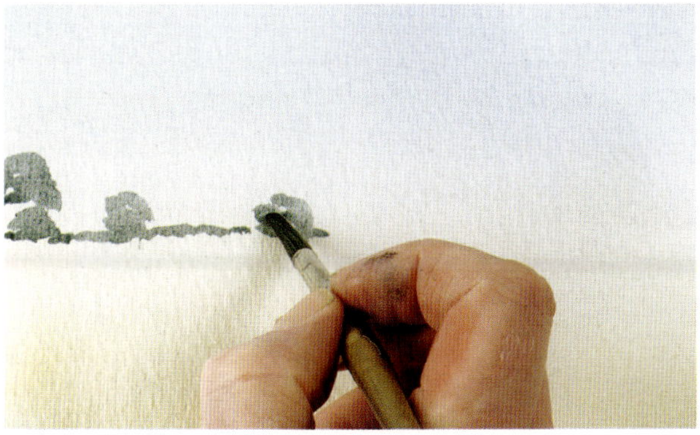

**5.** Work across the paper, adding a horizon line – which doesn't have to be dead straight – and some more blobs for trees. Leave a little background visible in the trees to give the birds gaps to fly through.

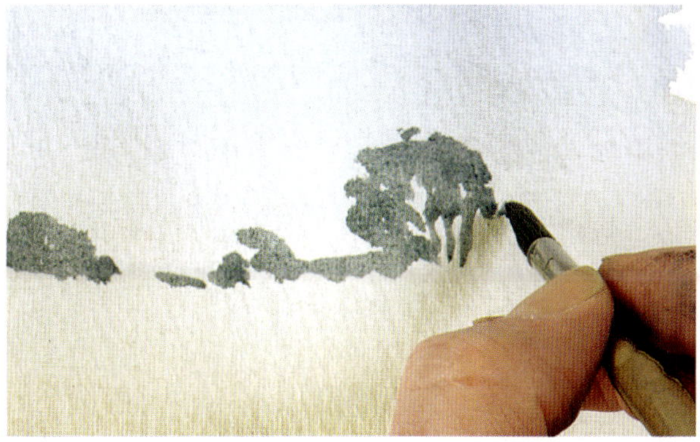

**6.** Distant tree trunks are easy: just use the tip of the brush to add a few lines from the leaf canopy to the ground. Note that you don't have to paint the horizon across the whole paper – you're only concerned with the trees, and the 'lost line' adds interest.

**7.** Make up a very watery, diluted wash of the tree colour, and stroke the tip of a flat wash brush to make gentle contours across the land. Don't try to cover the whole of the yellow area, just show the shadows. You've just painted a landscape!

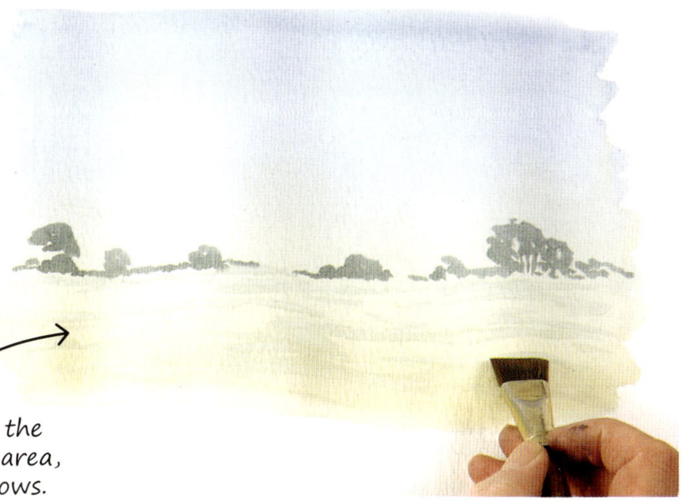

*Don't try to cover the whole of the yellow area, just show the shadows.*

# Moorland at dawn

This project, a desolate moorland dotted with telegraph poles, uses variegated washes for the sky, which takes up most of the painting. Make sure that the horizon line isn't exactly halfway up this kind of composition, as it will split the painting in half and lose the interest of the sky; note how the path meanders through the painting for the same reason.

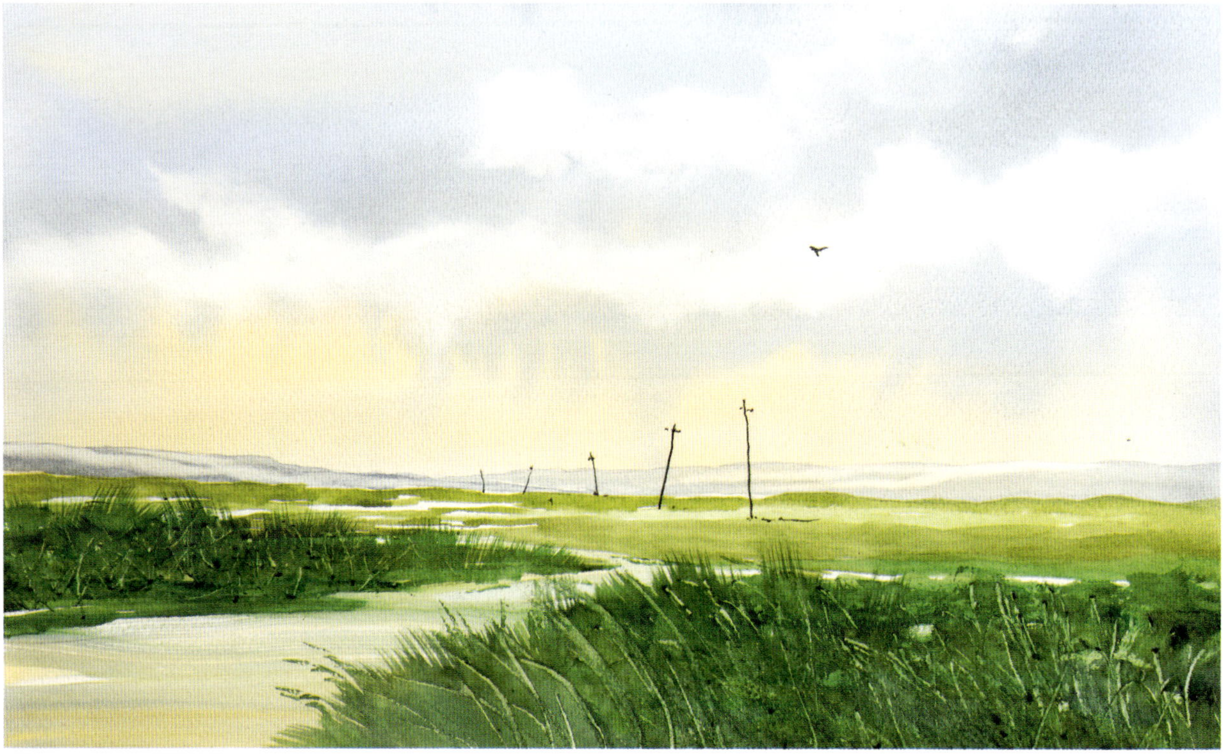

### PRELIMINARY DRAWING

The pencil outlines show the basic and very simple shapes of the landscape – the sky will form itself as you paint it. Note how the path, appearing narrower as it leads away into the distance, helps to create the effect of recession, which I'll look at in a bit more depth in the next project.

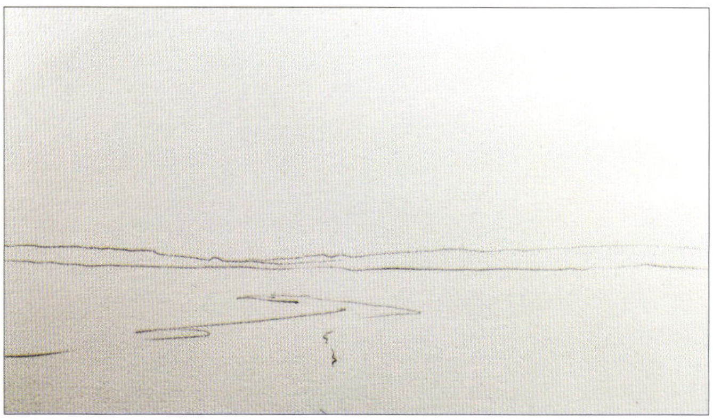

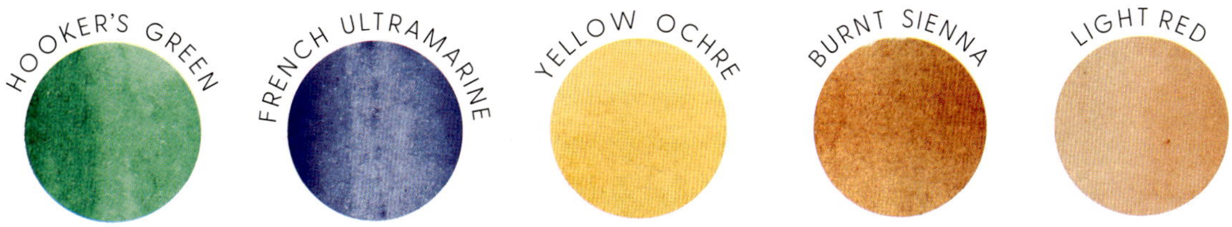


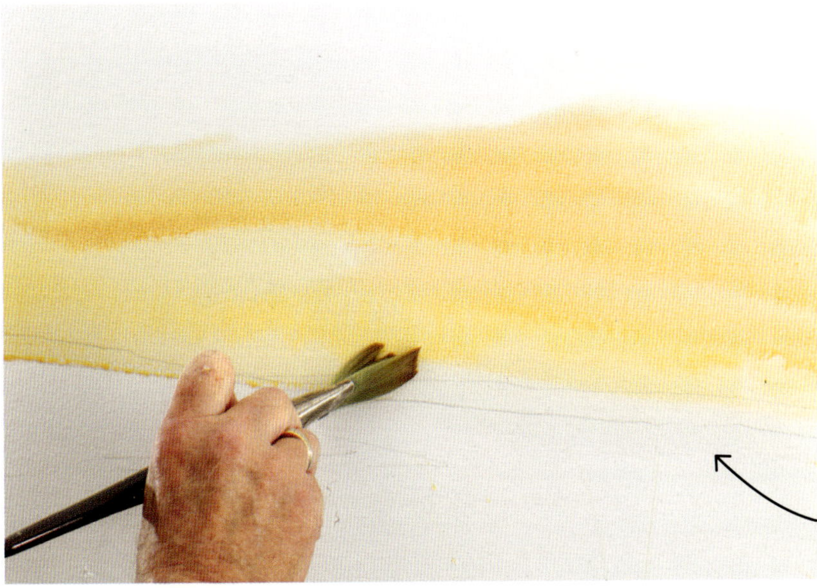

**STEP 1**
Thoroughly wet the sky area with clean water, then use a 38mm (1½in) flat brush to stroke a wash of yellow ochre across the bottom of the sky. Now add a little bit of burnt sienna above the yellow ochre.

*Keep mopping up along the bottom of the sky to control the water.*

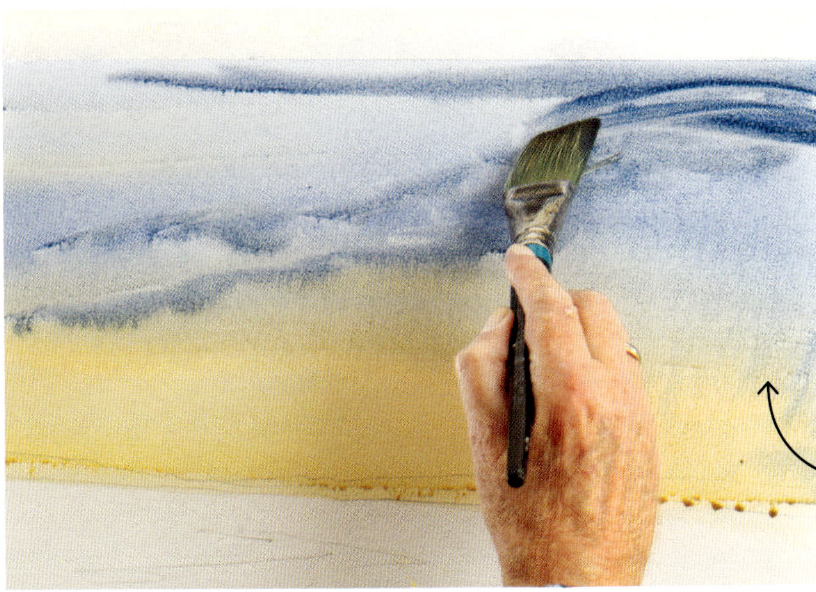

**STEP 2**
While this is wet, add a watery wash of ultramarine mixed with burnt sienna from the top and blend it into the yellow for a variegated wash. Use the side of the brush to add a few darker areas with a stronger mix, using more burnt sienna and less water.

*When painting on pre-wet paper, remember that it's going to dry about 30 per cent lighter, so allow for that.*

**STEP 3**
Now it's time to add a few soft-edged clouds. While the sky is still wet, rinse and squeeze out the brush and use it to suck the paint out of the wash, moving the brush around on the paper. This is such an effective technique that's it tempting to use it more than you need – do your best to resist the temptation.

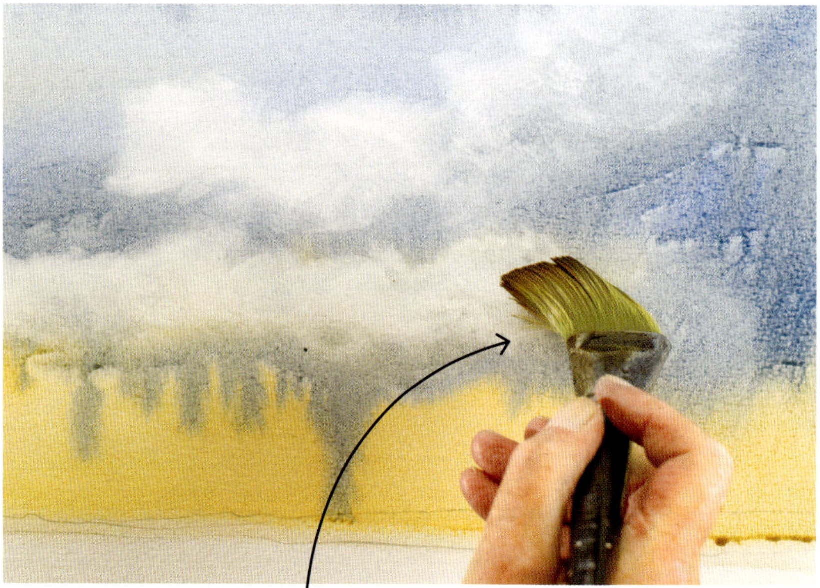

*Use a clean brush rather than tissue or paper towel to suck out the paint to achieve a softer finish.*

**STEP 4**
With a 19mm (¾in) wash brush use a mix of ultramarine and a touch of light red with plenty of water to block in the distant hills. Rinse and squeeze out the brush between your fingers, and use the tip to suck out some paint to give a little bit of movement and light to the hills. Use the same mix but slightly weaker for the distant hills, sucking out a little bit of paint again for depth.

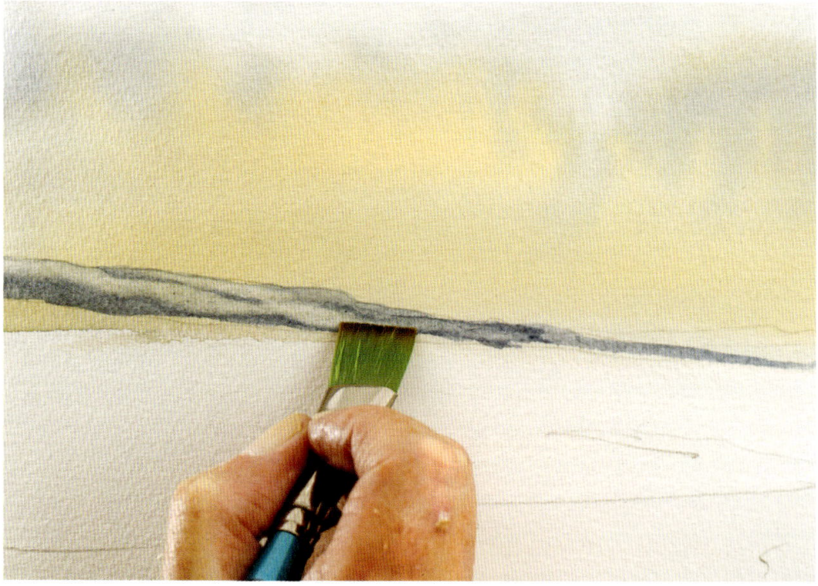

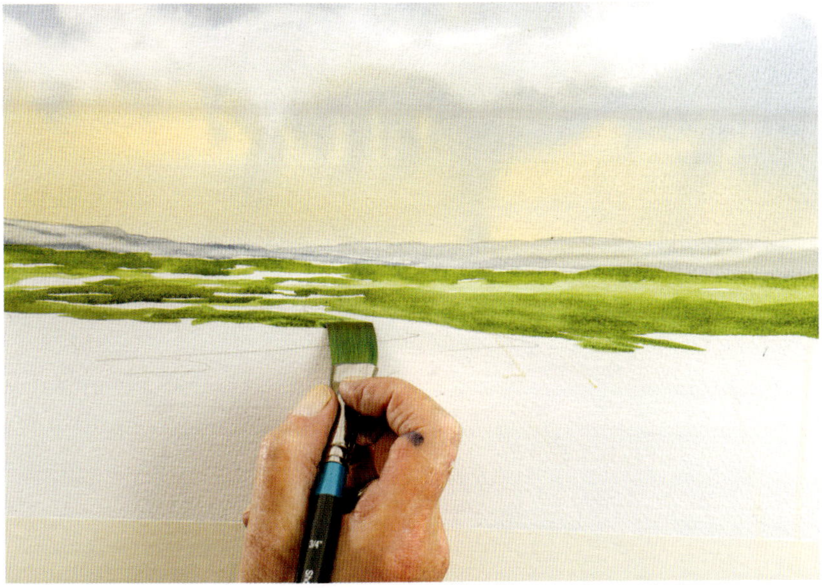

**STEP 5**

Using a mix of Hooker's green and a lot of yellow ochre, still with a 19mm (¾in) flat brush, go all the way across under the hills. Leave a few little bits of white paper showing through here and there to capture some light. Add more water to the mix to get different tones of the same green within that area too.

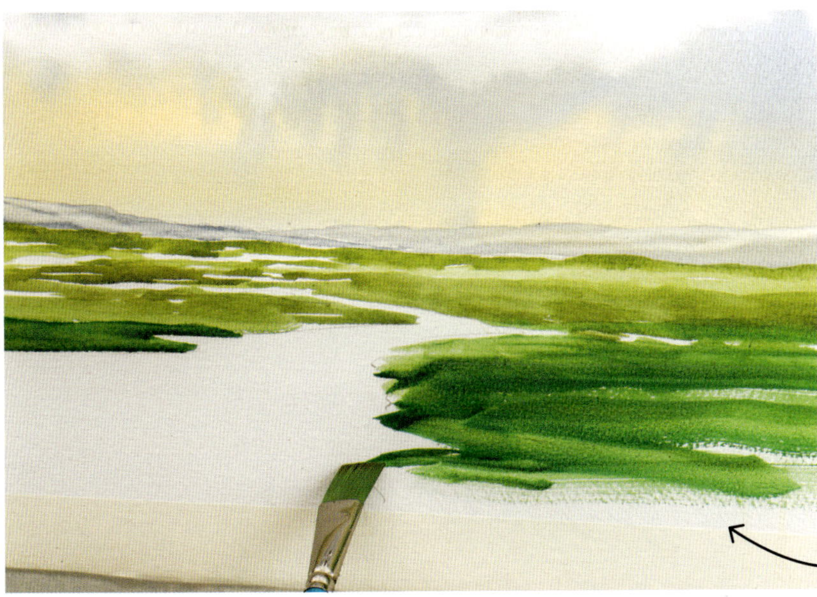

**STEP 6**

For the closer grassy areas use Hooker's green again but this time with burnt sienna, so this is an altogether stronger mix. At this stage, thinking back to the pencil drawing, this is where we need to go around the path too. Allow to dry for a couple of minutes before filling in the path.

*The colour should get slightly stronger as you come further forward in the landscape.*

**STEP 7**

Lightly stroke over the path with a little bit of yellow ochre first of all. Skip over the surface of the rough paper, picking up a little bit of the green from either side. Leave that for a second. Now mix ultramarine and burnt sienna with plenty of water and, again, stroke lightly over the surface of the paper across the path.

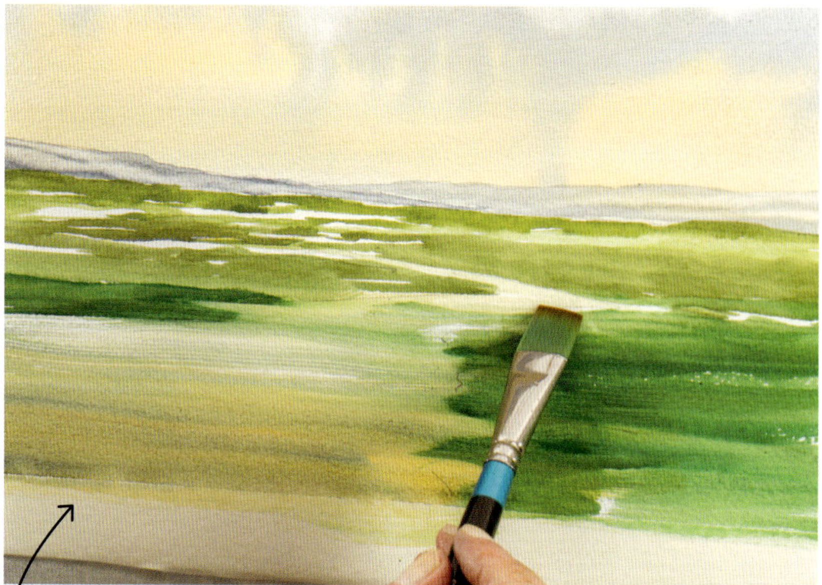

*Bring all the colours from the landscape into the path.*

*You don't need to paint individual blades of grass – push the flat brush on to the paper and flick it up to create tufts of grass.*

**STEP 8**

Now it's time for the big, strong grasses in the foreground. With a 19mm (¾in) flat brush and a mix of Hooker's green and burnt sienna, literally whack this on. As you get to the edge near the path, start to flick up with the same brush for grasses. Likewise, on the other side of the path, edge the path with that dark green mix, which helps to pronounce it, and again, flick up.

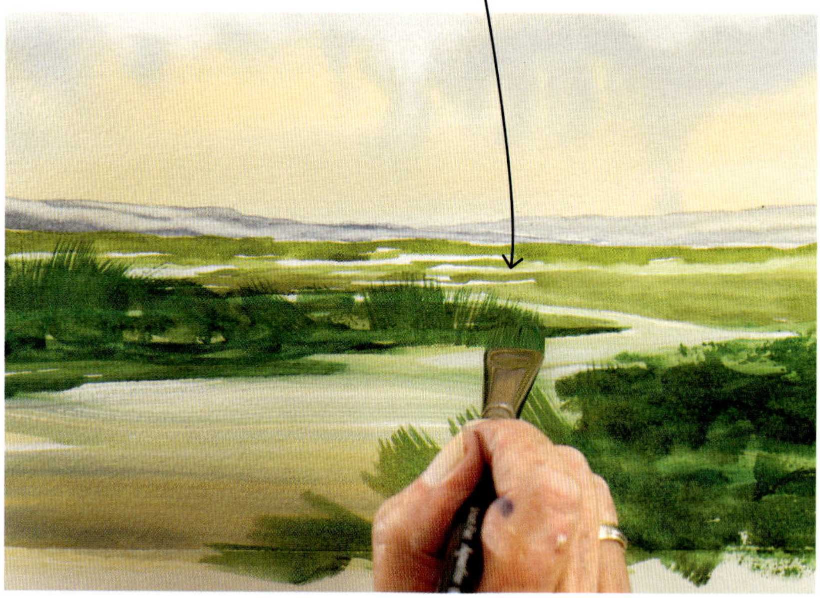

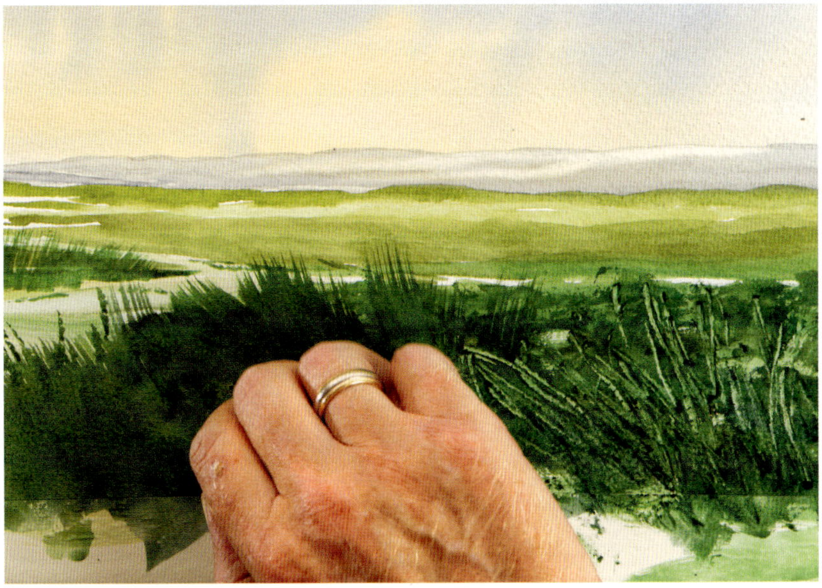

**STEP 9**

Use a mix of ultramarine and burnt sienna to add a few sharp bits of grass with the edge of the brush. And add more grasses by flicking up yet again. Then use your fingernail to scratch away some paint for more texture. Allow that to dry.

*Don't make the poles all perfect and straight – this is an old moorland and everything's windblown!*

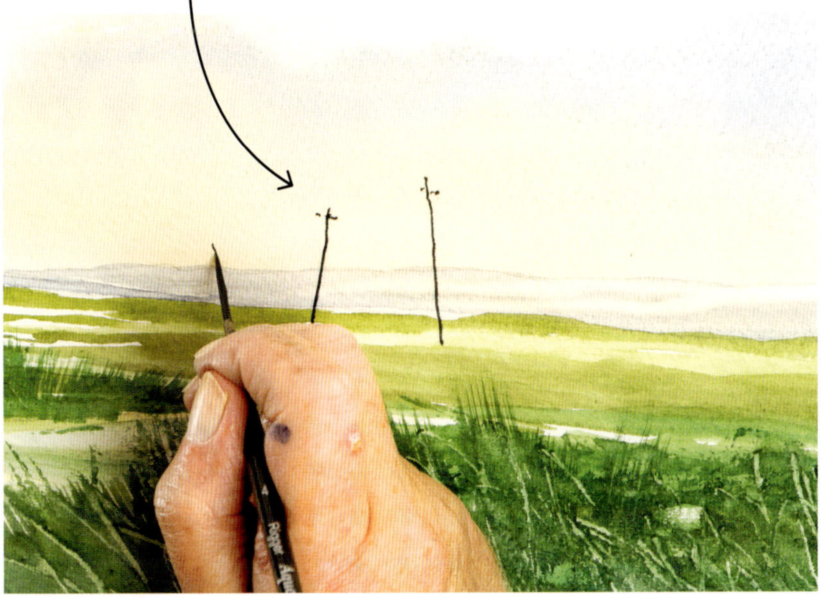

**STEP 10**

Now for a few telegraph posts in the distance using a No. 4 rigger brush and a strong mix of ultramarine and burnt sienna. Keep in mind that the posts are going further away, so make them smaller in the distance. Finally, add a buzzard flying in the sky.

# Mountains and lakes

In this project, the lake in the foreground reflects the mountains that stretch away up to the sky. Reflections and recession are explained in the step-by-step exercises, and the project painting brings together all the techniques looked at so far.

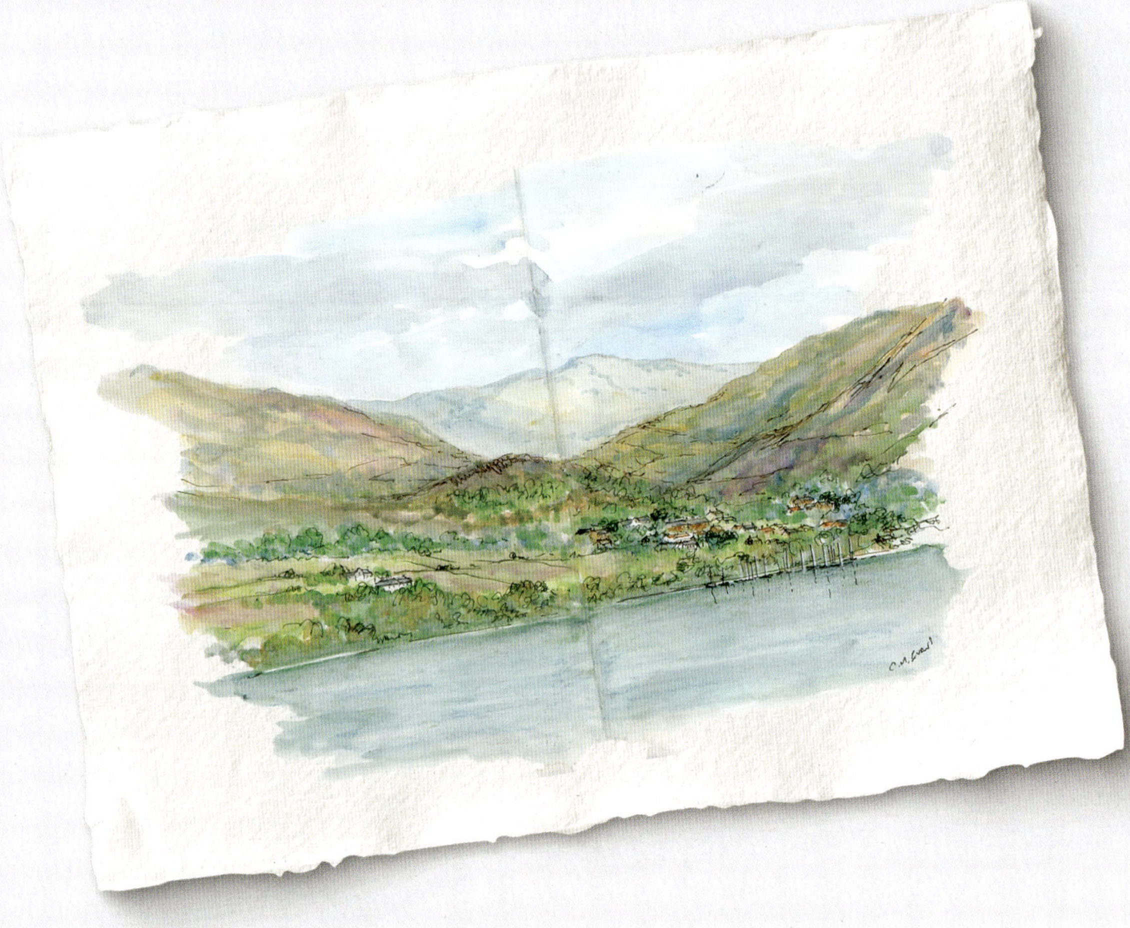

**REFERENCE SKETCH**
Working from life, I included all the houses in the village on the right and a number of boats, but dropped them from the final painting.

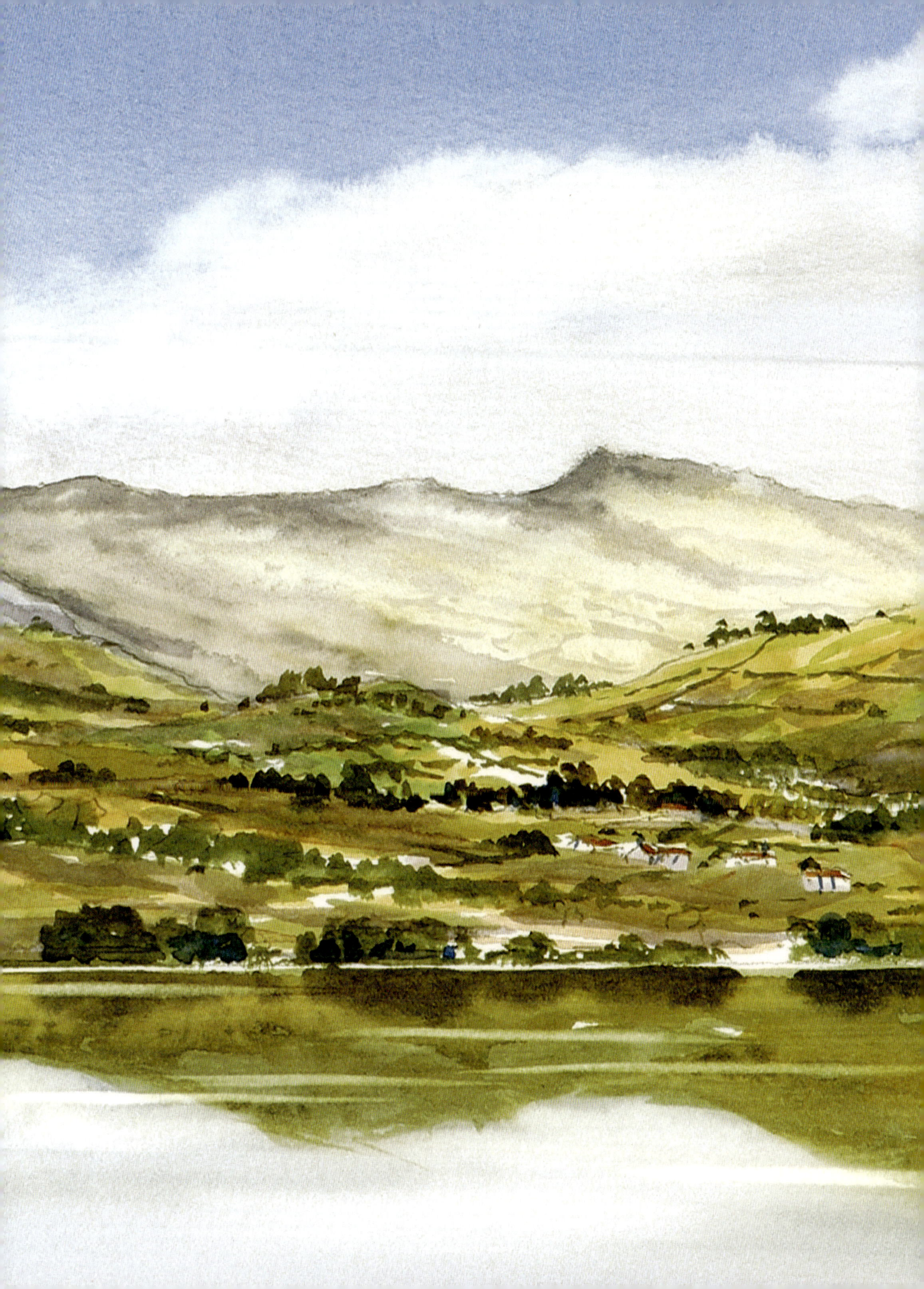

# EXERCISE: RECESSION

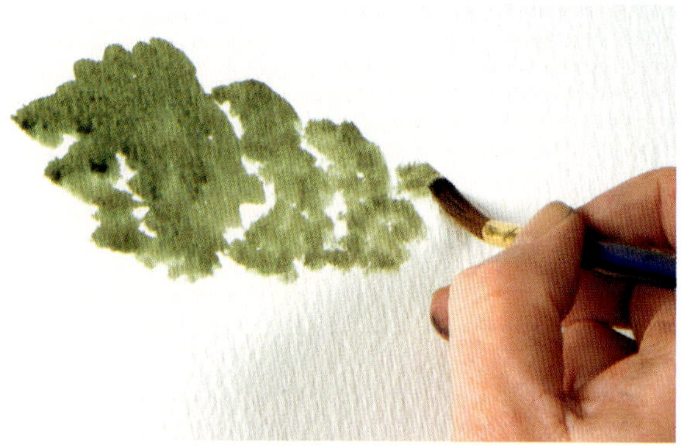

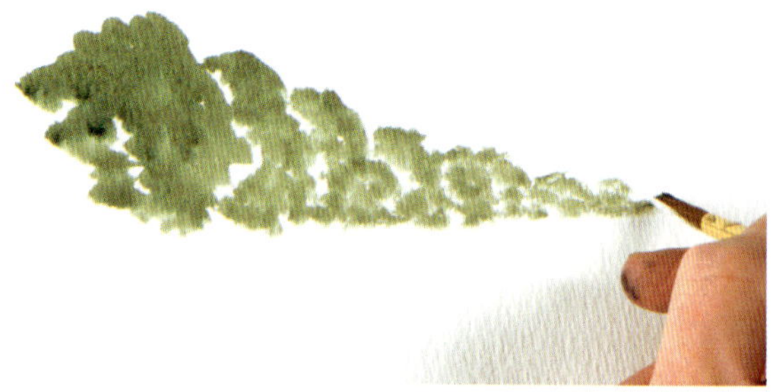

**1.** Recession is linked with perspective (see Buildings) in that similar objects appear smaller as they become more distant – if they are vertical make them shorter, and if they are horizontal make them narrower. With tonal recession, the colours get fainter the further away they are. Use a green mix and No. 8 round brush to paint clumps of trees, starting large in the foreground with a fully loaded brush.

**2.** As you move away from the first tree, replicate the shape but make the next one shorter at the top – and don't refill the brush, but let the colour get weaker as you go along. Dip the brush into clean water as you approach the end of the line of trees. Don't forget to leave some white between the clumps for shadows and a few gaps in the leaves.

### TRY IT YOURSELF

Paint a very flat piece of land, using your own colour option, followed by a line of fence posts or telegraph poles that get smaller as they go into the distance. There, you have just created recession!

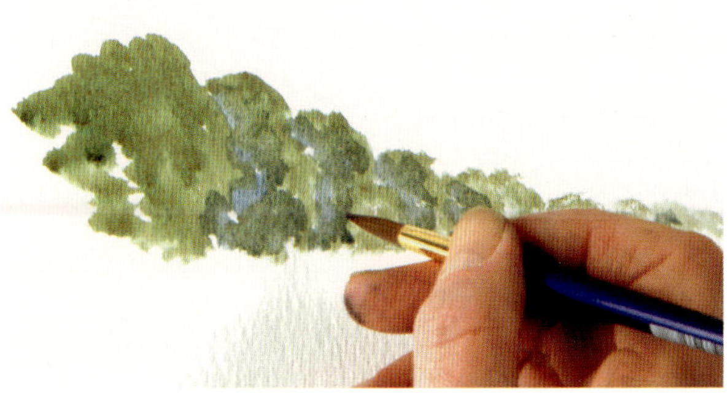

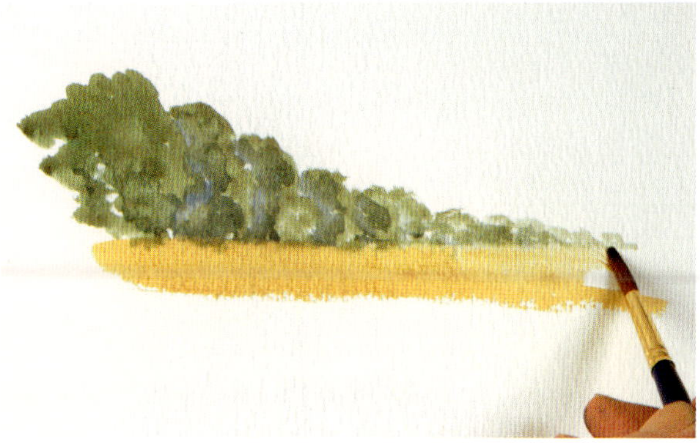

**3.** Let the green dry a little, then add ultramarine for the shadows, again starting with a strongish wash in the foreground and dipping the brush into clean water as you get further away.

**4.** To aid the feeling of recession, don't leave the trees floating in mid-air – attach them to the ground. Add a field of yellow ochre, this time painting a graded wash upside down ...

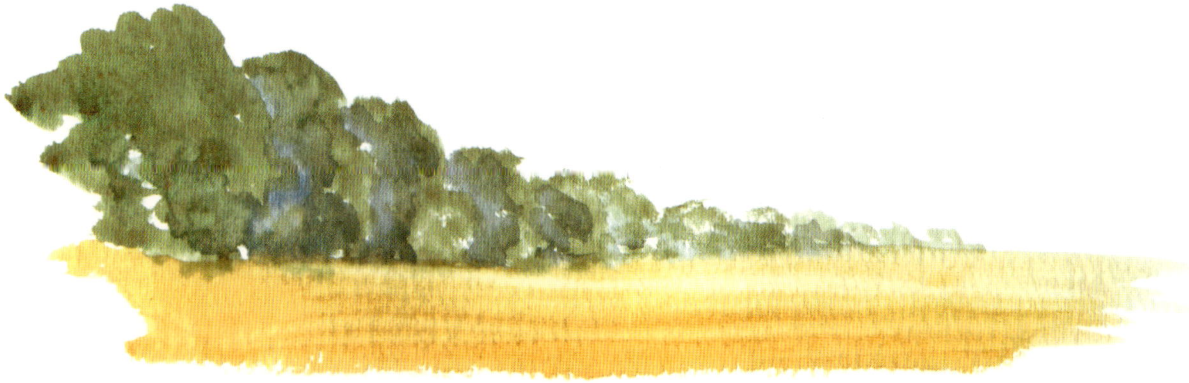

**5.** ... stronger and darker in the foreground and weaker and lighter as it goes into the distance. Remember: warm, strong colours come forwards and cool, pale colours recede.

# EXERCISE: REFLECTIONS

## STILL WATER

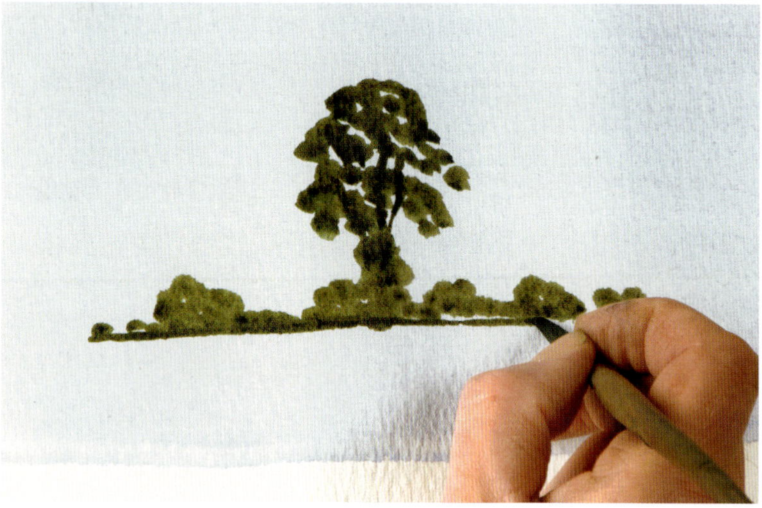

**1.** Paint a flat wash (see Sky and land) for the background and let it dry completely. Use a No. 8 round brush to make a few daubs and blobs of a mix of Hooker's green and burnt sienna for a tree (see Trees and foliage). Add some bushy blobs at each side and make a fairly straight line at the base for the edge of the water.

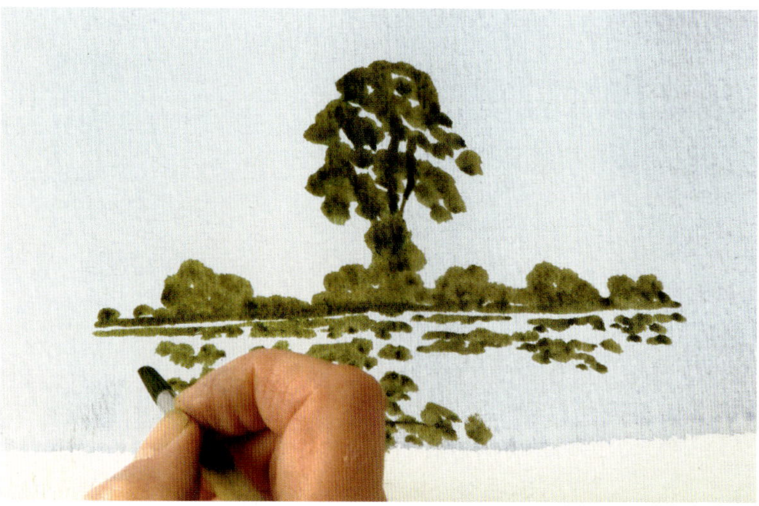

**2.** The secret of painting still reflections is to invert what's above the water, while leaving parts of the underwash showing through to break up the solidity of the reflected objects. If your viewpoint is close to the surface of the water the reflections are going to be a little longer than the actual trees, coming out further towards the foreground, while remaining as wide as the originals. Don't try to make an exact copy in the water.

## MOVING WATER

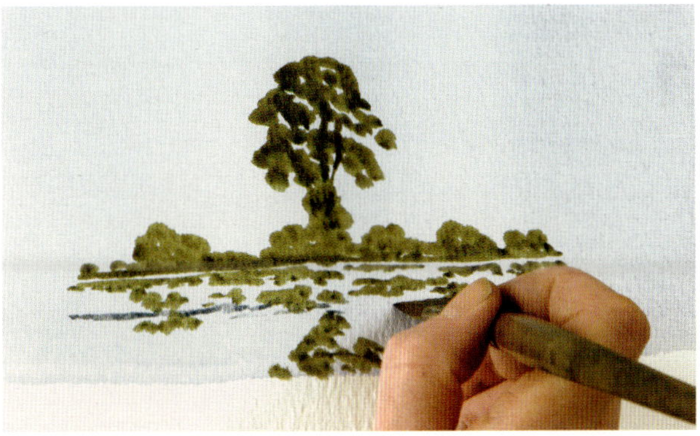

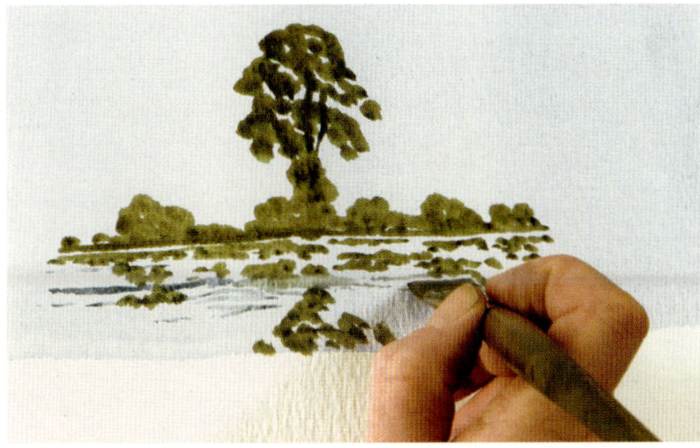

**1.** Use the same technique to paint the trees and bushes; this time break up the reflections a bit more and allow to dry.

**2.** Use a flat wash brush to stroke some ripples in a strong ultramarine wash to show the movement of the water.

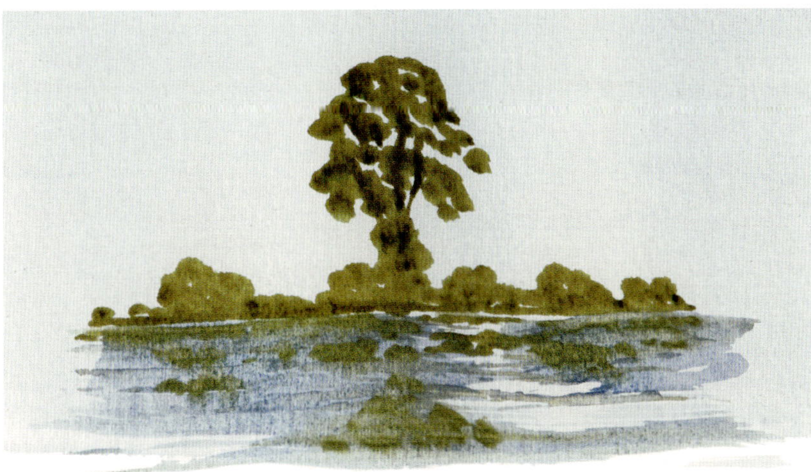

**3.** Stroke a diluted blue wash over the reflections, making the movement of waves and ripples and leaving the underwash to show as highlights here and there. Add a few stronger ripples, and there you have moving water.

# Lakeside view

This view of Coniston Water in the English Lake District is slightly more difficult than the last project – but not scarily so. It's a view from John Ruskin's house, and looking at this you can understand why he never wanted to leave the place. The painting combines the basic themes of sky and land with the step-by-step exercises in this project to create a complex finished picture.

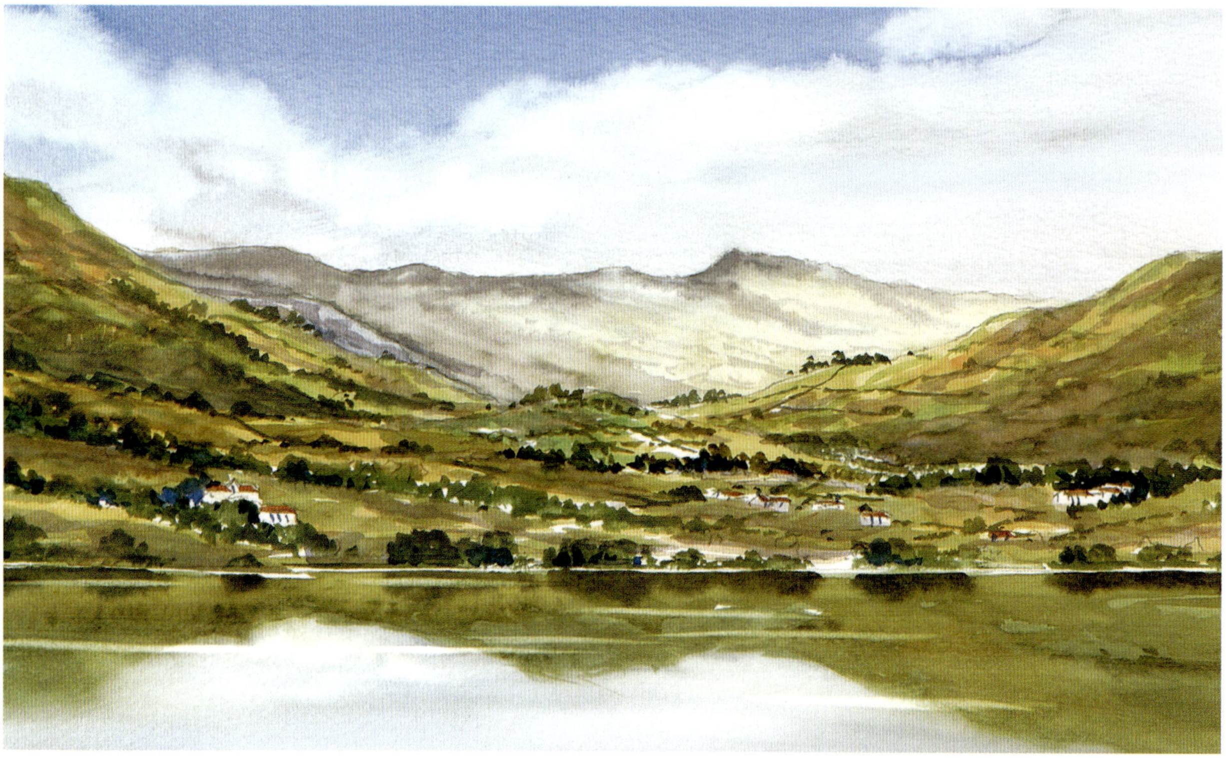

### PRELIMINARY DRAWING

The drawing here takes up only the middle third of the paper, from the tops of the mountains to the edge of the lake – the reflections will be based on the results of painting the scene on land. I've indicated just a few houses and the darkest clumps of trees here and there.

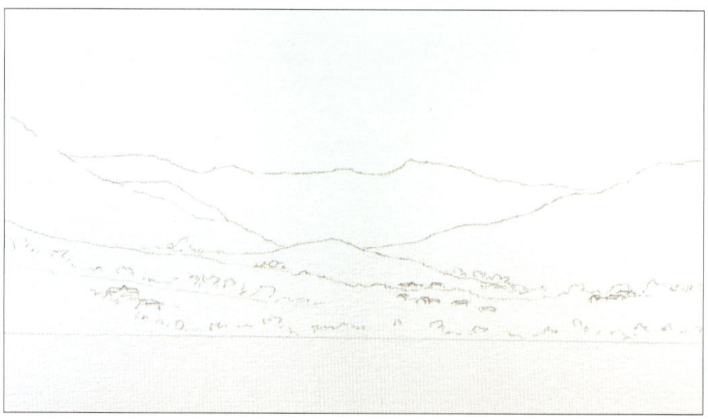

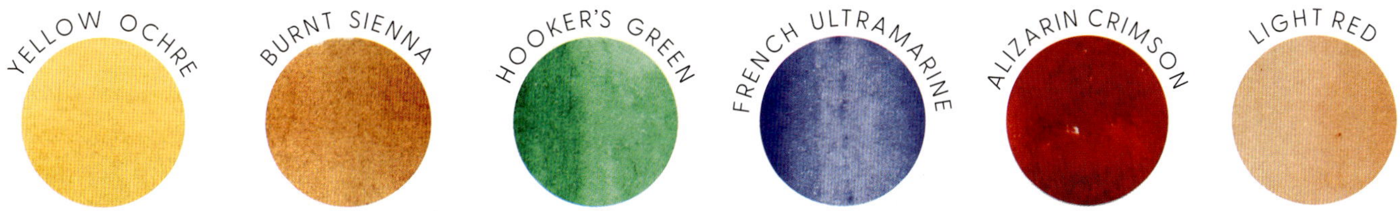


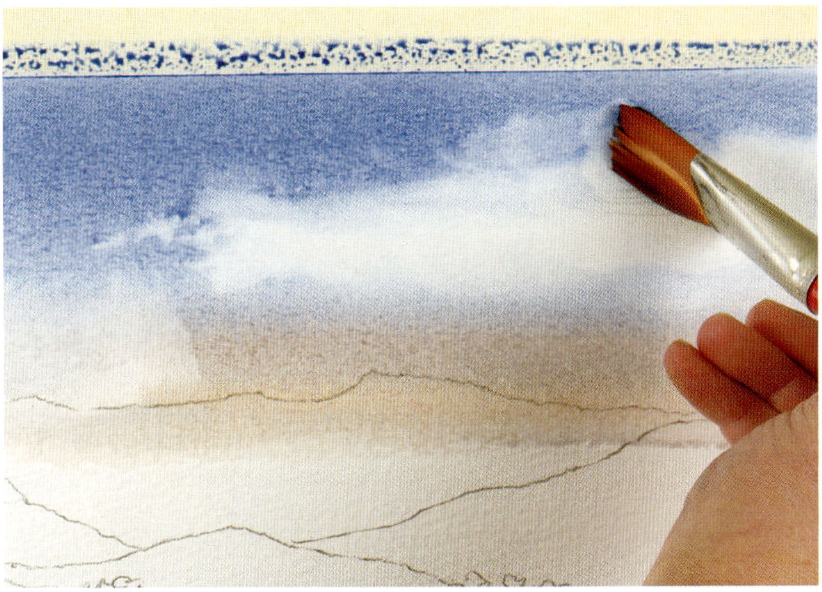

**STEP 1**

Wet the sky area with clean water, then use a 38mm (1½in) flat brush to stroke a wash of yellow ochre with a little alizarin crimson into the bottom third. Then work down from the top with ultramarine to make a variegated wash. Squeeze out the brush and suck out the paint to make soft clouds before adding a few cloud shadows in the white areas with a watery mix of ultramarine and burnt sienna.

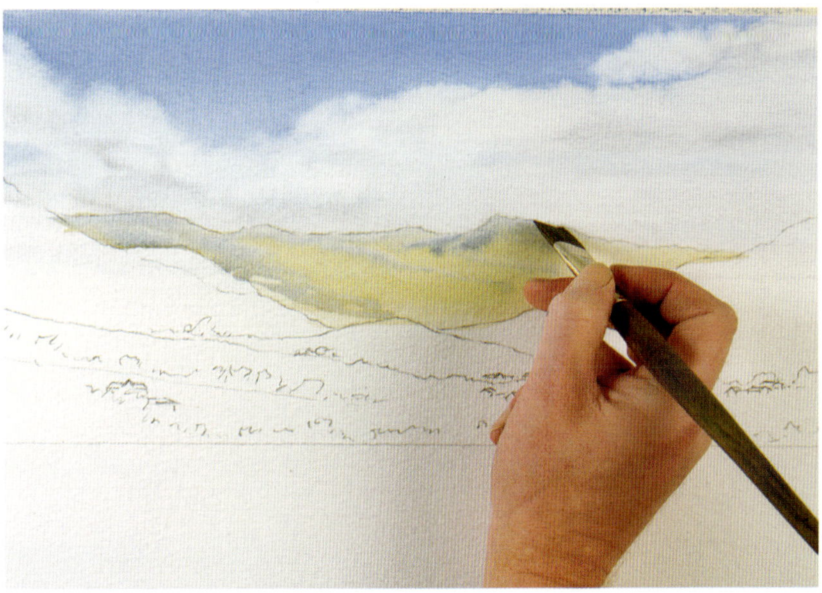

**STEP 2**

With a 19mm (¾in) wash brush block in the most distant mountains with diluted yellow ochre. While they are still wet, lay a watery mix of ultramarine and burnt sienna on top, allowing the yellow to show through in places. Leave this for a while to dry.

Don't make the distant hills too strong. Use a fainter colour to indicate tonal recession.

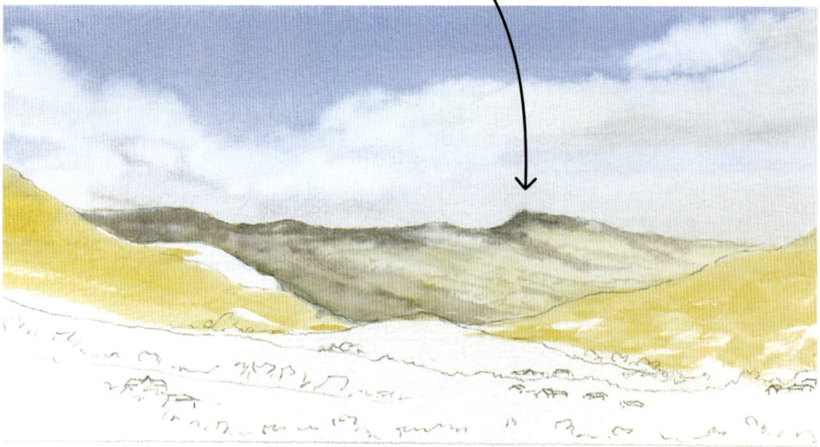

**STEP 3**

Stroke a slightly stronger wash of yellow ochre into the mountains on the left and right, leaving some white areas, and allow this to dry. Go back to the now dry distant central mountains and follow the contours with a darker shadow mix of ultramarine and burnt sienna, using a No. 8 round brush.

**STEP 4**

Block in the small area on the left between the two ranges with the same colour. Now mix Hooker's green and yellow ochre with lots of water and stroke this on with the larger wash brush – once again, don't go over all the first wash, and let some of the white paper still show through. While this is wet, warm it up in the same way with a watery wash of burnt sienna. Allow everything to dry just a little.

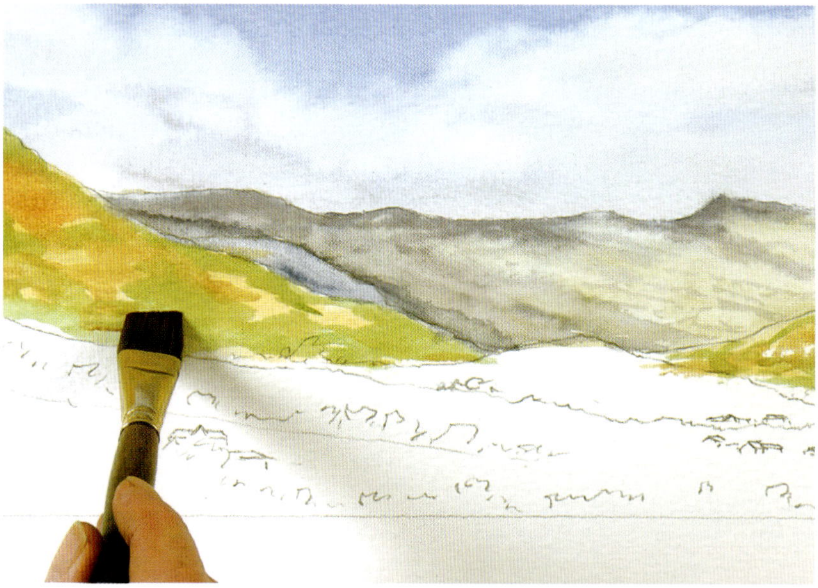

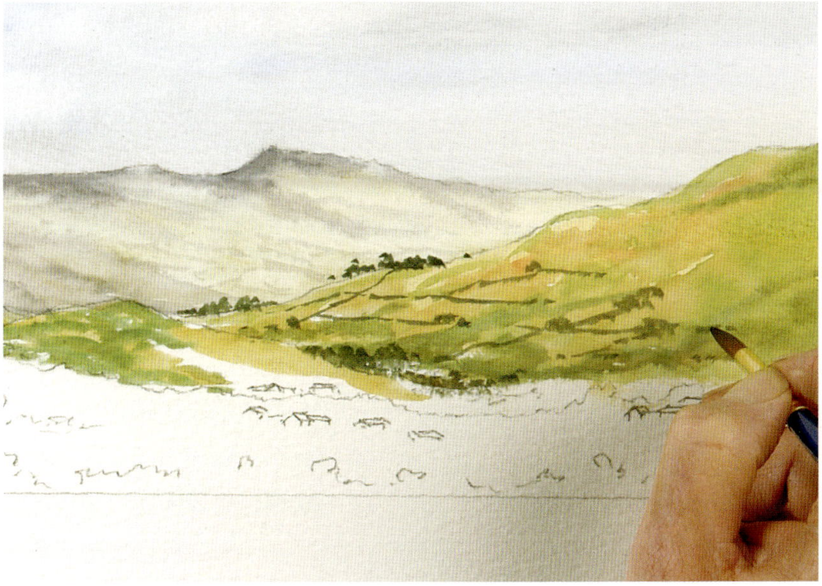

**STEP 5**

Start the hills and fields in the middle distance with the yellow ochre and Hooker's green and burnt sienna washes used before. Add a touch of ultramarine to the mix and use the No. 8 brush to put in some woodlands and boundaries for the field shapes – these follow the contours of the ground and have no verticals or horizontals. Bring the green and sienna mix into the nearest hills, again leaving some white areas.

*Make the tree 'blobs' different sizes to add variety. Dab and stipple them on.*

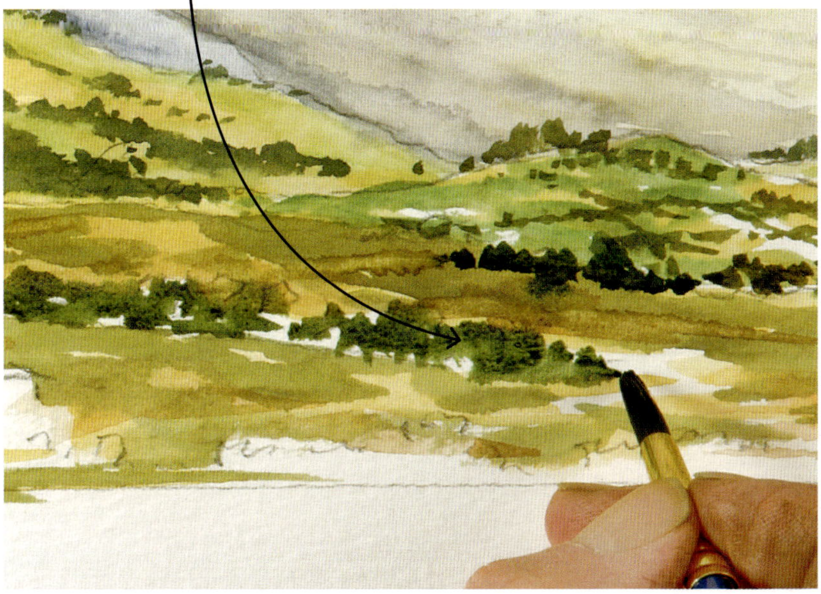

**STEP 6**

Come into the foreground with the yellow and green and sienna washes, using the larger wash brush; go around the buildings to give yourself the option of leaving them white. While this is wet, use the No. 8 round brush and a mix of Hooker's green and light red for the nearest woodlands, bringing them down to the shoreline. Use a darker mix of Hooker's green and burnt sienna for the trees around and behind the buildings.

**STEP 7**

While these washes are drying, put in literally just a few tiny strokes of light red for the roofs, leaving the white underneath – and there are the buildings with a minimum of fuss. A touch of ultramarine around some of the buildings, but not all, darkens the greens and makes each building stand out more. Allow to dry completely.

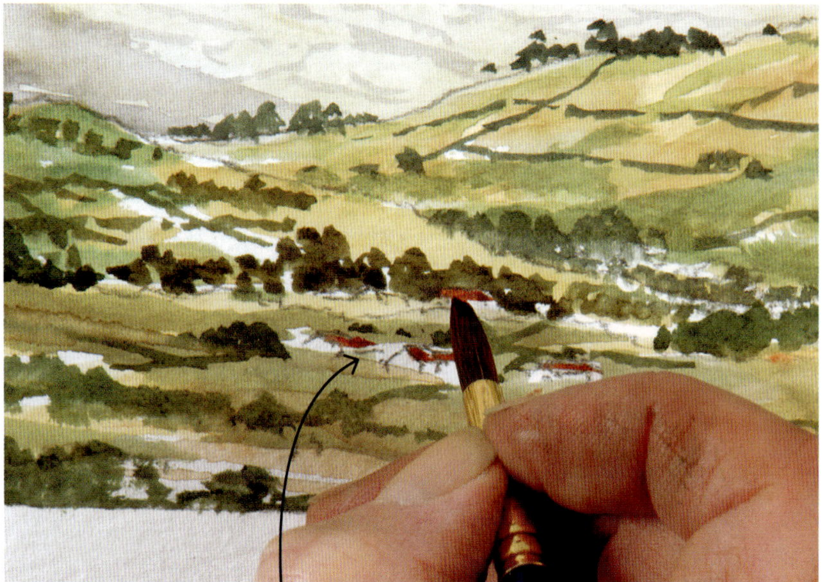

*These buildings are a long way off. You don't need to see sash windows and net curtains! They are just blocks.*

**STEP 8**

Now for the scary bit. Make up a mix of ultramarine and alizarin crimson with no more than a touch of burnt sienna, using lots of water, for a purple shadow colour. Use the smaller wash brush to put the shadows across the hills and into the valleys. You have to be quick and brave here – if you prevaricate or mess around you'll disturb the washes underneath, so use big, simple diagonal strokes for this.

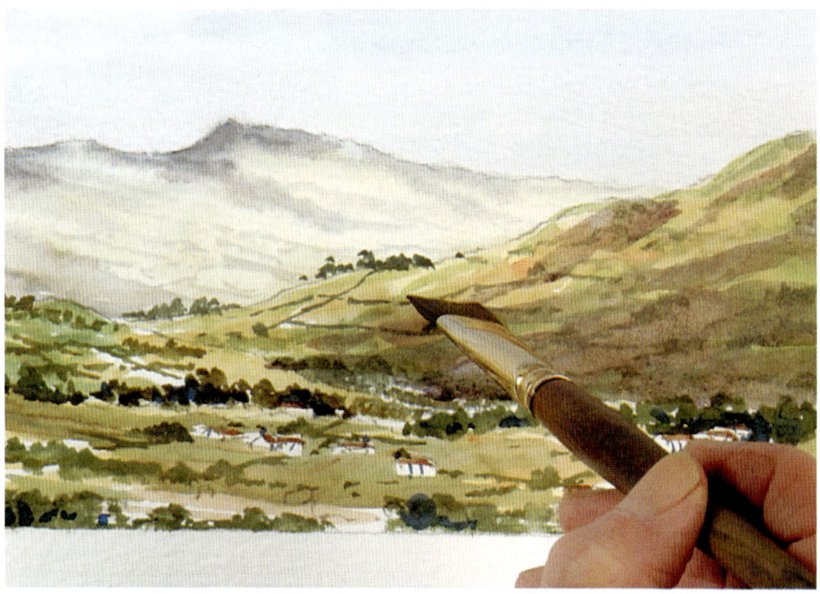

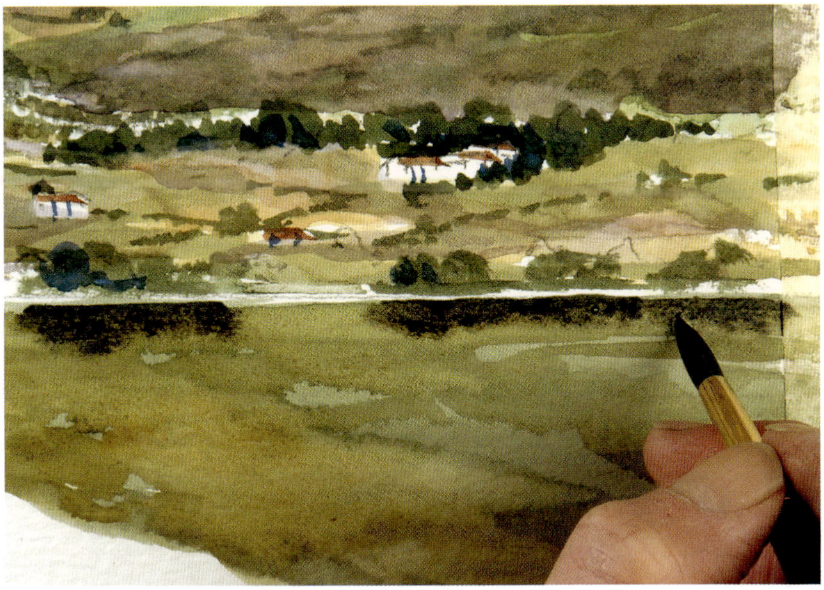

### STEP 9

Start the water with the reflections of the land, using the Hooker's green and burnt sienna mix again. Don't aim for a perfect reproduction, rather match the big shapes from above, leaving a narrow white strip between the land and the water. While this is wet tap on a little yellow ochre, then with the No. 8 brush add ultramarine to the green mix for the groups of trees near the shoreline. Make sure this is dry before going on to ...

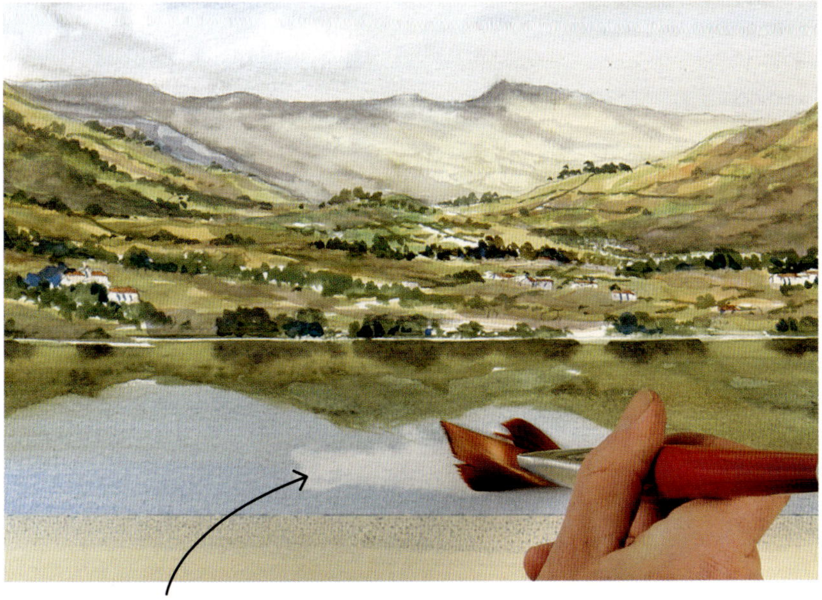

*Remember, the water still needs to be wet as you are taking out. Don't spend too long on this.*

### STEP 10

... the reflection of the sky. Use the larger wash brush to stroke on a very quick wash of watery ultramarine, then rinse and squeeze out the smaller wash brush to suck out lines reflecting the clouds: for smaller shafts of light use the tip of the brush. And voilà – a still lake with a vista of mountains reflected in it.

# The sea

Just as with lakes, painting the sea doesn't mean simply putting a series of washes on the paper to represent a stretch of water. In a seascape it's all the other features that make the scene come to life – sea, shore, dunes, harbours, boats and seabirds all combine to create the atmosphere. And, of course, taking a sketchbook and some pencils and paints makes a visit to the seaside even more interesting.

**REFERENCE SKETCH**
This simple sketch uses just a few washes to establish the horizon line and the basic colours of the scene.

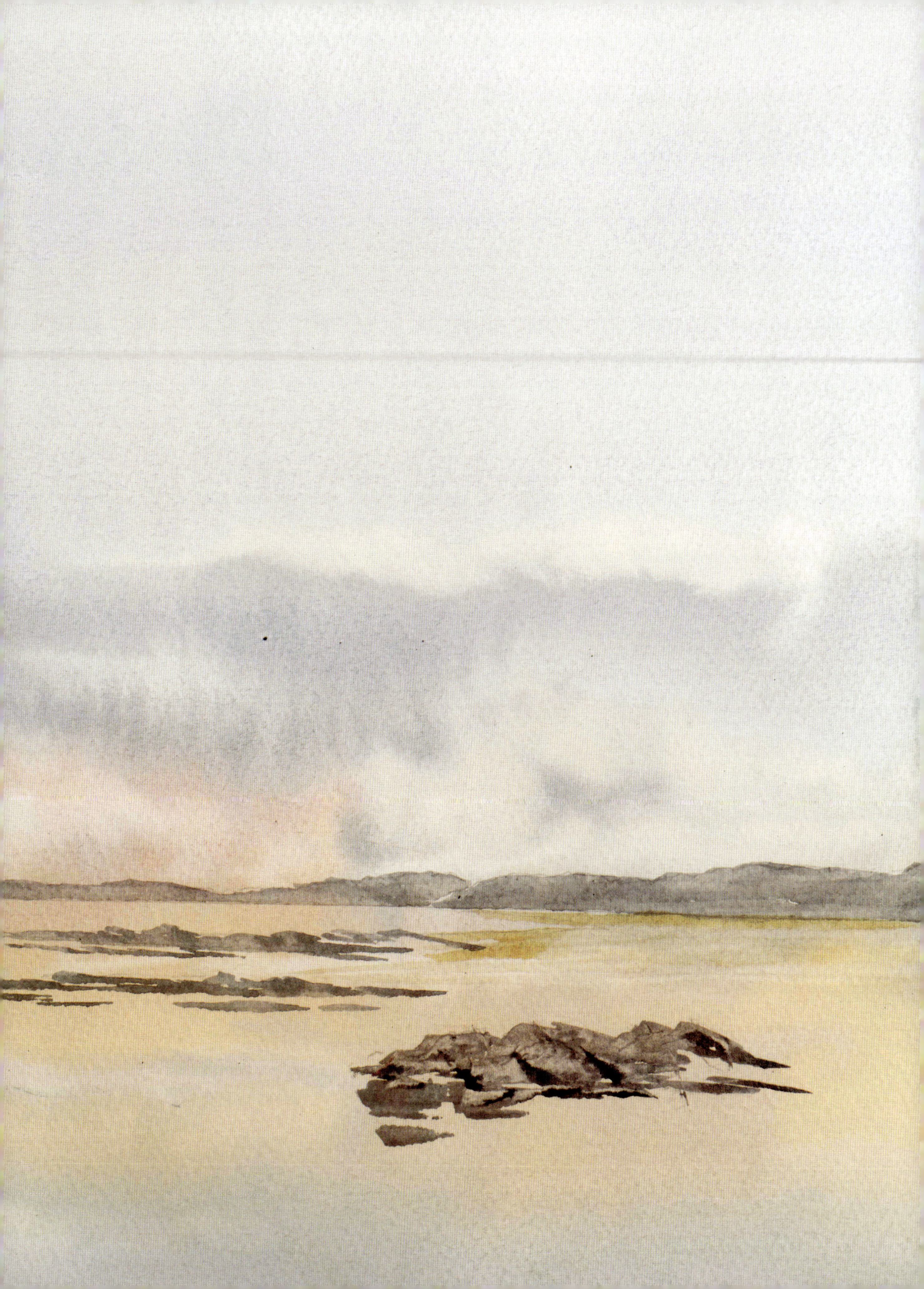

## EXERCISE: HIGHLIGHTS AND WAVE TOPS

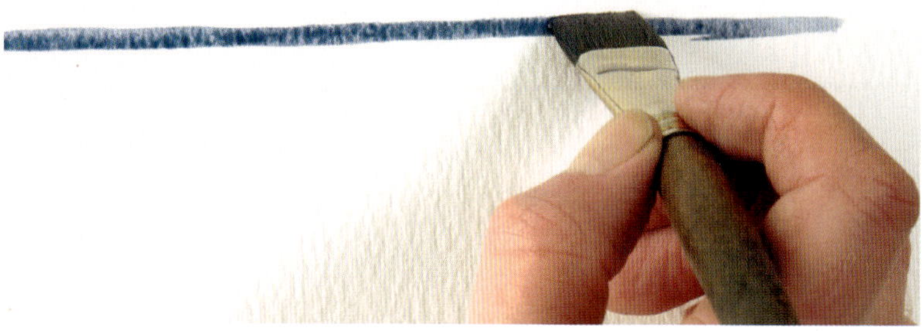

1. Let's start painting the sea with a fairly simple little exercise that gets some life into the surface as the sea comes in to the shore. Make up a mix of ultramarine with tiny touches of Hooker's green and burnt sienna to warm it up. Use the tip of a 19mm (¾in) brush to stroke a line across dry paper.

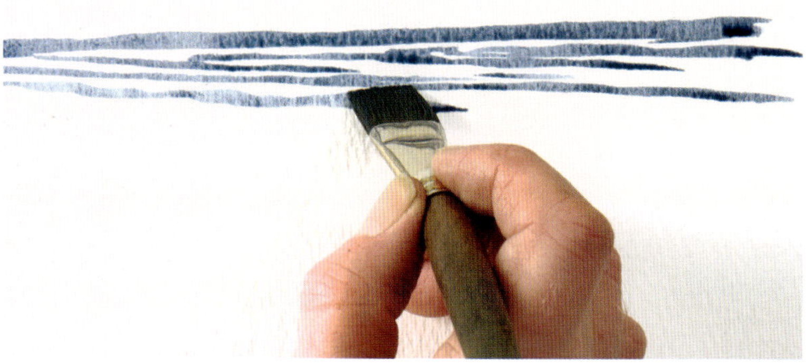

2. Go back and forth across the paper, making sure you leave squiggly bits of white paper showing through for the highlights and 'white horses'. Press a little harder to get slightly wider lines.

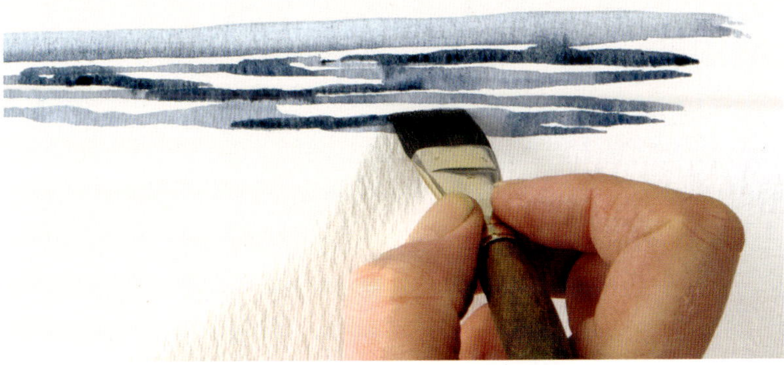

**3.** To get some sense of distance, paint the furthest areas of the sea using a diluted wash of the same colours. Let this first wash dry out, then make up a darker version of the mix and stroke this just under the white highlights to give a sense of motion.

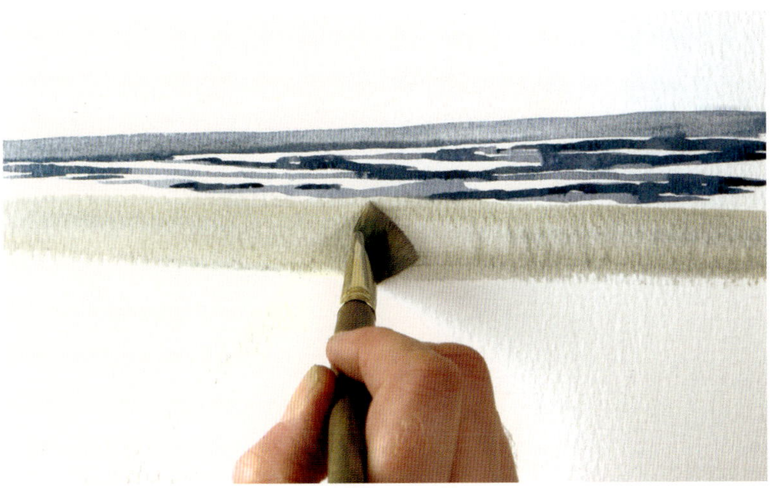

**4.** Now you need to put the sea into context. When the washes are completely dry, make up a watery wash of a beach colour and paint in a strip of beach that meets the edge of the sea.

## EXERCISE: MOVEMENT IN THE SEA

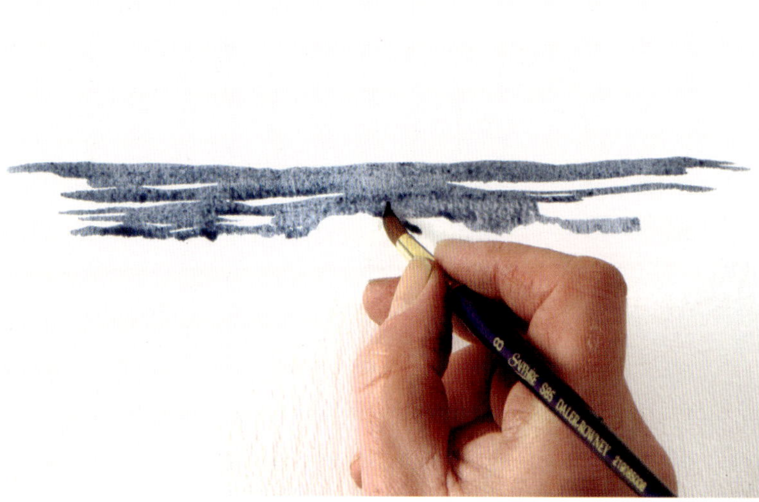

**1.** To add some movement to a fairly simple large expanse of sea, start with the same sea wash used on the previous pages. Using a No. 8 brush, apply this quickly, again without wetting the paper beforehand. Start in the distance and bring the wash forwards, using the point of the brush to form the tops of the waves.

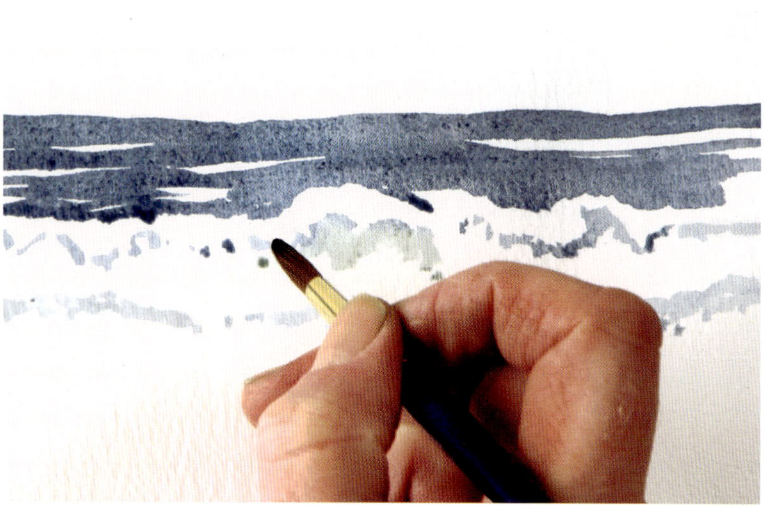

**2.** As you come closer to the shore, make the mix a little stronger. Then add a touch more Hooker's green and plenty of water and start to stroke in some shadow in the foam under the wave tops, still leaving plenty of white paper.

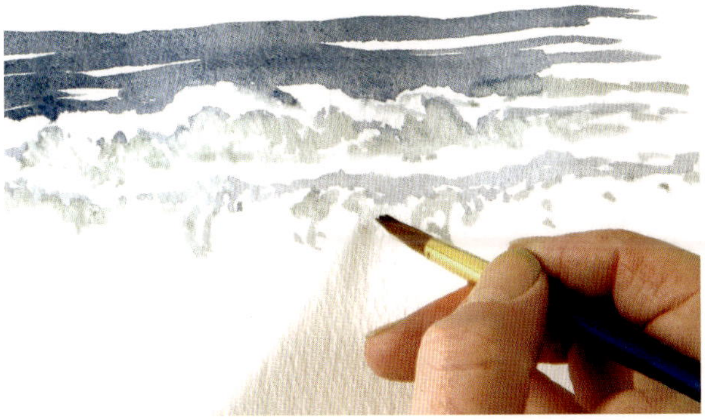

**3.** As you bring the shadows in the foam towards the shore, vary the strength of the washes to bring in both darker and lighter areas. Keep all the washes very watery and make sure you don't overwork the paint – less is more here.

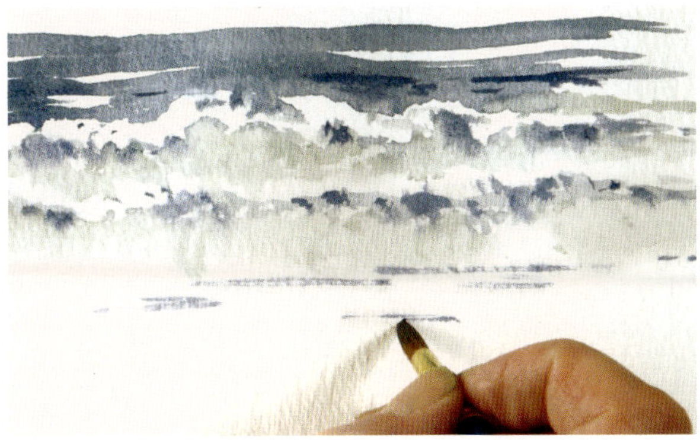

**4.** Still keeping everything simple and using the same mix, add a few horizontal lines of a fairly strong wash for the water on the shore. As with the shadows in the foam, use a very watery wash to fill in this area, but again leave some patches of white paper.

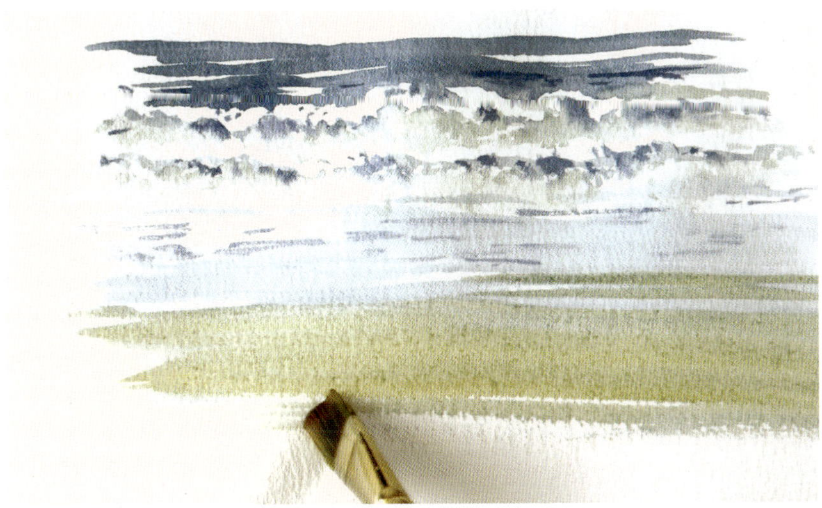

**5.** While this is still wet, switch to a 19mm (¾in) wash brush and use both the flat and the side to stroke on a light wash of yellow ochre for the beach. Blend this lightly with the blue, aiming for freshness, and stop sooner rather than later.

# Rocky coastline

This project is mainly just big washes, the sky and the ground. The predominant features are the rocks. When scraping out the rocks, the paint should still be wet and the card held at an angle to move the paint.

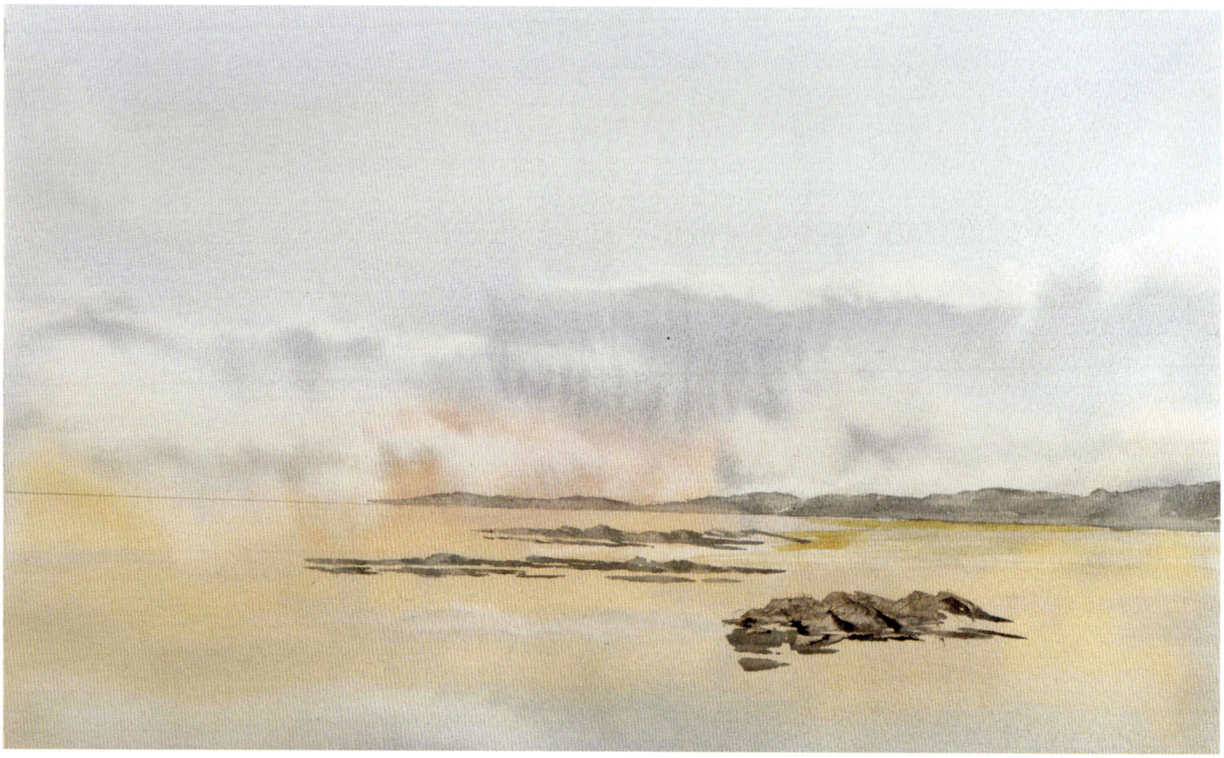

### PRELIMINARY DRAWING

This simple outline for the painting establishes the positions of the rocky outcrops as they recede into the distance. The horizon line is well below the middle of the paper, and the distant sand dunes stop short of the left edge of the composition to avoid too much regularity.

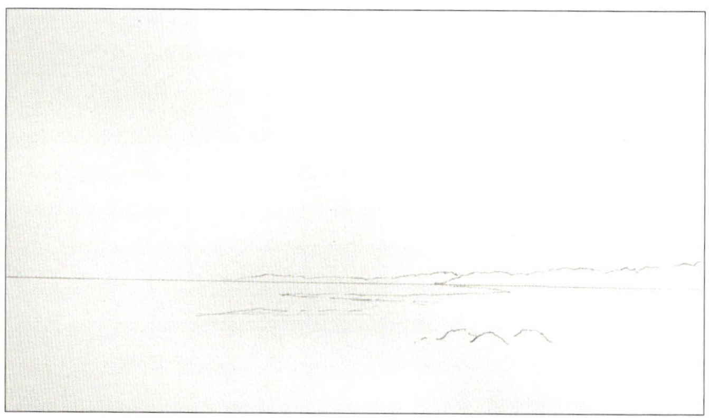

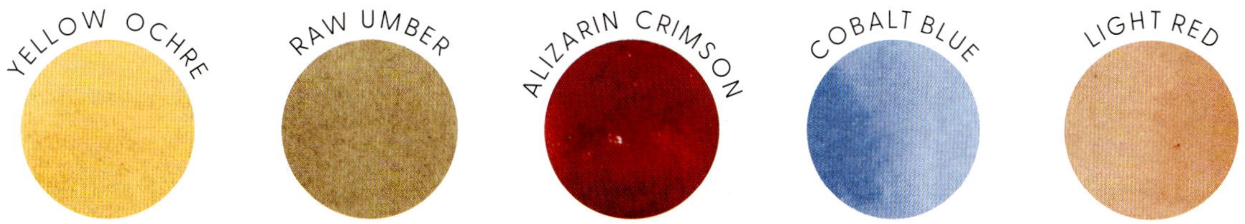


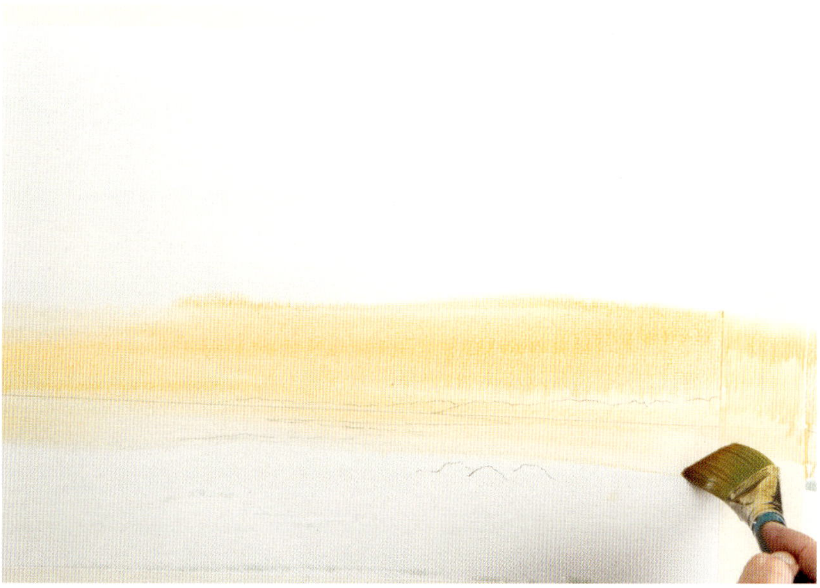

**STEP 1**

Here I'm using a little bit of cobalt blue, which is slightly milder than ultramarine, for the sky. With lots of water, fill the entire painting with sky using a 38mm (1½in) wash brush, all the way down to the bottom. Mix a little bit of yellow ochre with light red and plenty of water. Paint over the bottom half of the picture, leaving touches of the sky showing through.

**STEP 2**

Add a touch of alizarin crimson in the centre. Then a slightly stronger wash of cobalt blue to the top and bottom of the painting.

**STEP 3**

Now, with more cobalt blue, this time mixed with light red, paint some loose strokes across the sky. Add some in the sea as reflections as well. Let that run ever so slightly, mopping up a bit if needed.

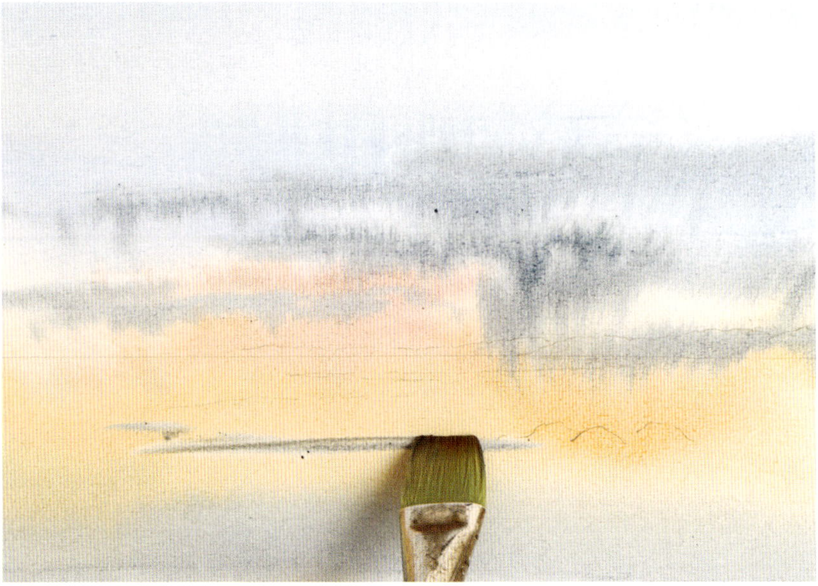

**STEP 4**

Wash the brush, squeeze out, and suck a few clouds from the darker mix, including the lines in the sea. This creates a lovely soft effect for the background. Leave that to dry thoroughly before carrying on.

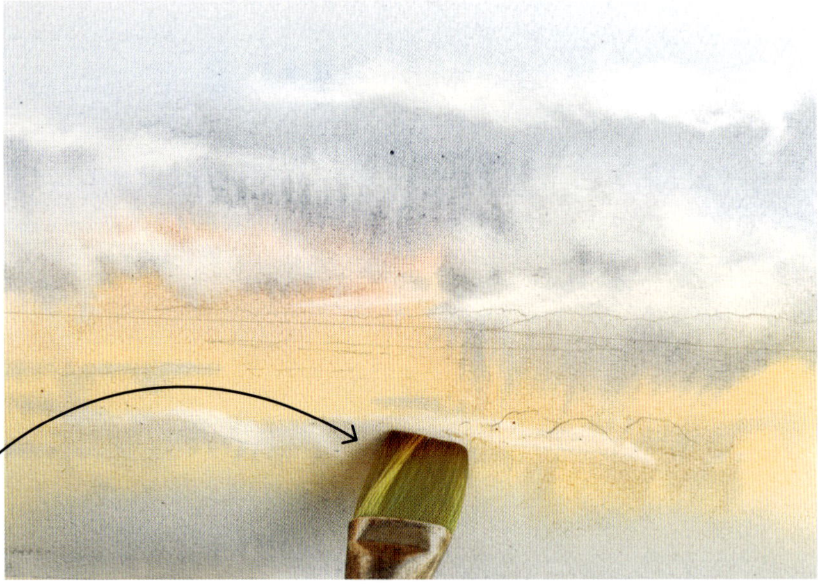

*Make sure your brush is damp for taking out, not dry!*

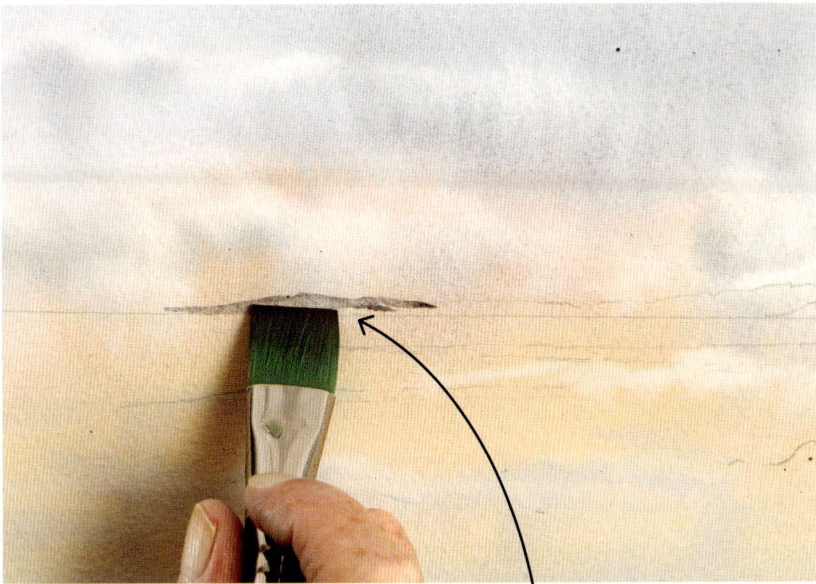

The sharp edge of your brush will give you a lovely straight line so make sure that it is flat by squeezing it between your fingers before you start.

**STEP 5**

Because of the time of day, everything is more or less silhouetted. So, with a 19mm (¾in) flat brush and a mixture of cobalt blue and light red, just fill in the pencil lines. Do this carefully to make sure that it stays flat and level at the bottom of these sand dunes.

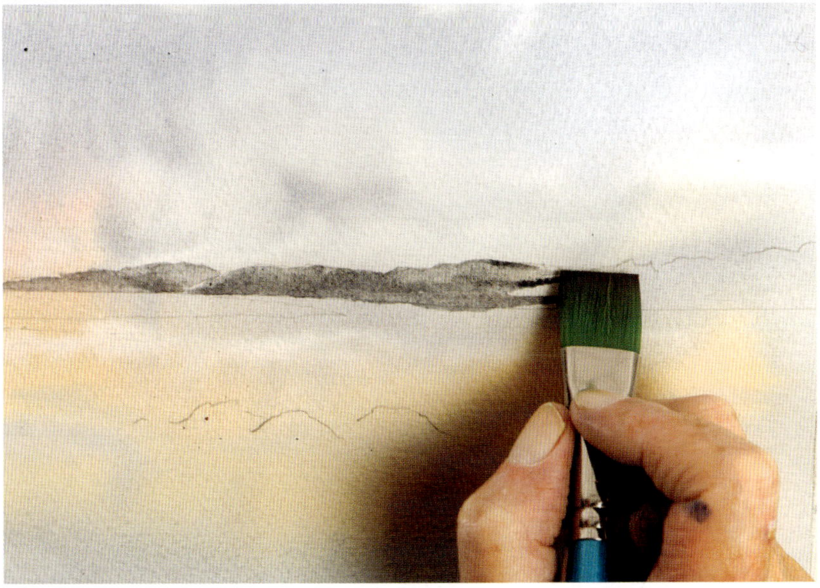

**STEP 6**

Use slightly less water in the mix for the closer ones. Leave a tiny sliver of under paper showing through in between the two clumps of sand dunes, again keeping sharp and flat to the base. I'm not going to take any light out of those – I'm leaving those as they are.

Keep in mind your recession so the clumps of rocks are smaller and less impressive the further away they go.

**STEP 7**
Likewise for the couple of rocky outcrops. Again, a little bit of cobalt blue and light red here, but the mix is slightly stronger. Remember that these are supposed to be rocks in the middle distance, so don't make them flat along the top – they need to have a bumpy edge.

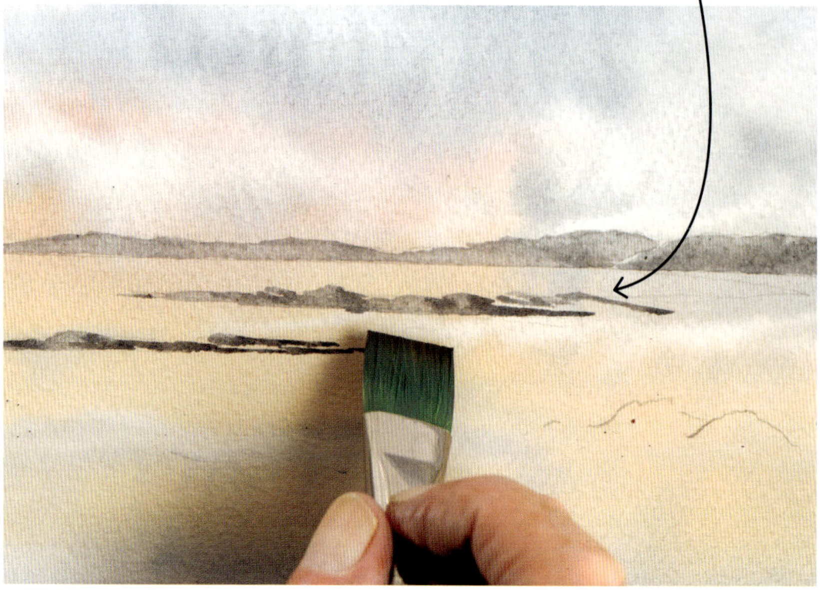

**STEP 8**
Now repeat some of that underneath where you just painted those outcrops so that you've got reflections. Then, with the same stronger mix of cobalt blue and light red, paint in those rocks in the foreground. Again, reflect slightly underneath.

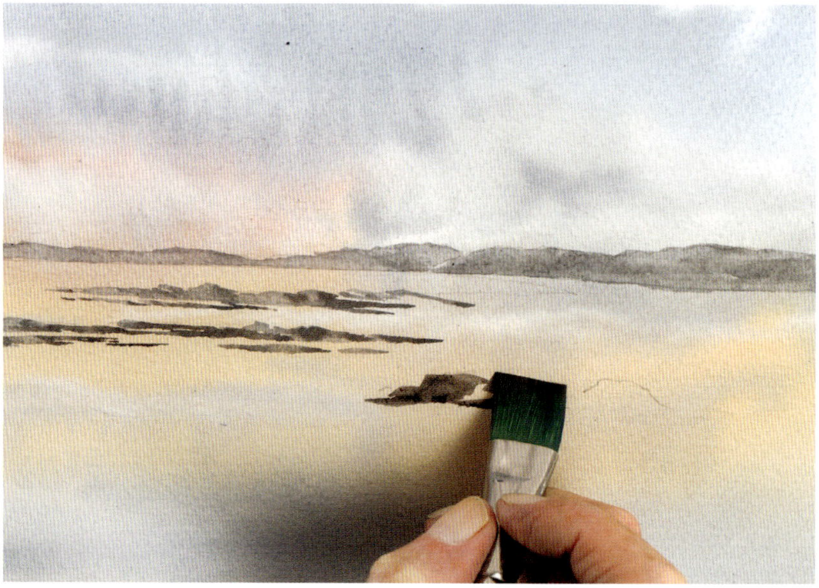

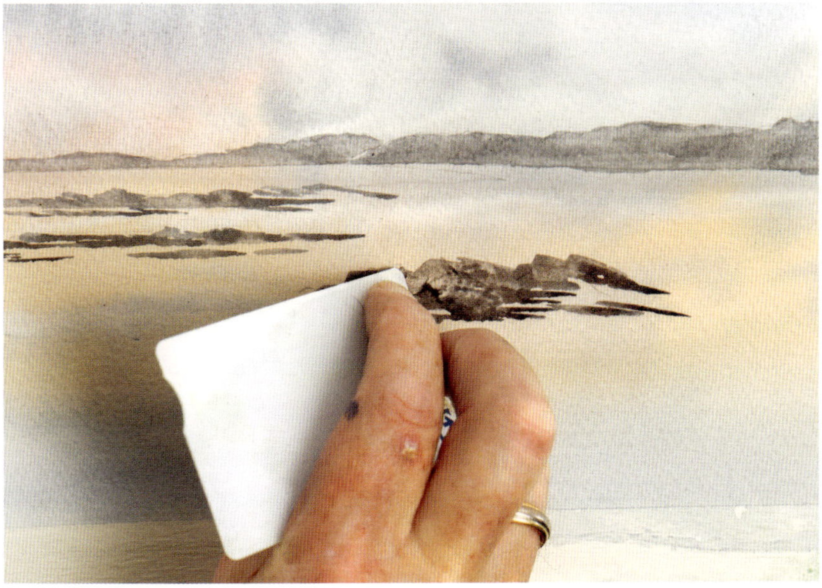

### STEP 9

Then use an old credit card to scrape across the paint on the rocks and add texture.

*Don't mess about with this process – it's a couple of very quick strokes.*

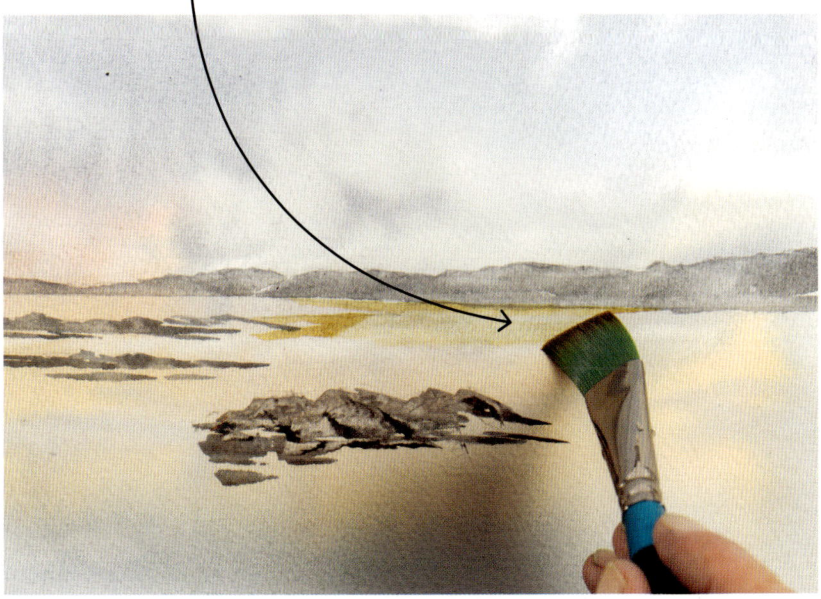

### STEP 10

And, finally, for the little bit of beach in the distance, use a little bit of raw umber mixed with yellow ochre. Once you've put the paint on, clean with a damp brush and move it across.

# Trees and foliage

If you live inland you'll need to make a journey to paint the sea, as in the last project, but no one is ever far from a tree. In this section we're going to look at autumn and summer trees, when the leaf canopy is at its strongest – and there's an extra small project that concentrates on the bare, stark outlines of winter trees.

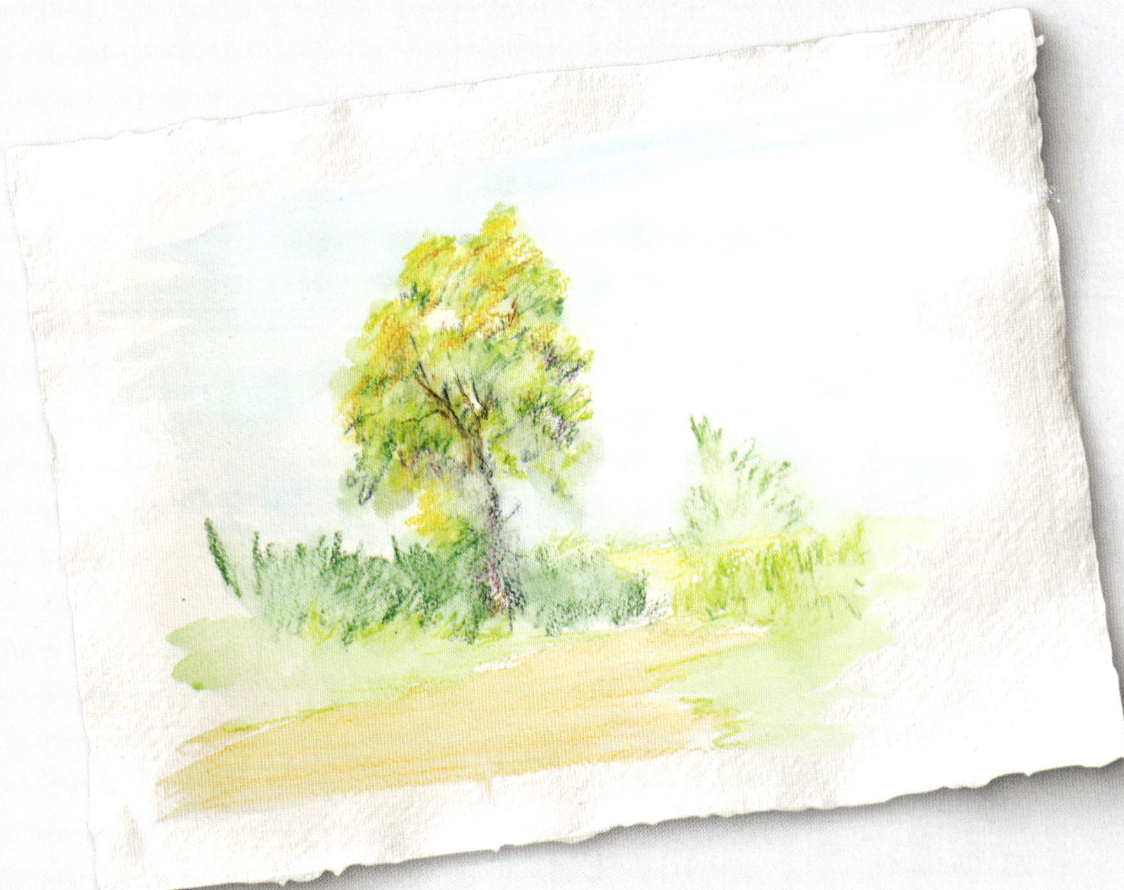

REFERENCE SKETCH
Make lots of studies of trees in your sketchbook so you have a basic reference library of shapes and leaf canopies; you can also see how trees work in different landscapes.

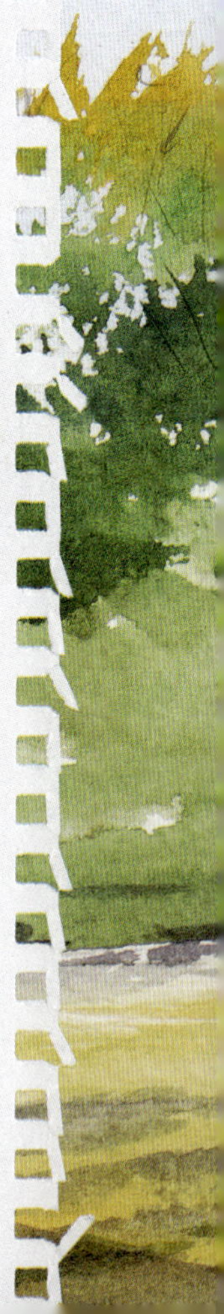

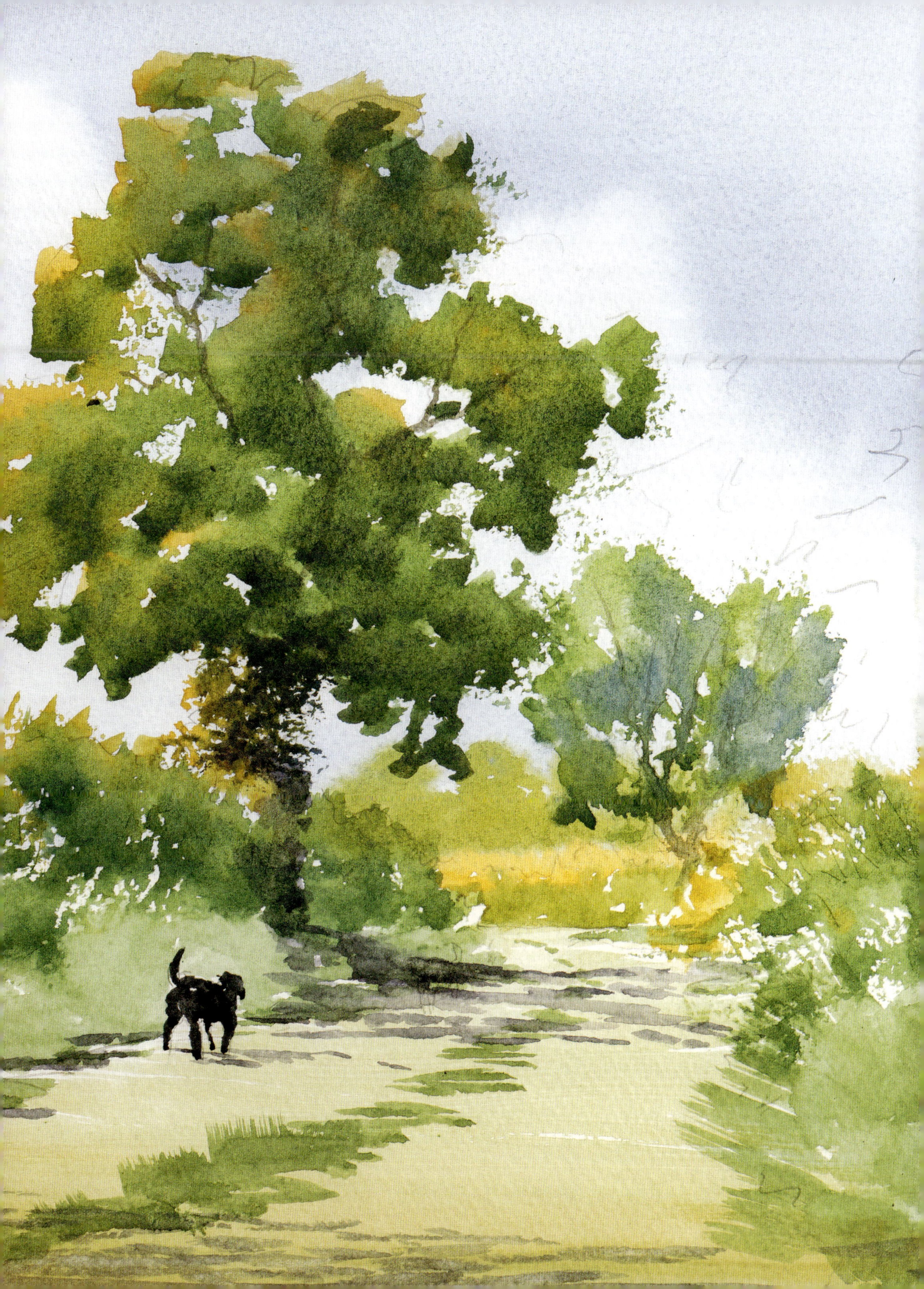

# EXERCISE: AUTUMN TREES

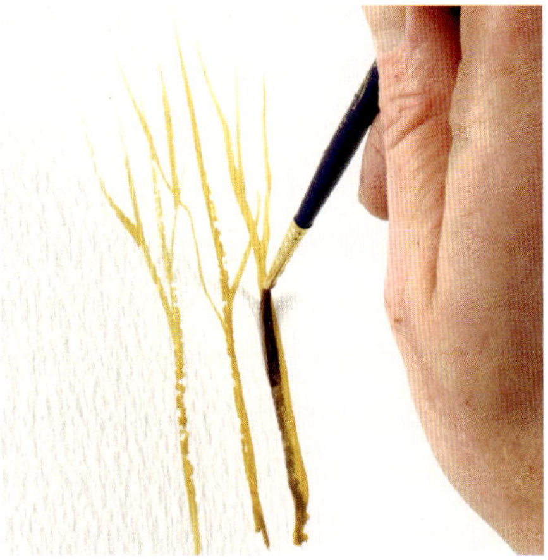

**1.** Start the trunks and main branches with yellow ochre applied with a No. 4 rigger brush. Work quickly and roughly, and don't think about detail at this stage. The light is coming from the right, so the shadows will be on the left ...

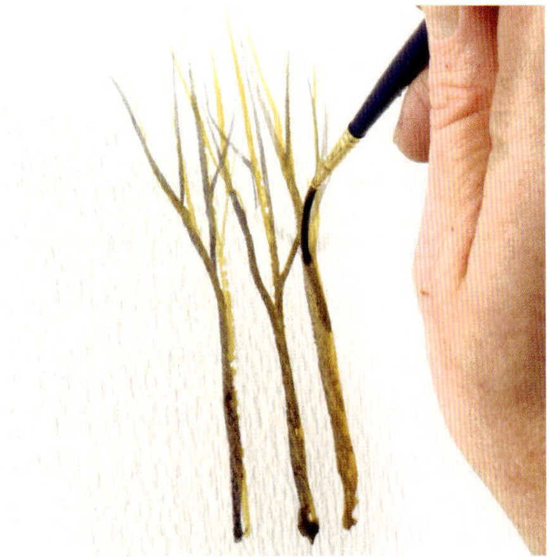

**2.** ... and these are done with a mix of ultramarine and light red on the wet ochre so the edges blend softly and give a rounded look. Go over the shadows where they take up a lot of the trunks and branches, but leave some of the yellow showing through.

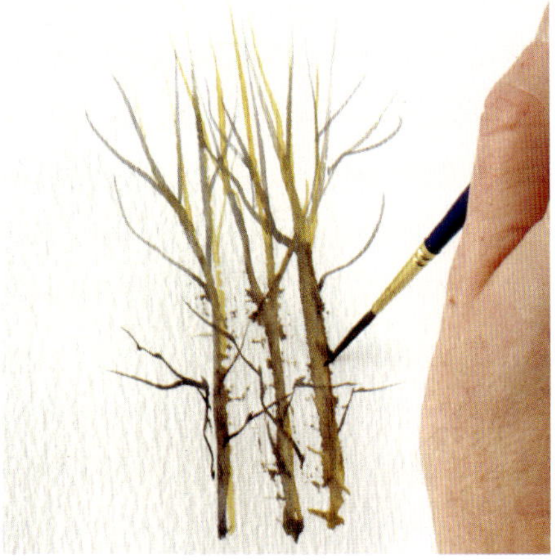

**3.** Make up a darker mix of the shadow colour and use the rigger to flick on some twigs, mainly coming out from the trunk. Don't forget to dab on a few burrs on the trunks – but, as with the twigs, don't overdo the effect.

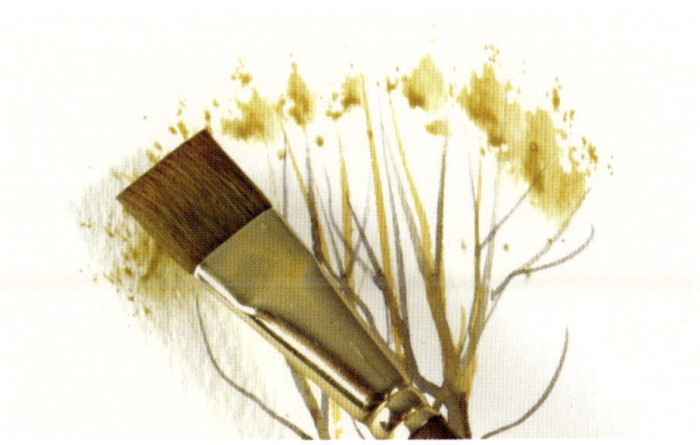

**4.** Let everything dry, then load a 19mm (¾in) wash brush with yellow ochre and get ready for some fun: hold the brush like a decorator's brush, not a pencil, and tap the flat of the brush on to the top parts of the branches to give some leaf cover. If you're pushing the bristles hard on to the paper, you should hear the metal ferrule slap down on it.

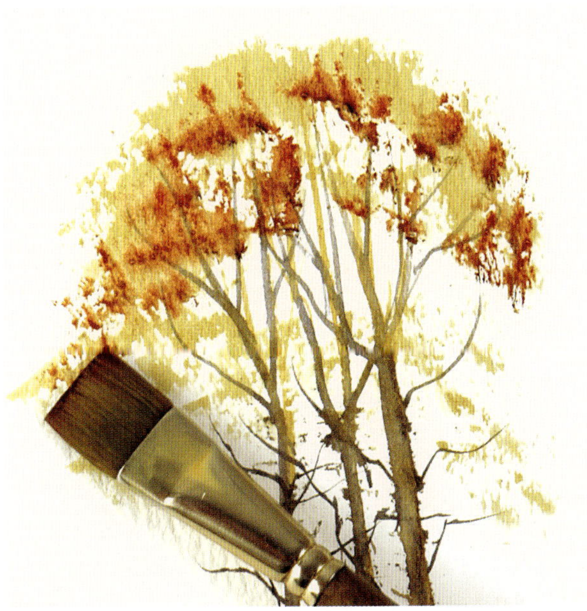

**5.** While the yellow ochre is wet, do the same with some burnt sienna, and then with the shadow mix, each time making sure that the earlier washes can be seen.

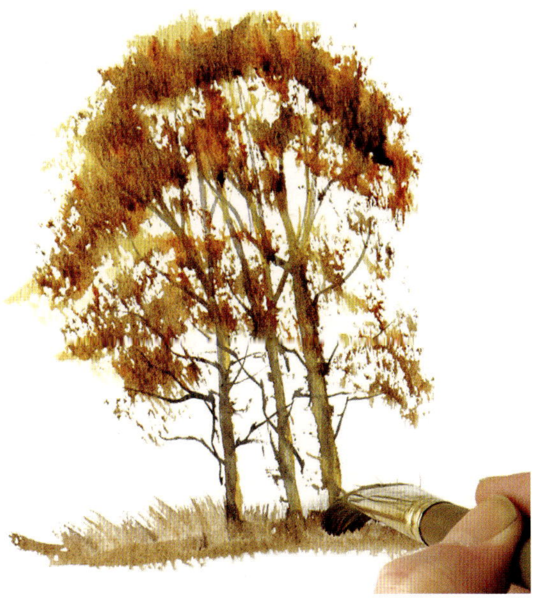

**6.** To ground the trees, use the diluted shadow mix to flick up some grass around the bases of the trunks.

# EXERCISE: SUMMER TREES

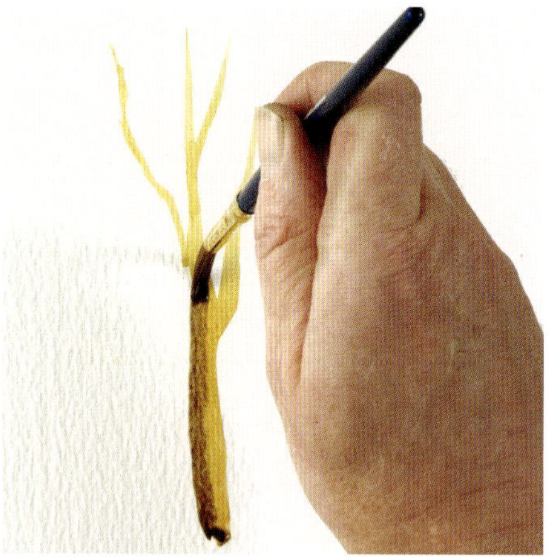

**1.** Start the trunk as you did for the autumn trees on the previous pages, using yellow ochre and a No. 8 round brush to give a broad, rough outline. While the ochre is wet, add some raw umber on the left, allowing the edges to blend.

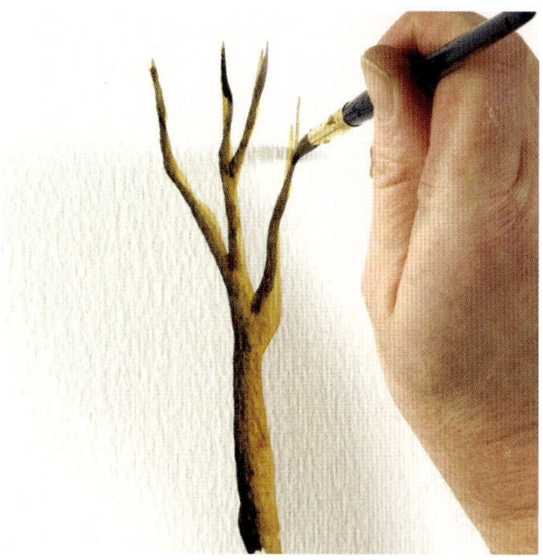

**2.** You can get an even more rounded feel on the trunk and branches by going over the wet umber with a mix of ultramarine and burnt sienna, again letting the colours blend and soften. On the lower part of the trunk, flick in a few twigs and burrs with a No. 3 rigger brush and the ultramarine and burnt sienna mix.

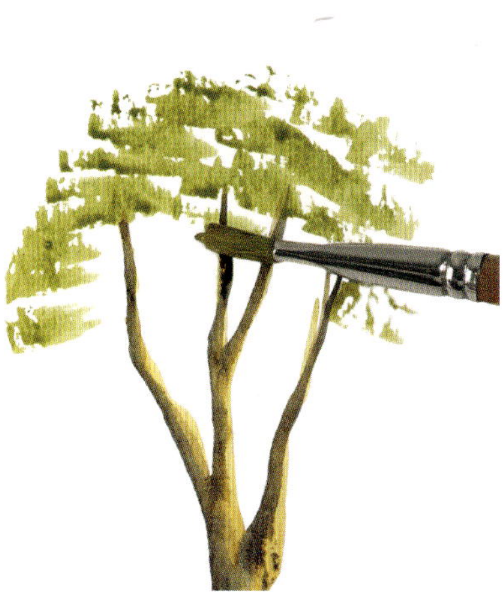

**3.** Make up a light green mix of Hooker's green and yellow ochre, and use the side of the round brush to tap this on. Resist any temptation to try to paint individual leaves – this way is far more effective (and quicker).

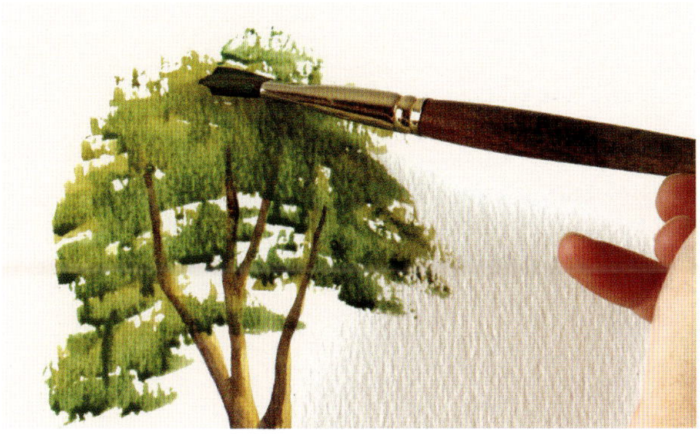

**4.** While the first green is still wet, make up a darker green mix of Hooker's green and burnt sienna and tap this on in the same way, not forgetting the leaves on the twigs lower down. Leave some of the first green to show through, and keep some gaps in the canopy.

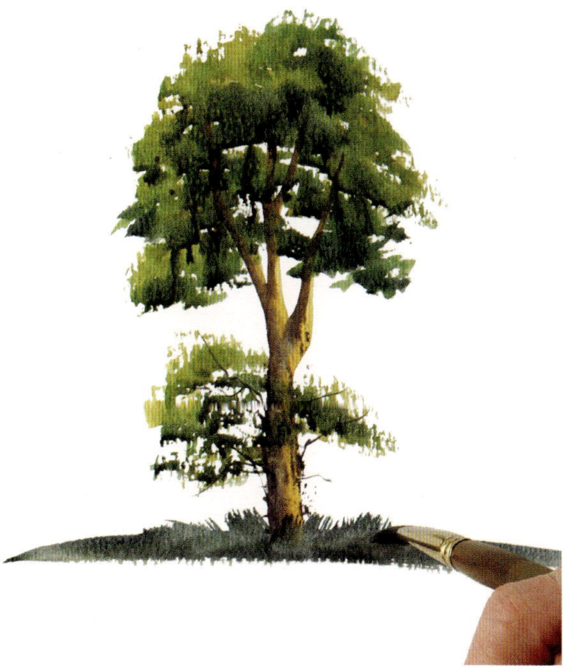

**5.** Tap on some ultramarine for the shadows in the foliage while the green washes are wet – you can make these quite dark in places. Then use a lighter wash of ultramarine to block in and flick up some grasses to ground the tree in the earth. Hey presto! You have a quickly and cleverly painted summer tree.

#### TRY IT YOURSELF

Use a simple graduated wash for the sky. Let it dry and then paint a single tree in full foliage with a few flicks of grass under the tree trailing off into the distance, creating recession.

# Countryside walk

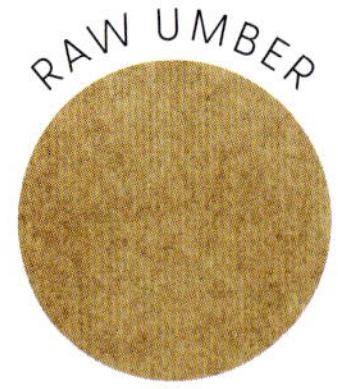


In this nice, simple little scene I've opted for a portrait (upright) format, which emphasizes the height of the main tree in the middle ground. This painting combines the techniques used for foliage in the exercises with the quick methods for painting skies and land.

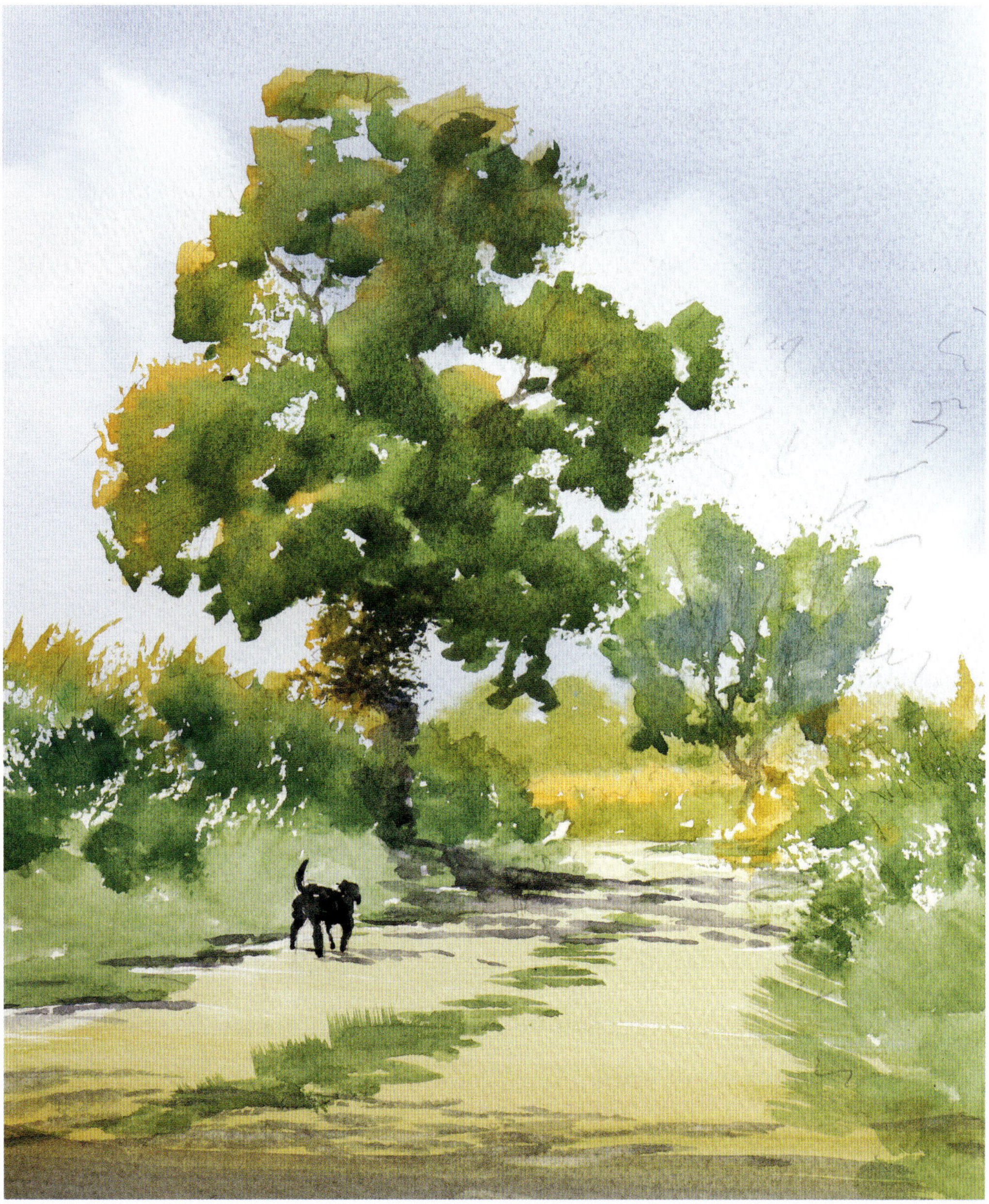

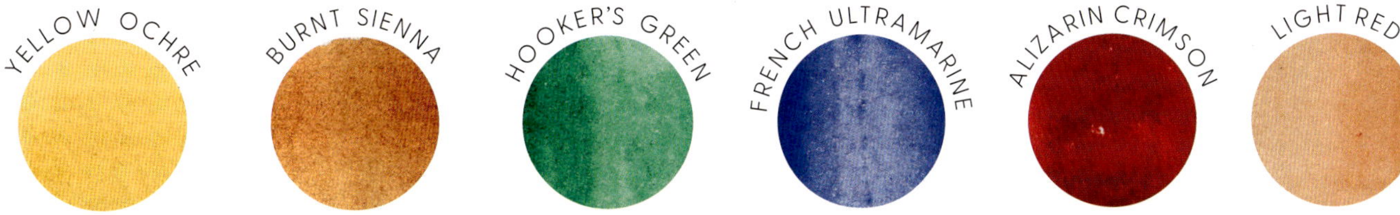


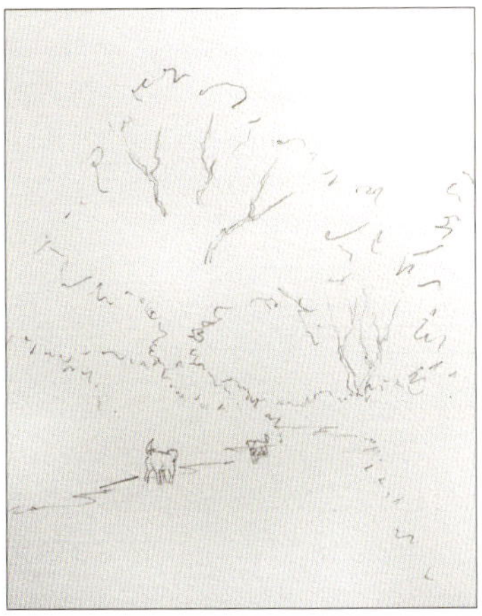

### PRELIMINARY DRAWING

Once again, the drawing is kept very simple, and is really no more than a framework for the paint. Note how the bushes get smaller as they go round the corner. I haven't drawn any of the canopy of foliage on the main tree, just the outline structure of the trunk and boughs.

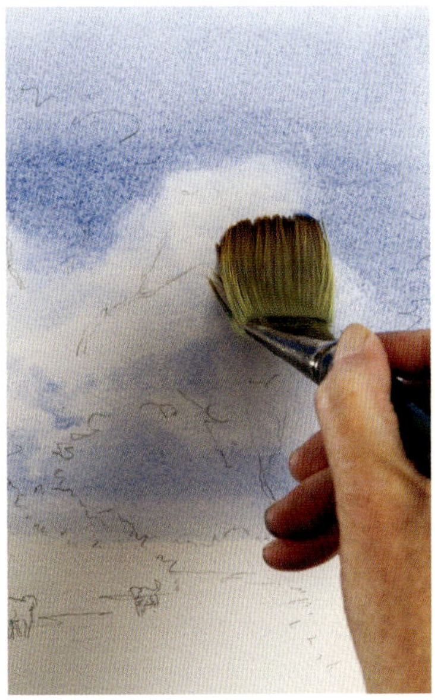

### STEP 1

Wet the paper and paint a wash of ultramarine for the sky. When you're painting trees, make sure you take the sky all the way through the trees because you want to see sky colour through gaps in the foliage, not white paper! Then take out a couple of clouds, but drop a little bit of paint back in again to create shadow within the clouds. There we go ... a very simple sky.

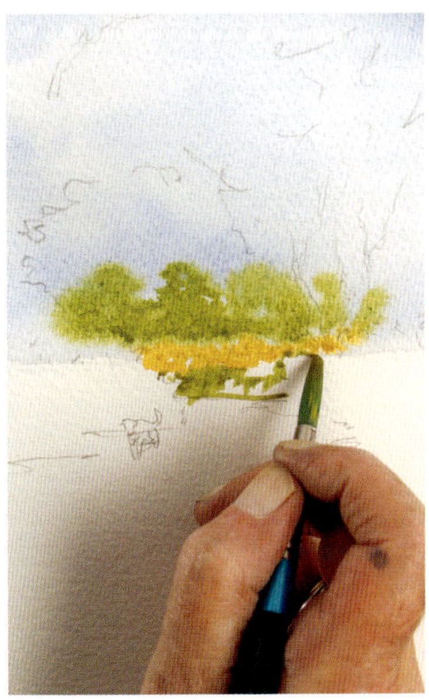

### STEP 2

While the base of the sky is still ever so slightly damp, with a No. 8 round brush use a mix of Hooker's green and a lot of yellow ochre, with plenty of water, for the tops of the distant trees and bushes. Drop yellow ochre underneath those bushes, and then back to the Hooker's green and yellow ochre mix to fill in the grasses on the other side of the path. Leave to dry.

### STEP 3

With a No. 4 rigger brush, using raw umber with a touch of French ultramarine mixed into it, pull the brush upwards to paint the boughs. For the foliage on top of that, use a fairly strong mix of Hooker's green and yellow ochre. Using the side of a No. 8 round brush, just tap on to get a rough edge. Then a touch of French ultramarine on top to add shadows. Use your fingers to soften and merge.

*The light is coming from the left, so I'm putting the darker bits to the right-hand side.*

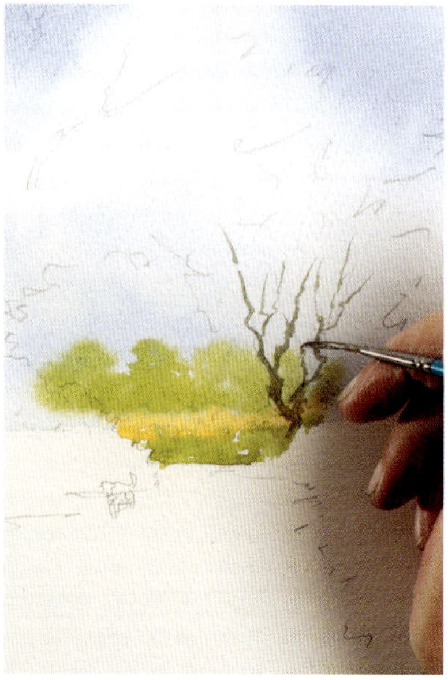

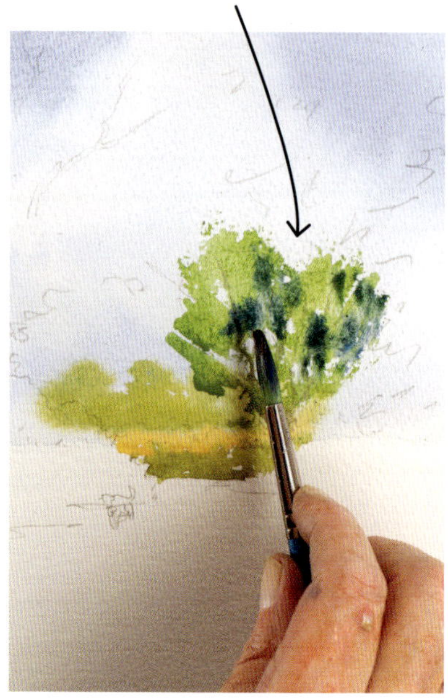

### STEP 4

Add a few boughs to the big tree using a No. 4 rigger brush before putting the foliage in. Now split a No. 8 round brush with yellow ochre and dab on to the trunk. Then the same process with a strong mix of Hooker's green and burnt sienna, followed by a touch of French ultramarine mixed with burnt Sienna. Remember that the light is coming from the left, so add darker shades on the right.

*Don't paint loads of twigs, because you're going to cover them up with the foliage! Just have a few of the major boughs.*

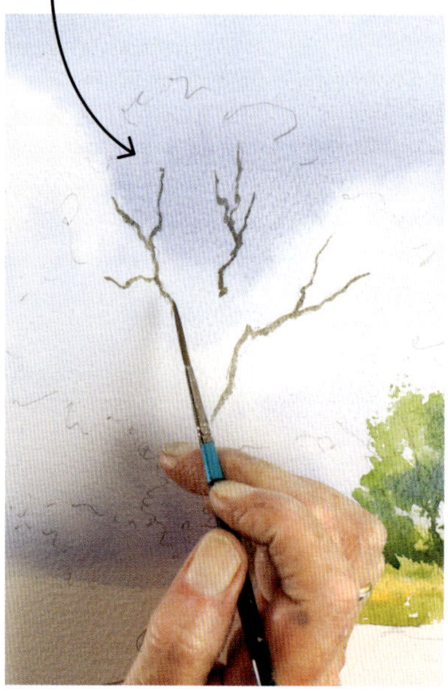

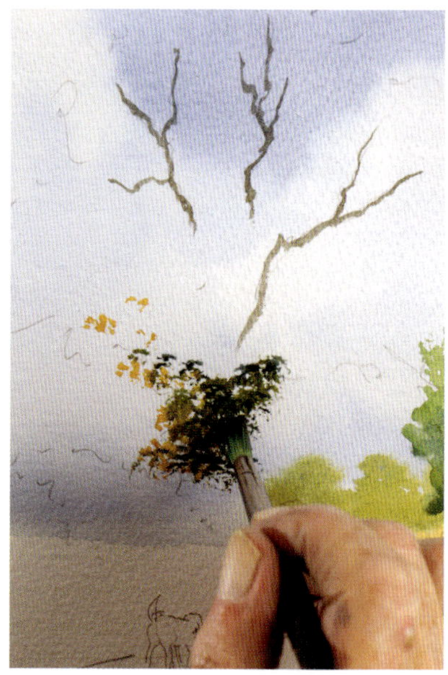

*Always think about seeing some sky through the foliage – if you fill it all in you end up with a lollipop on a stick!*

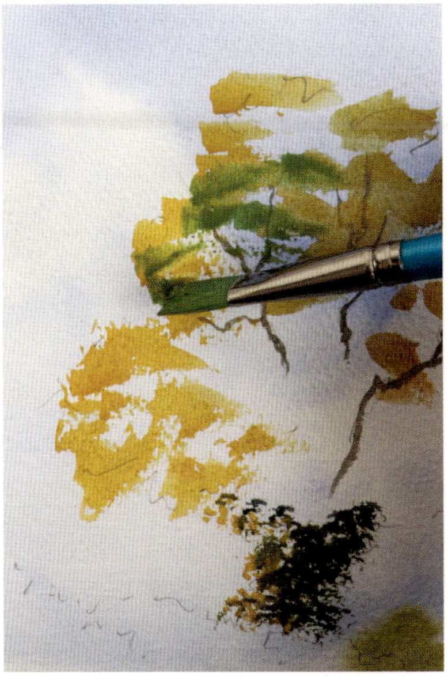

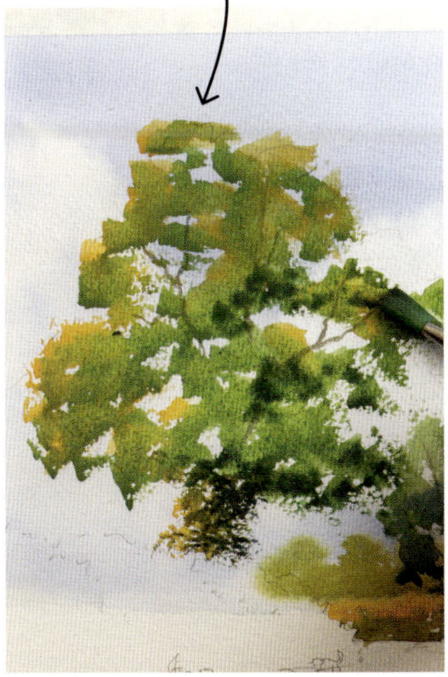

### STEP 5

Using the side of a 19mm (¾in) flat brush with yellow ochre, tap on to the paper around the boughs to create the impression of leaves. Then, using Hooker's green mixed with a lot of yellow ochre, tap on top, bearing in mind the light is coming from the left. Mix Hooker's green and burnt sienna to make a nice strong green. And finally a touch of ultramarine into that last green mix, still with the 19mm (¾in) flat brush, just tapping.

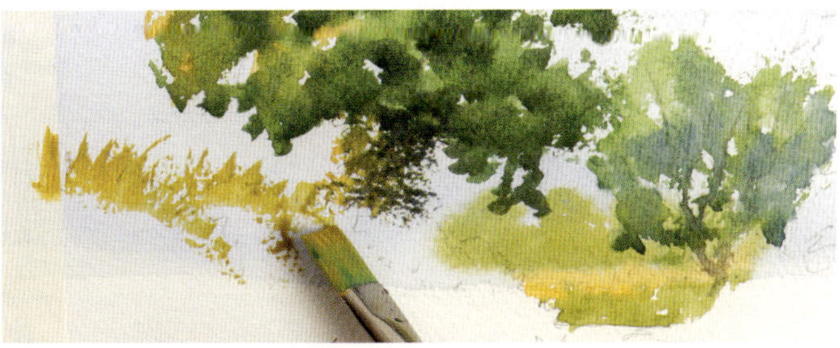

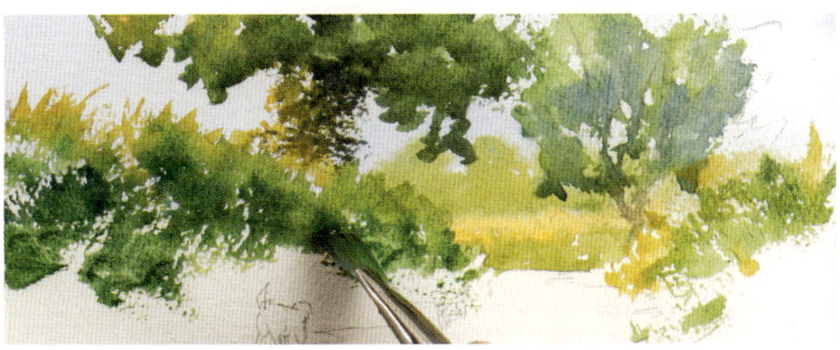

### STEP 6

For the hedges on both sides of the painting use the side of a 19mm (¾in) flat brush again and drag up with a little bit of yellow ochre. Now Hooker's green and a lot of yellow ochre, and again dragging up the side of the 19mm (¾in) flat brush, leaving little bits of the yellow ochre showing through in between. Then a mix of Hooker's green, yellow ochre and French ultramarine for the darkest bits at the bottom.

**STEP 7**

While all that is drying, move on to the path. Using yellow ochre and a touch of raw umber with a 19mm (¾in) flat brush, stroke across from side to side. Add in a little bit more water as it goes further away. And again we'll let that dry.

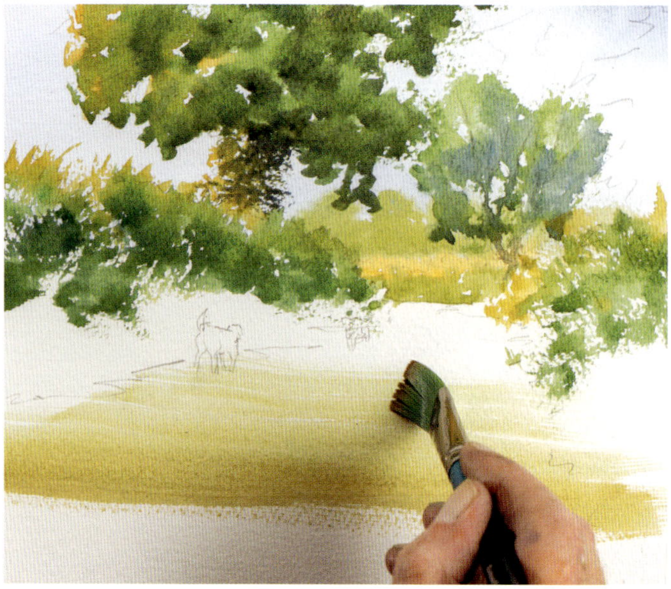

**STEP 8**

Still with a 19mm (¾in) flat brush, use a mix of Hooker's green and light red to bring the foliage up to the edge of the path, following the outline around the dog. With that same colour, flick up in front of the path and also with a tiny corner of the 19mm (¾in) flat brush tap on to the paper. As you come further forward lay the brush more on to the paper to get a wider stroke. Then add a little bit of grass down the centre of the track.

*I decided to drop one of the dogs at this point, as I didn't like the composition.*

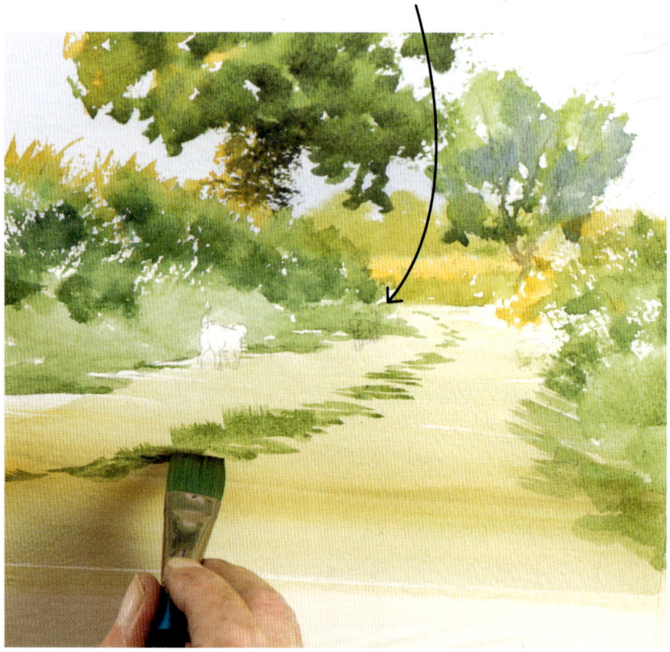

*Don't use manufactured black – make your own using French ultramarine and burnt sienna for more depth. Another good way of making black is alizarin crimson and Hooker's green.*

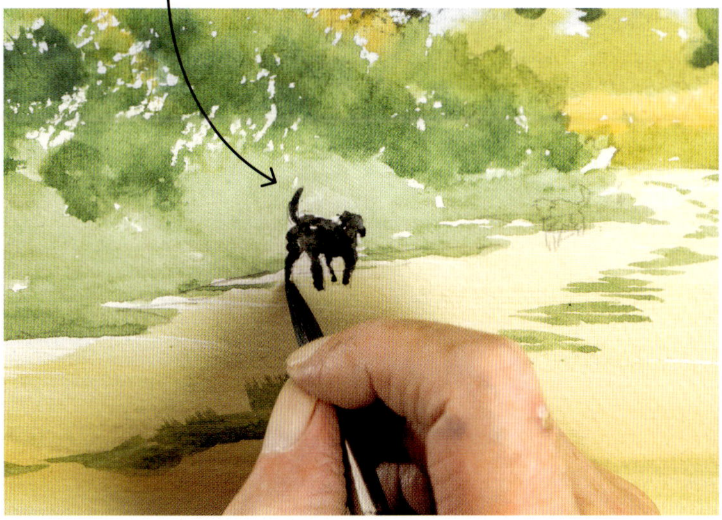

### STEP 9

For the black labrador use a mix of French ultramarine and burnt sienna and fill in the outline with the tip of a No. 8 round brush. Let that dry thoroughly.

*Always stick to the same shade of blue as the sky for your shadow mix, as otherwise it won't sit well.*

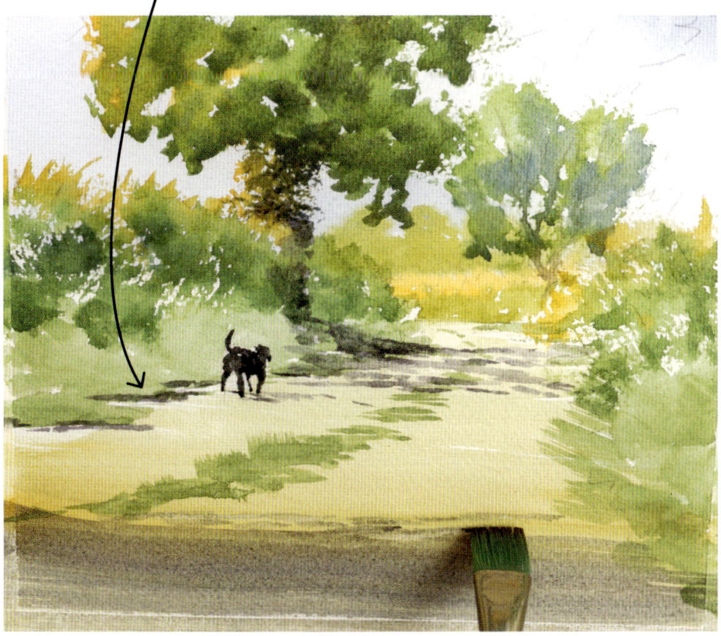

### STEP 10

Mix ultramarine with alizarin crimson and then tone it back with a touch of burnt sienna to create your shadow mix. Whatever is casting a shadow, touch that thing with the shadow mix. So, a little bit of the shadow into the base of the tree, bring it down slightly and then across the path. Tap the brush on the paper to get a more dappled type of shadow. Add shadows to the bottom of the bushes on the left side and invent another tree out of shot to create a large shadow at the base of the painting, again tapping to create a dappled shadow.

# Winter field

As a contrast to the preceding painting, this winter scene has no leaves or rich colours – you just have to concentrate on the shapes of the trunks and branches, and paint the background trees as a mass. This is a very simple painting, so don't spend time fiddling about with it: keep it loose.

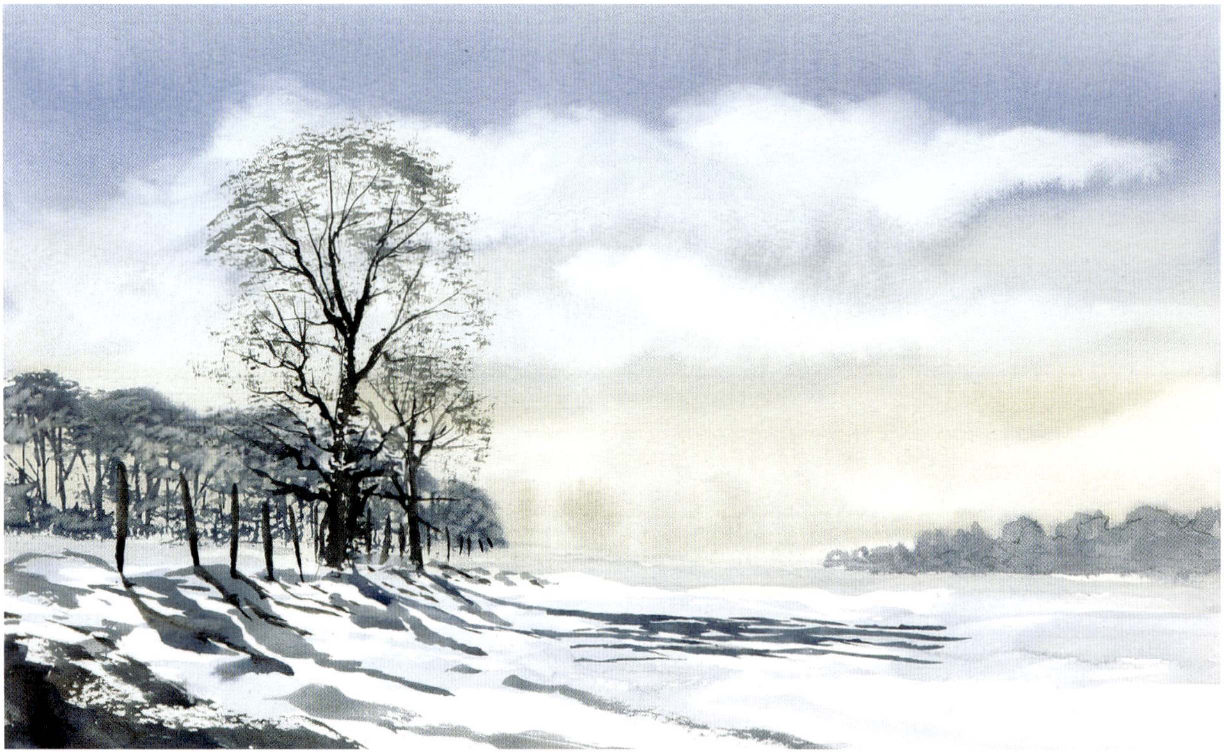

### PRELIMINARY DRAWING

The simple outlines take in the whole scene: far distant trees on the right, a clump of trees to the left in the middle distance, and two foreground trees, one slightly further away and therefore smaller. And that's all there is to it.

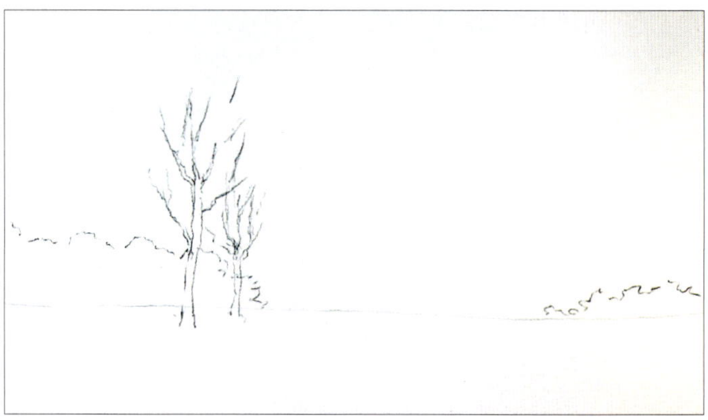

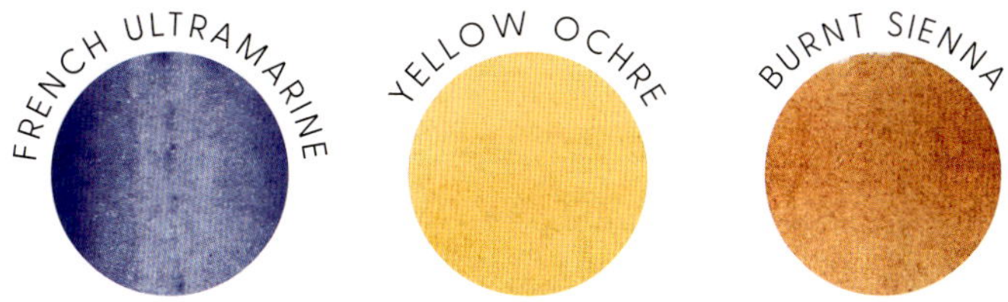


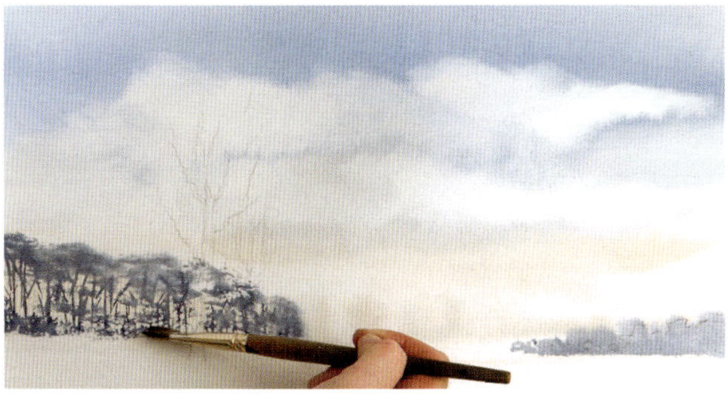

**STEP 1**

Wet the sky, then use a 38mm (1½in) wash brush with a mix of yellow ochre and burnt sienna in the bottom third, and watery ultramarine for the rest. Suck out the clouds. While this is damp, use a No. 8 brush for the distant trees with a mix of ultramarine and burnt sienna; use a stronger mix and a 19mm (¾in) wash brush to tap on the trees in the middle distance. Flick in their bases.

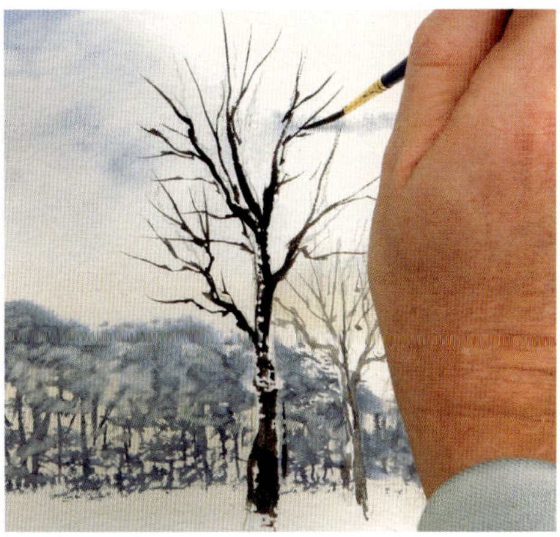

**STEP 2**

Use a No. 4 rigger brush and the same mix for the further foreground tree – just a few squiggly lines that let the paper show through. For the nearer tree use a stronger mix, laying on the side of the brush and stroking through. Add a few boughs and twigs with the rigger, then use the wash brush to tap on the smallest twigs, still working very dark.

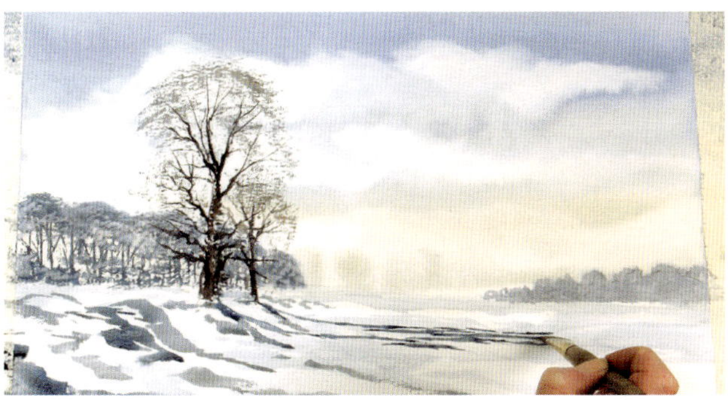

**STEP 3**

To tint the contours of the snow, use the same wash very, very weak, using the wash brush; then strengthen the mix a little for the shadow areas, and build this up for the shadows cast over the snow by the trees. Increase the strength of the mix to almost black for the fence posts, which give a sense of recession. Simple – and how few colours you've used!

# Buildings

Street scenes and buildings often seem daunting – and terms such as 'perspective' and 'vanishing point' only increase the fear factor. But a few exercises will help you create effective perspective and shapes, and knowing how to add textures will take your paintings further.

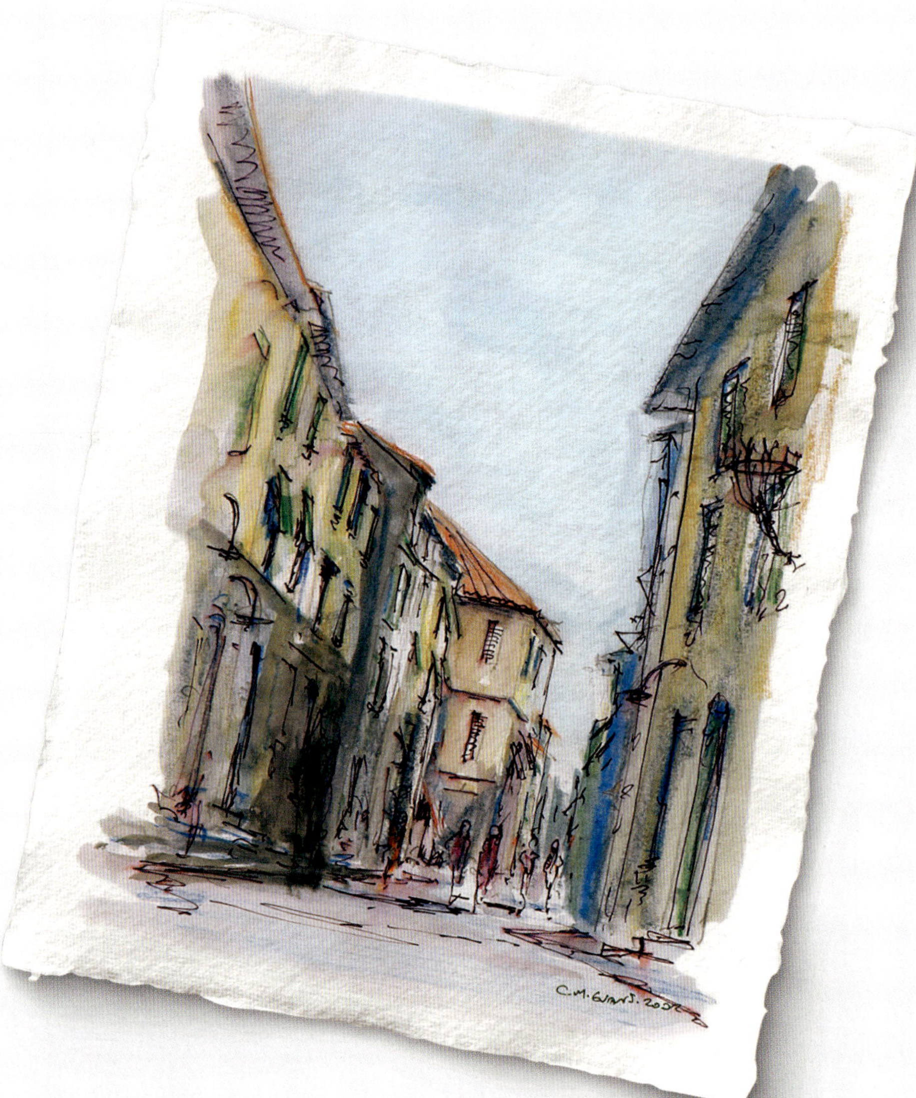

REFERENCE SKETCH
Combining watercolour washes with pen and ink lines is a great way to suggest shapes and details quickly in your sketchbook.

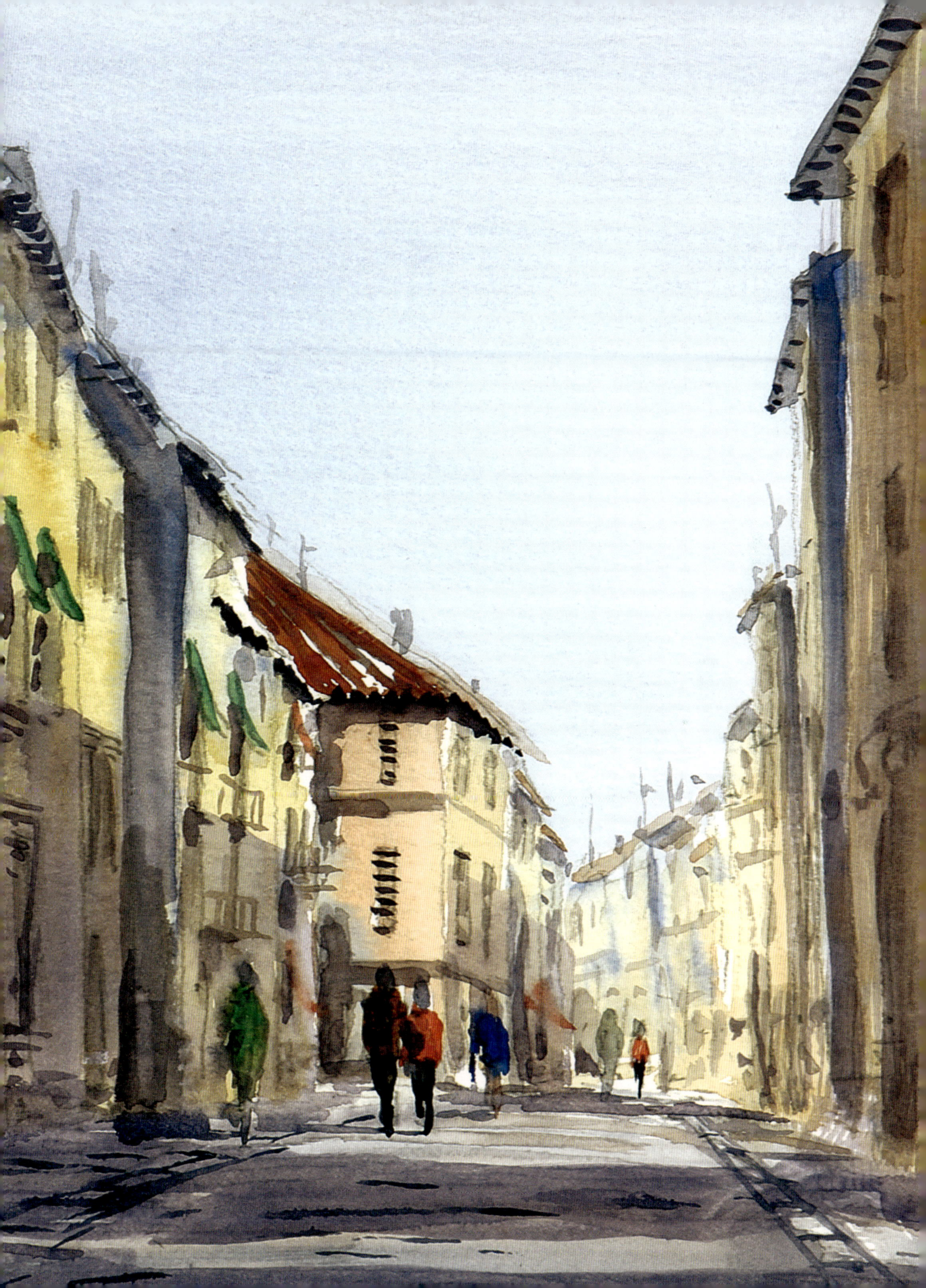

# EXERCISE: PERSPECTIVE

## COTTAGE

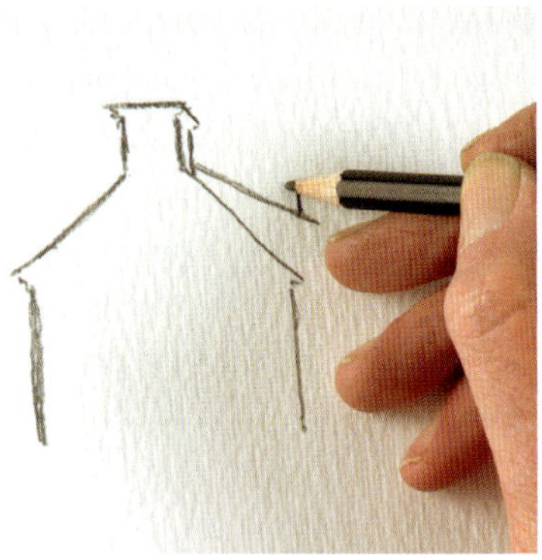

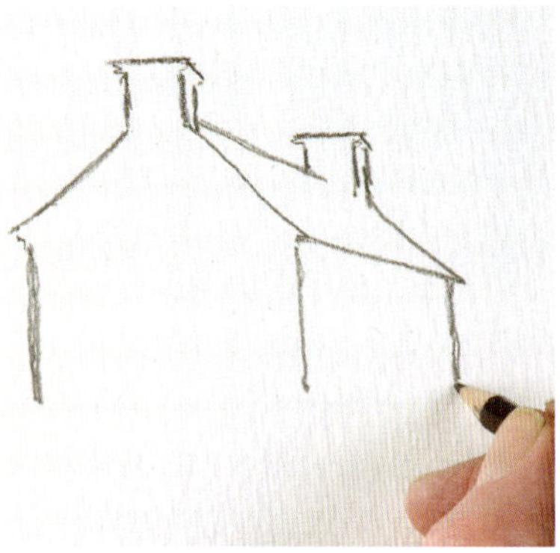

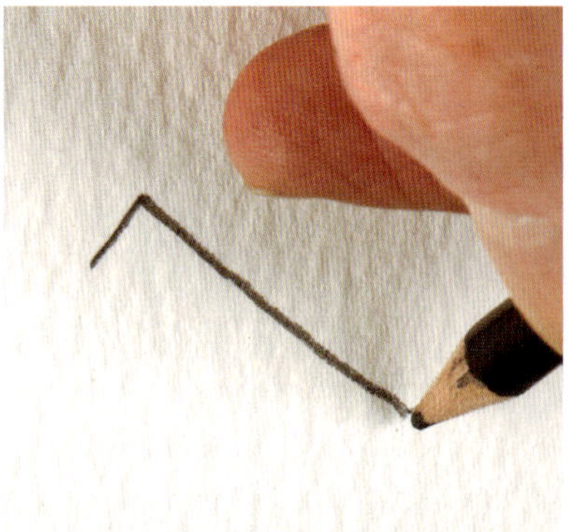

**1.** For a cottage, draw the side wall and chimney. Draw a diagonal line from the top of the chimney and show the front, then use the same angle to draw the ridge of the roof.

**2.** Draw the far chimney and sloping edge of the roof at the same angles only smaller, as they are further away, then join the two roof lines.

**3.** A simple tick is all you need to draw windows, doors and ledges. Following the roof line, put the tick on its end for windows and doors, and on its side for ledges.

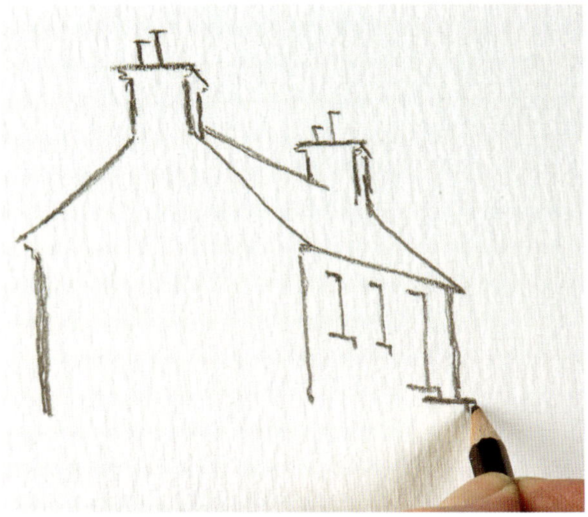

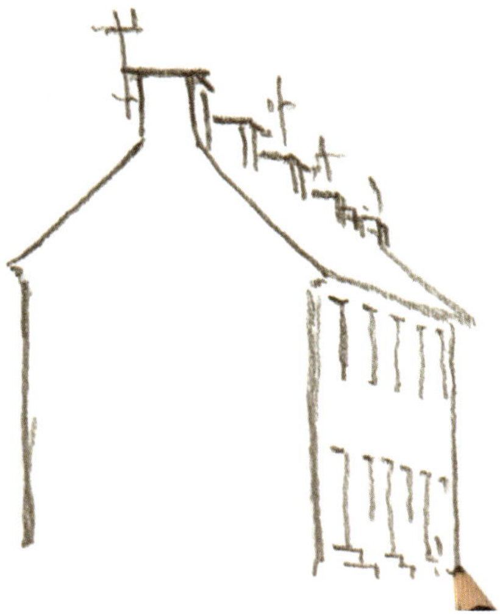

**4.** Without adding much detail, you can create an effective building at an angle by just following the basic guidelines.

**5.** To draw a row of buildings, work in the same way, adding more sets of chimneys before joining up the top roof line, each one getting smaller as it goes away from you.

## TELEGRAPH POLES

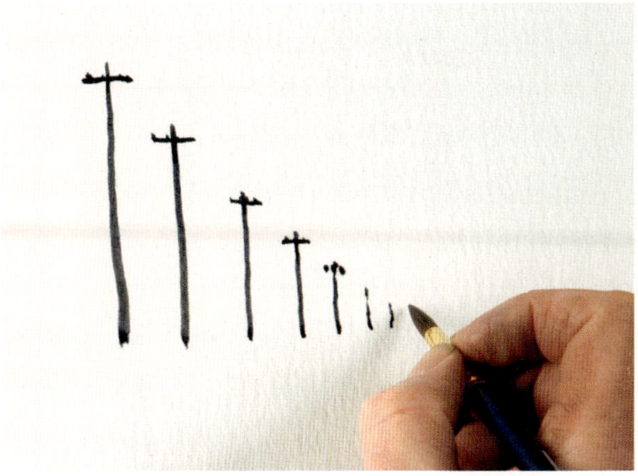

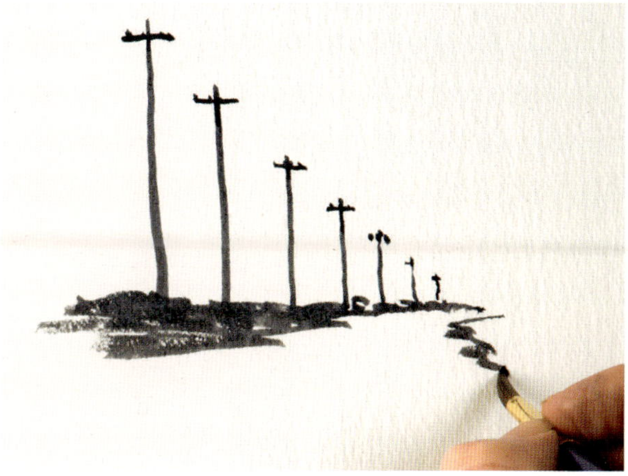

**1.** We've already looked at recession in the landscape; here's how to make it work without needing to use colour. Paint a row of telegraph poles that get progressively smaller as they go into the distance. Make sure the upright angles are the same, and keep the diagonal of the tops straight.

**2.** Now add the ground at the base of the poles, keeping this horizontal like the crossbars. Add the bank at the other side of the path with a squiggly line, remembering that the road will appear narrower as it runs into the distance.

**3.** A little bit of blocking in adds contours to the path, and there you are – a simple country lane that has a great sense of distance and space.

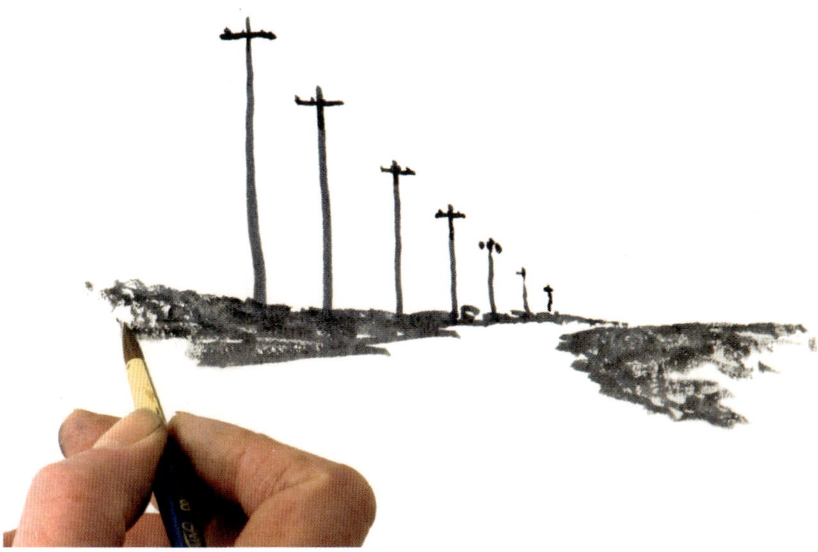

# EXERCISE: TEXTURES

## AT A DISTANCE

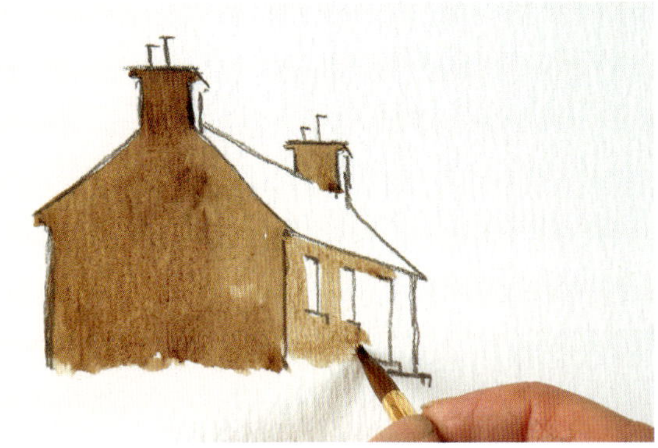

**1.** Using the drawing of a cottage from the previous pages, block in the side and far chimney with raw umber; dilute this for the front, which is facing the light.

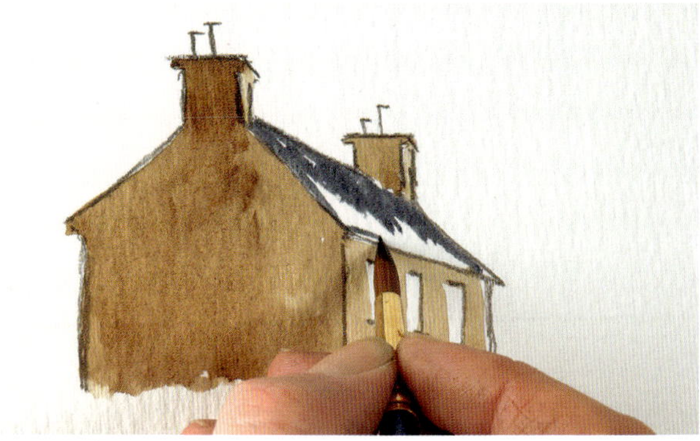

**2.** Mix ultramarine with burnt sienna for the roof and stroke it on following the diagonal angle. Leave a little white paper showing through for variation – roofs aren't all one colour.

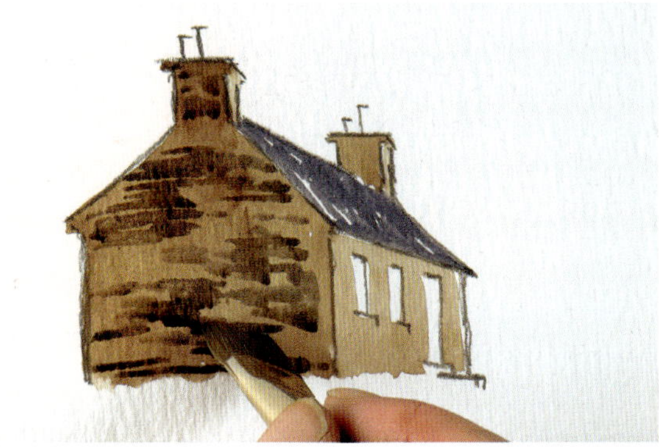

**3.** For the bricks or stonework on the side of the building, mix raw umber with ultramarine and use the edge of a wash brush to stipple this on. Vary the strength of the mix and don't try to put in too many details – leave the original colour to show through, and remember that watercolour washes dry about 50 per cent lighter than when applied.

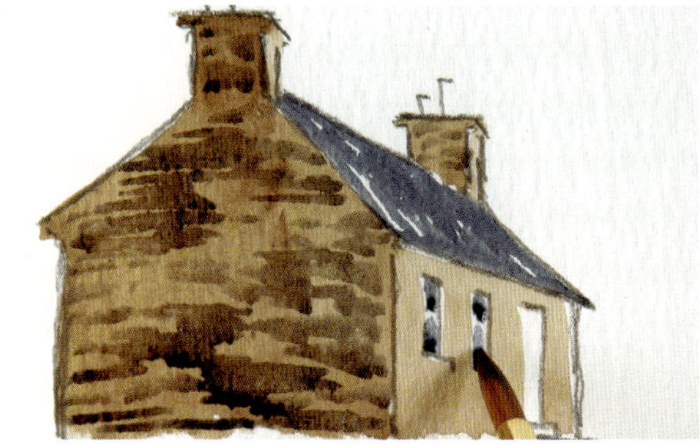

**4.** For the windows, mix ultramarine and burnt sienna darker than for the roof and use the tip of a round brush to dot in a couple of touches, leaving white between them for the window bars. Change colour and do the same for the door, which again isn't a flat colour.

## CLOSE-UP DETAIL

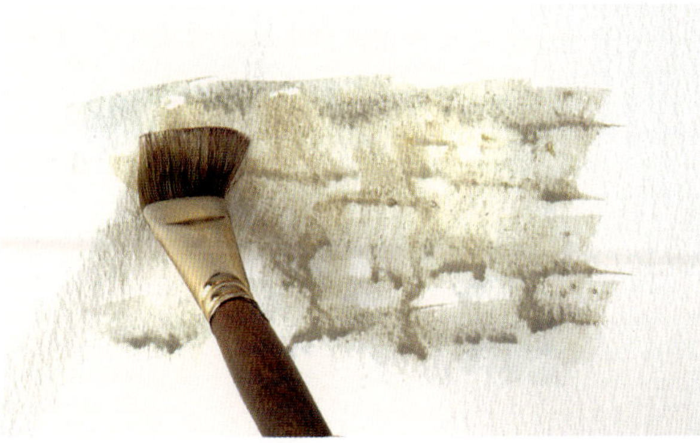

**1.** To add texture to stonework, start by stippling on a first colour – I used yellow ochre mixed with a tiny bit of raw umber – with a wash brush. Vary the strength of this wash to show the edges of the stones, but don't go into detail here.

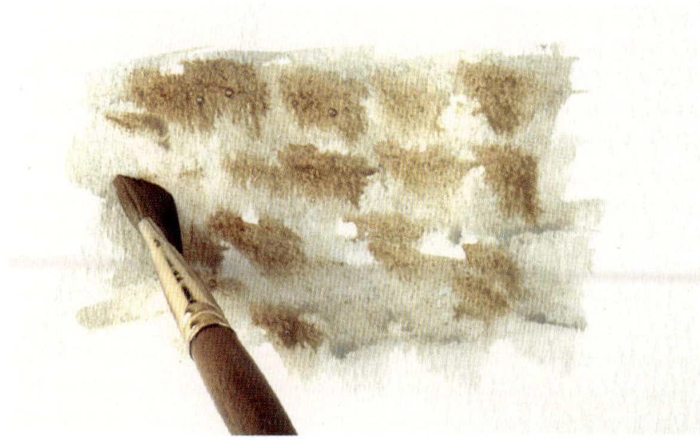

**2.** Add some more raw umber to the mix and stipple this on top of the wet wash in the same way, leaving some of the base wash showing through. It's all a bit of a mess at this stage.

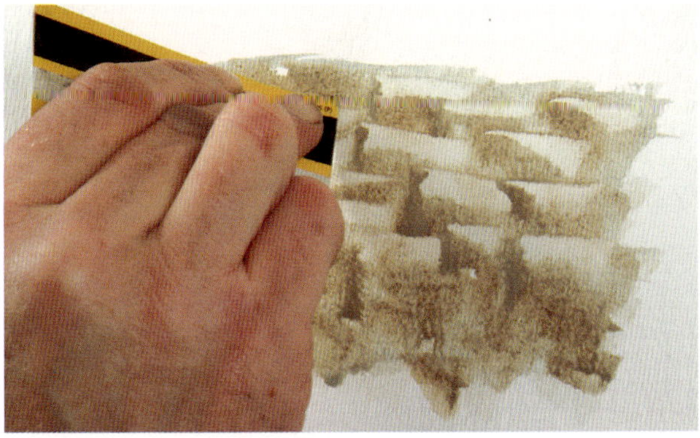

**3.** While the washes are wet, use the edge of a credit card to scrape them off to create stone shapes. Work in the same direction each time to reflect the directional light.

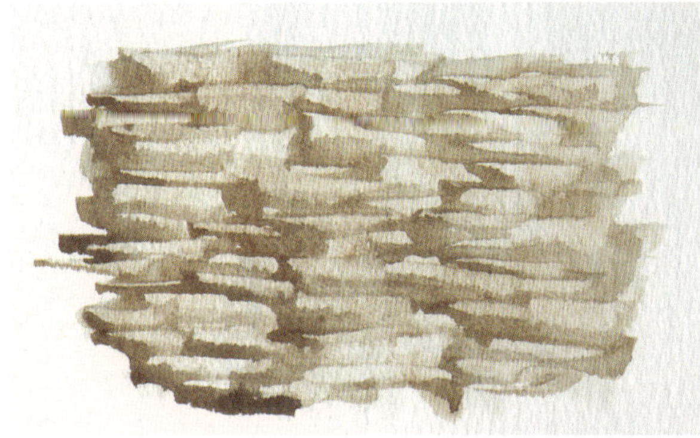

**4.** For smaller stones or rocks, you can cut up the credit card into smaller pieces – which will also save you money!

# Tuscan town

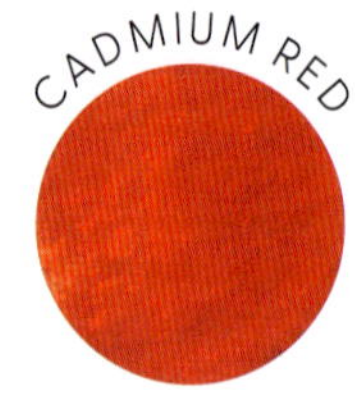


Here's a simple street scene in Lucca, a lovely town in Tuscany. The buildings are old and not all of the same height, so you have to treat each one separately and use the kerbs to provide the perspective lines. On the other hand, just a few details can bring the scene to life – and they aren't difficult to do.

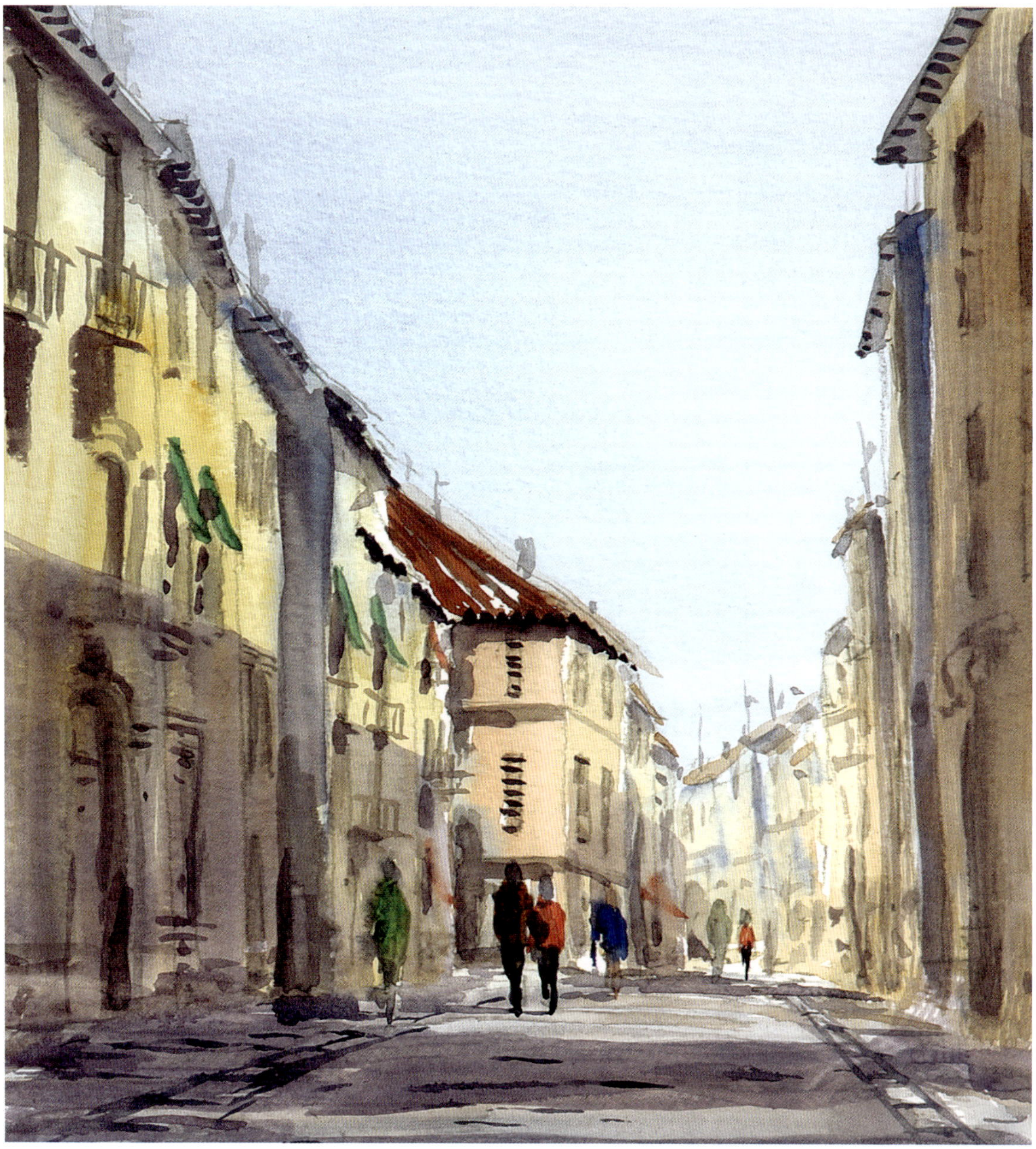

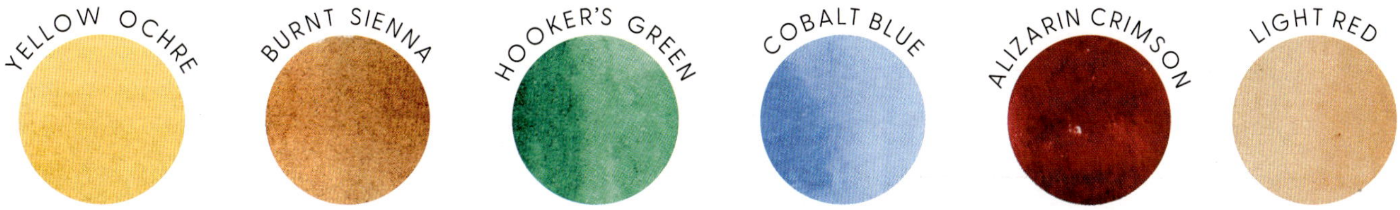


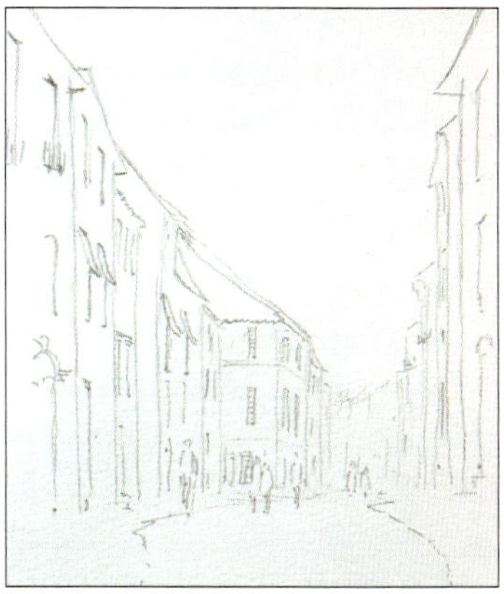

**PRELIMINARY DRAWING**

This is a slightly more complex drawing than in the previous projects, but it's still just the outlines, using ticks for the windows, doors and shutters. I sketched in the figures to give a sense of scale from the start, and decided to leave the sky as a plain flat wash so it wouldn't detract from the buildings beneath.

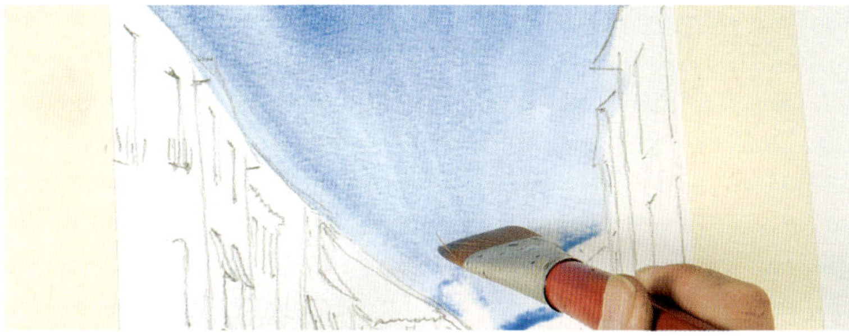

**STEP 1**

Wet the sky area with clean water, and use a 38mm (1½in) wash brush to block in the sky with cobalt blue. Squeeze out the brush and suck out any paint over the buildings – any that's left will add a sense of recession. Let this dry.

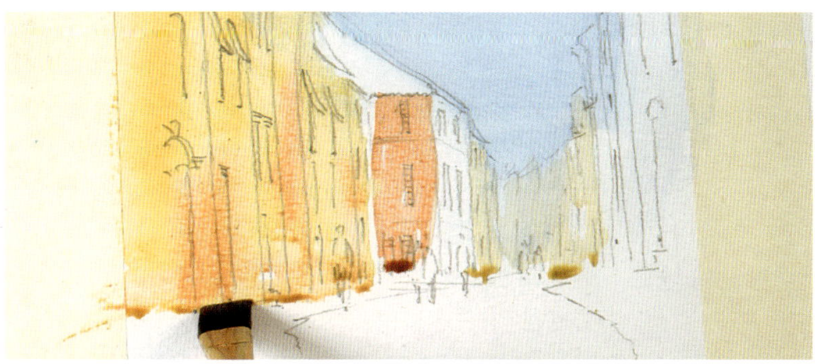

**STEP 2**

Start the buidings in the same way, wetting them with clean water and then dropping in a watery wash of yellow ochre with a 19mm (¾in) wash brush. While this is wet, add a little light red, letting the colours run into each other.

**STEP 3**
Mix light red and yellow ochre for the foreground building on the right – only a few strokes are needed. While the wash is wet, drop in some simple blobs and lines of cobalt blue, following the shapes and lines of the buildings.

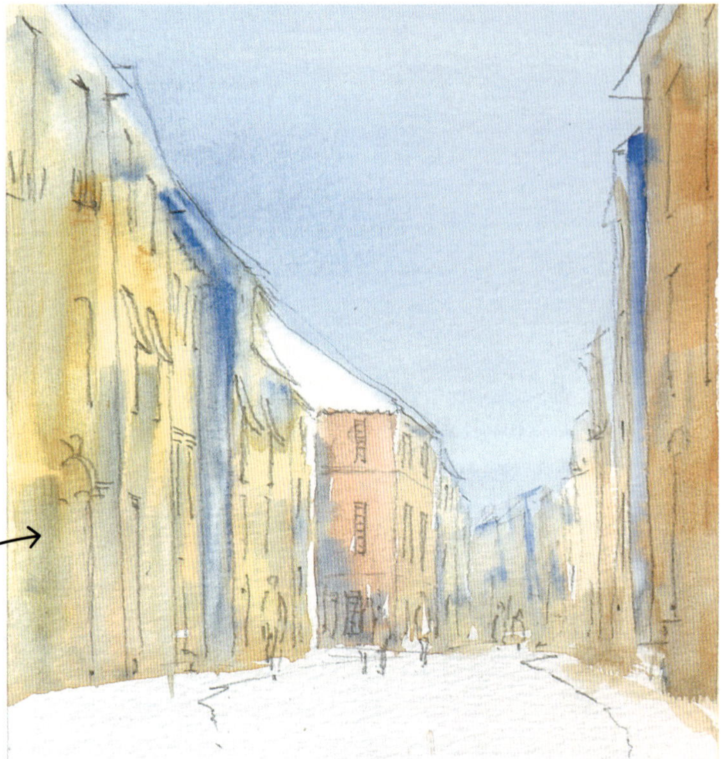

*This must all be thoroughly dry before carrying on with the next stage.*

**STEP 4**
Switch to a No. 8 round brush to block in the prominent roof in the middle distance with light red, being careful not to go over the buildings in front. Use a much weaker wash for the smaller front of the more distant roof, which can only just be seen, and even more watery washes for the roofs in the far distance.

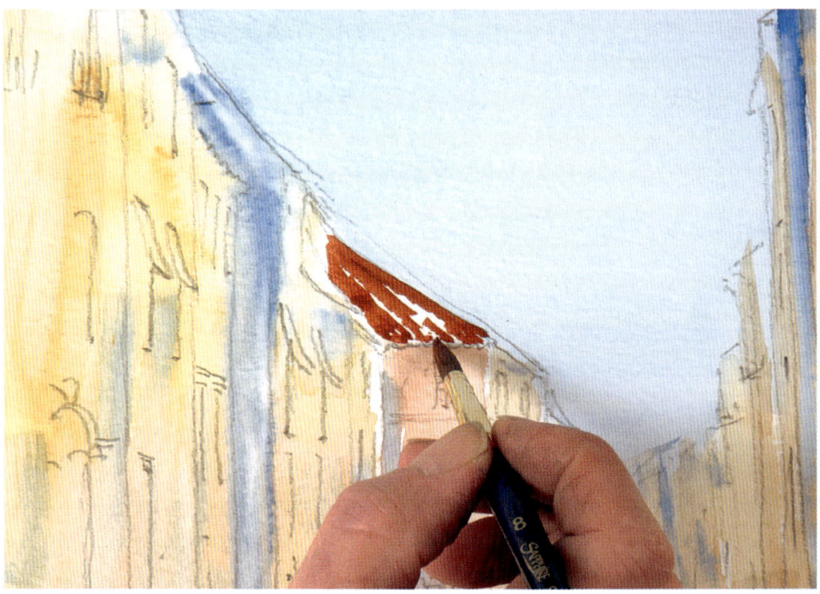

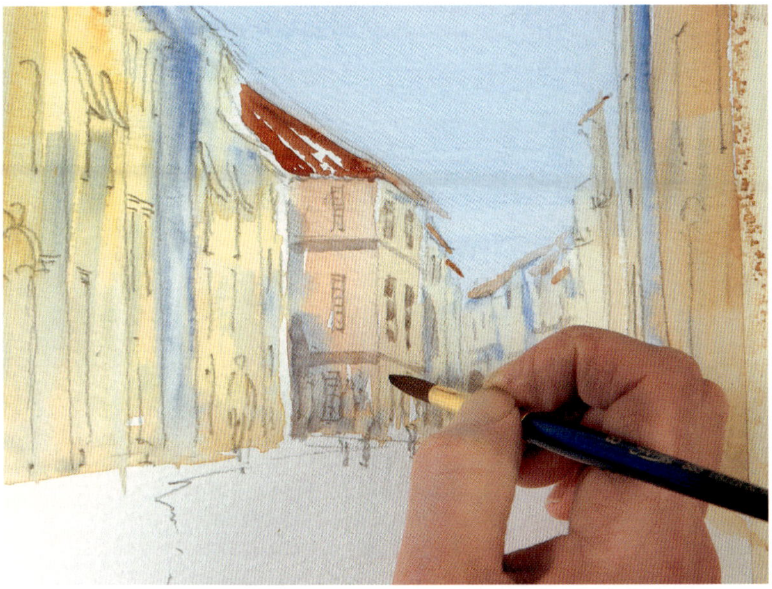

### STEP 5

Using a watery mix of light red and a little cobalt blue, put some tiny intimations of detail into the furthest buildings, without being too complicated. Come forward to the buildings in the middle distance and use a slightly stronger wash to paint the windows with three blobs, leaving lines between for the window frames. Use an even stronger wash for the windows in the foreground. Remember to keep everything simple.

*Remember to keep the mix good and strong before softening down.*

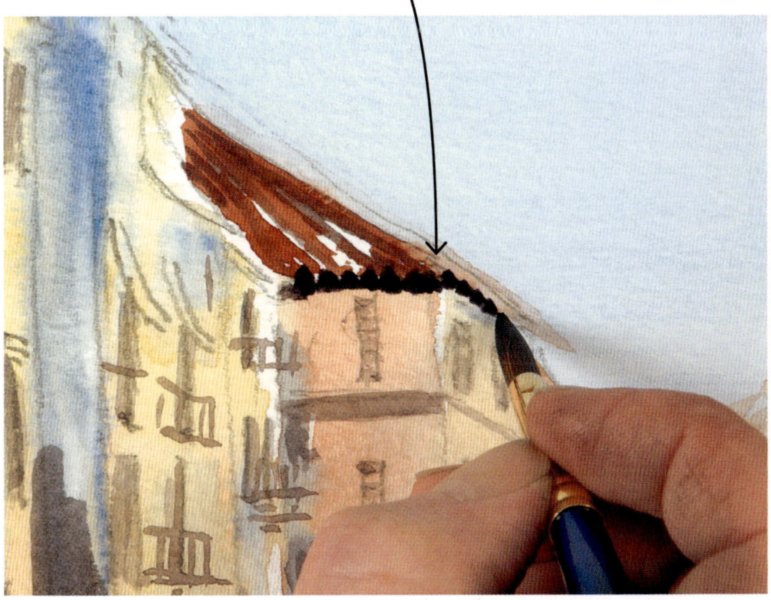

### STEP 6

Add a few hints of balconies using the same wash with a little more cobalt blue – all you need is a few lines for the bars and rails; let the eye fill in the rest from these impressions. Add more light red for some warm shadows here and there, particularly in the red roof, but leave a little white showing. Make up a dark shadow mix from cobalt blue, alizarin crimson and burnt sienna, and drop in blobs for the underside of the pantiled roof, then join them up.

Always remember where the light is coming from so that in the darker areas you can put more strength into the paint.

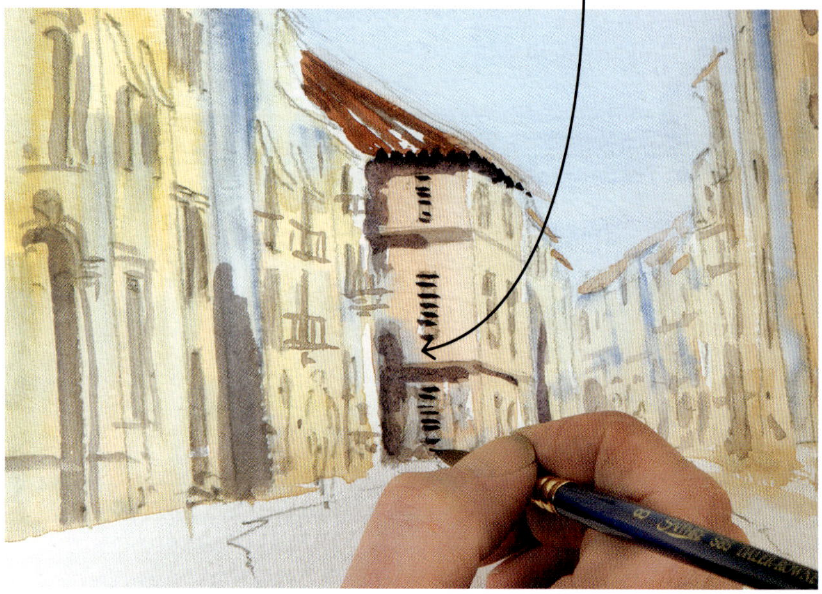

**STEP 7**

Add the shutters on the central building with the dark shadow mix – again, you're just hinting at what's there, rather than trying to paint in every detail. Use a diluted version of this mix for the lighter shadows throughout the buildings, adding more water the further into the distance you go.

**STEP 8**

For the upper window canopies on the left side use just one quick stroke of Hooker's green, and do the same for a couple of red canopies below with cadmium red. Return to the watery dark shadow mix for the underhangs below the canopies – look how easily little dibs and dabs with the brush can build up the scene and convey the character of this historic old town. Use a mix of light red and cobalt blue for the shadows and roof underhangs of the foreground buildings.

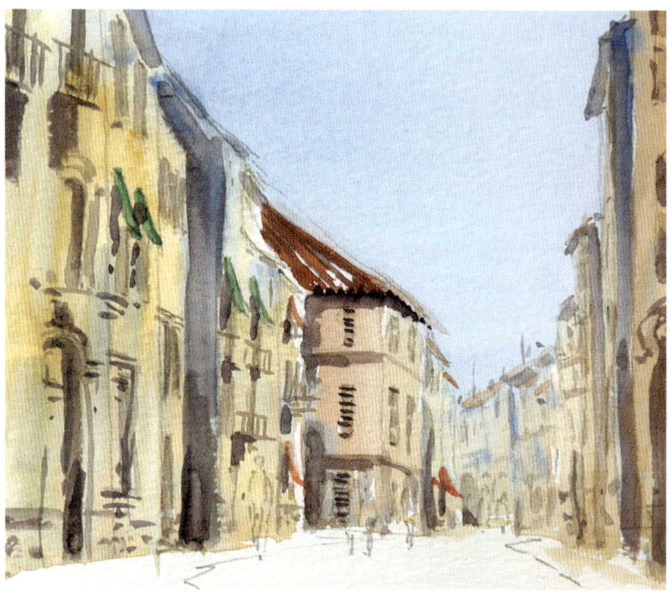

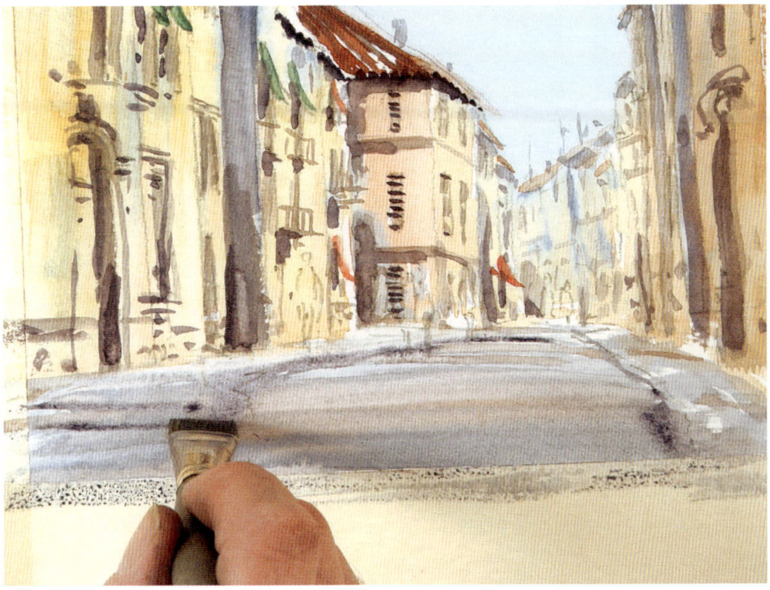

**STEP 9**

Touch in a little colour on the distant roofs with a watery mix of light red and alizarin crimson, still leaving some white showing. Then use the cobalt blue and light red mix for a few chimneys and aerials above the roofs. Stroke a watery version of this mix over the ground with the smaller wash brush, add a little light red while it's wet, and use a mix of cobalt blue and alizarin crimson to give the impression of a few kerb lines.

*Don't hang about with the brush strokes on the shadows. These are just a few simple broad strokes.*

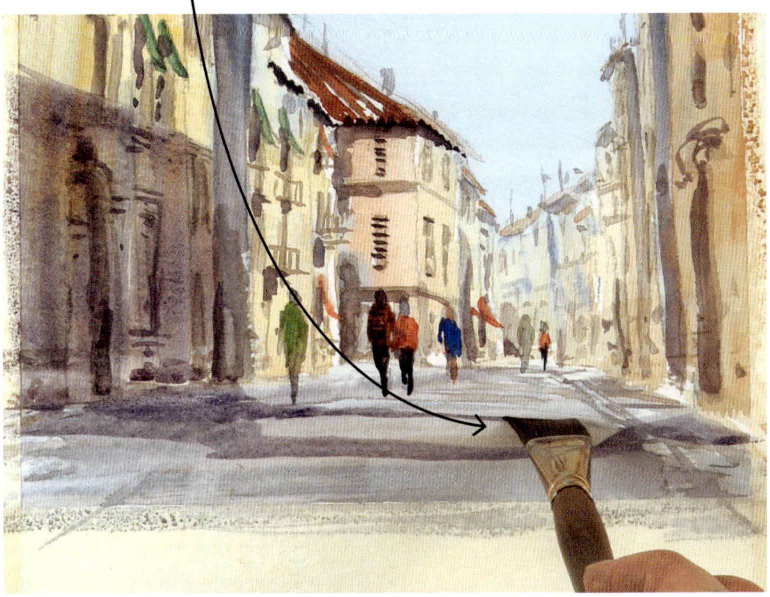

**STEP 10**

Let the picture dry a bit, then add a few people with the No. 8 brush – note how a little cadmium red in the coat of the furthest figure draws the eye into the distance. To get more light into the scene, you need to put in more dark: quickly stroke a very watery mix of cobalt blue and alizarin crimson with a little burnt sienna on to the left-hand foreground buildings, then bring this across the street – remember to indicate the kerbs. And there you have it: a classic Italian street scene.

# Flowers

Painting flowers is a great way to build up confidence – you can use really strong colours for some blooms, and you don't have to go into much detail for an effective impression. The techniques for this project – wet into wet, green leaves, lifting out and finishing touches – have been combined into a single set of exercises, although you can practise them one by one.

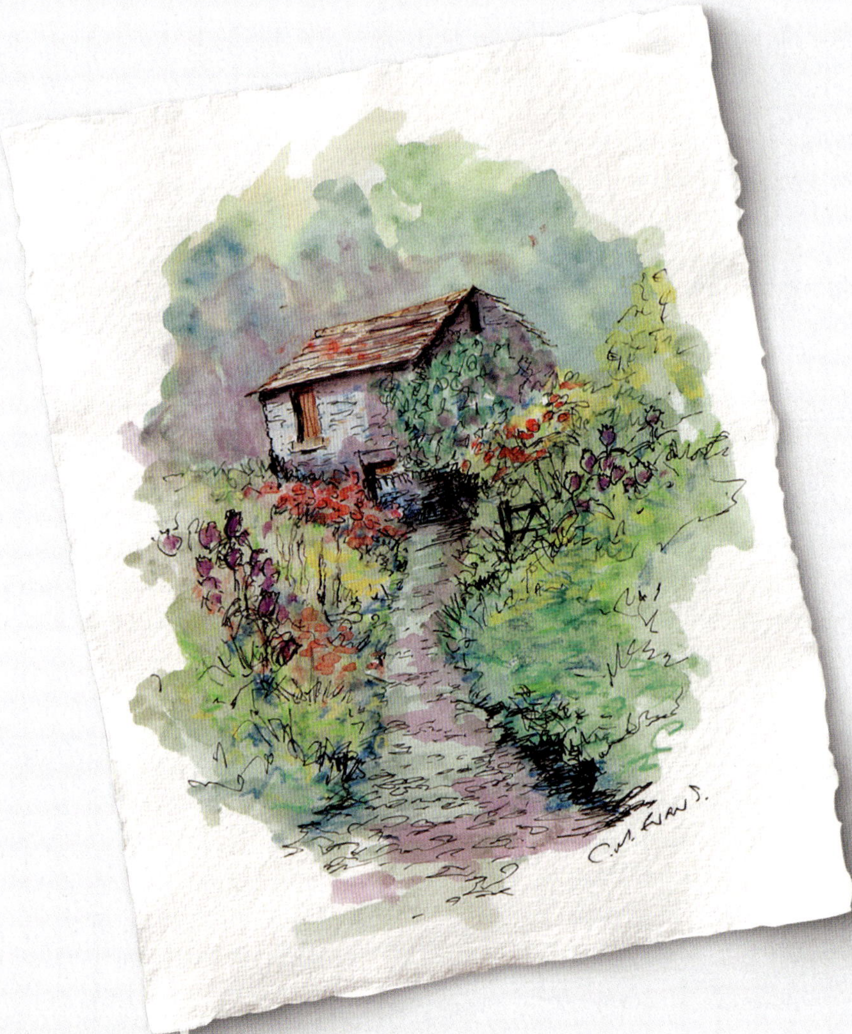

**REFERENCE SKETCH**
In the sketchbook study the flowers were clumped together closely; I decided to change the foreground to introduce more light into the scene.

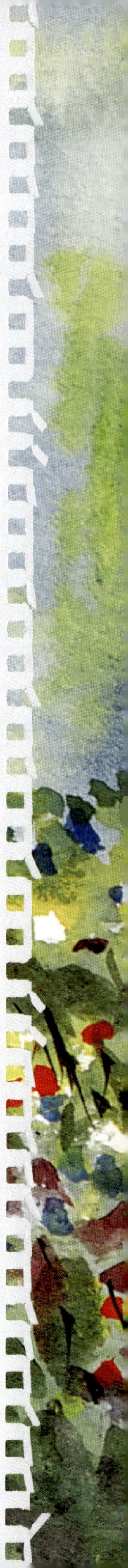

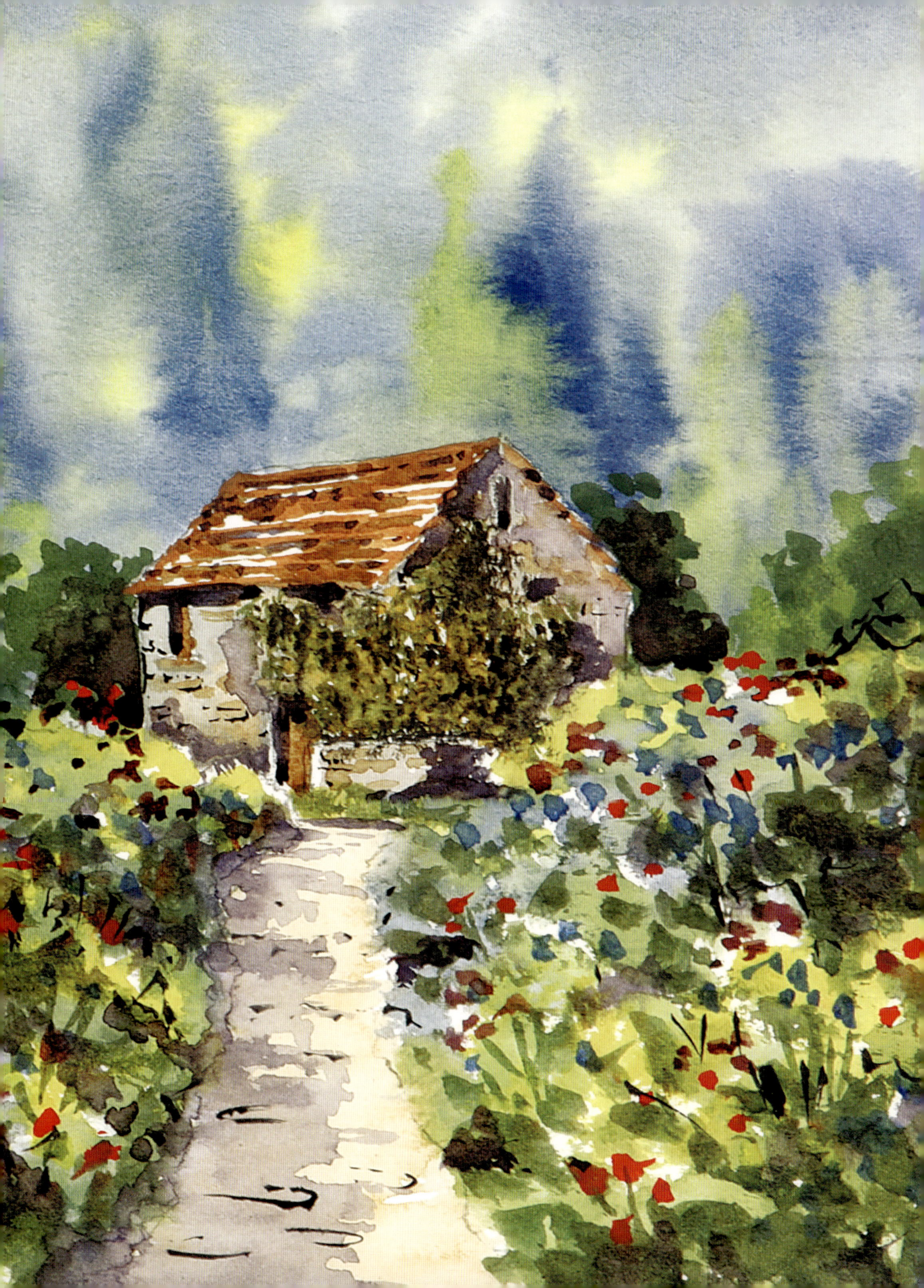

# EXERCISE: WET INTO WET

**1.** Wet the paper with clean water, then drop in a watery wash of cadmium yellow here and there; don't try to cover the whole of the wet area, and allow the colour to spread loosely.

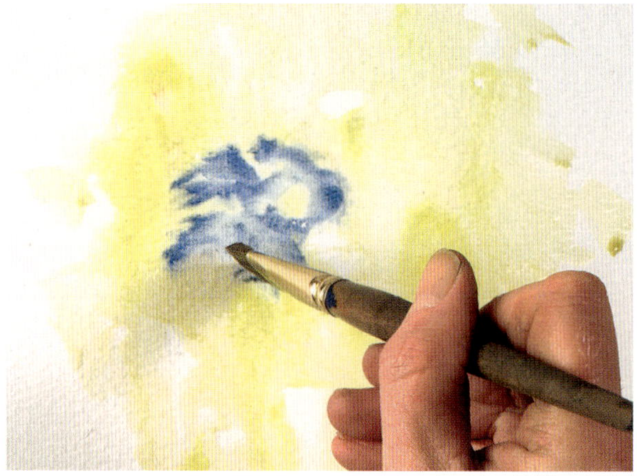

**2.** Working quickly, drop in some ultramarine – allow the yellow wash to show through. I used a 19mm (¾in) wash brush, which is broad enough to make largish marks.

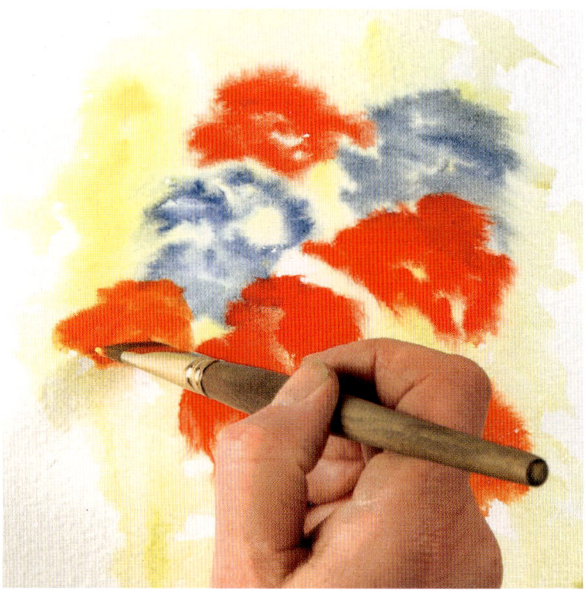

**3.** Drop in cadmium red and then cadmium yellow mixed with cadmium red for more blooms, again letting the colours blend into each other and creating soft edges.

# EXERCISE: GREEN LEAVES

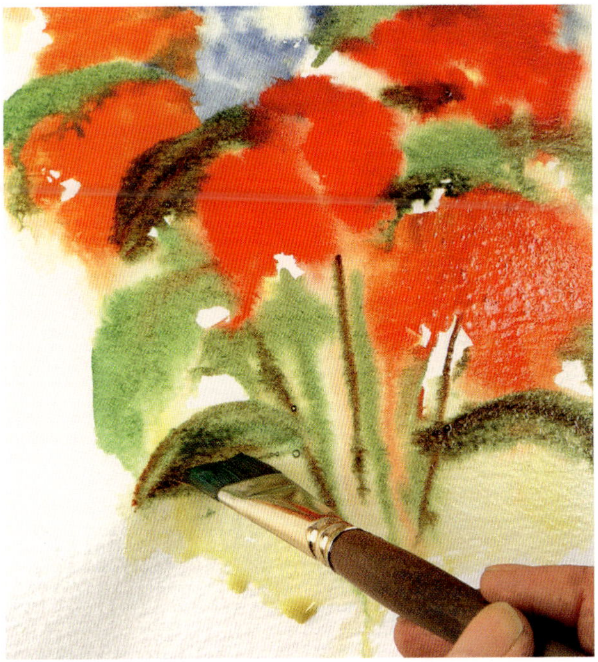

**1.** While the washes are still wet, add the first green mix of Hooker's green and yellow ochre – this is just to make the basic shapes of the leaves and stems. Keep the edges soft at this point and concentrate on working quickly. Use a mix of Hooker's green and burnt sienna to add a darker green for the foreground leaves and the stems (using the edge of the brush); this mix should blend with, but not obscure, the first green wash.

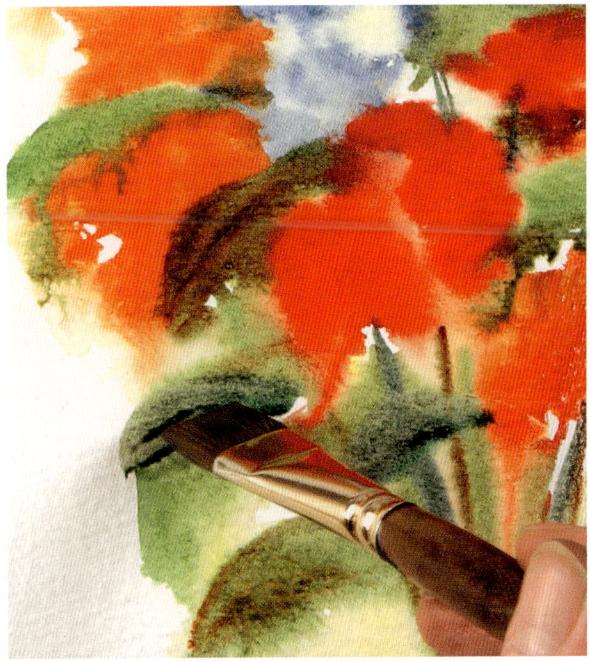

**2.** For the shadowed areas and veins use a mix of ultramarine, Hooker's green and burnt sienna, and vary the strength to pick out a few first details. At this stage the picture is a mass – you might say mess – of strong colours, with not much differentiation between the lightest and darkest parts.

### TRY IT YOURSELF

Explore a few different brush strokes, added wet into wet, and see what happens. See how you can move the paint around to change shapes.

# EXERCISE: LIFTING OUT PAINT

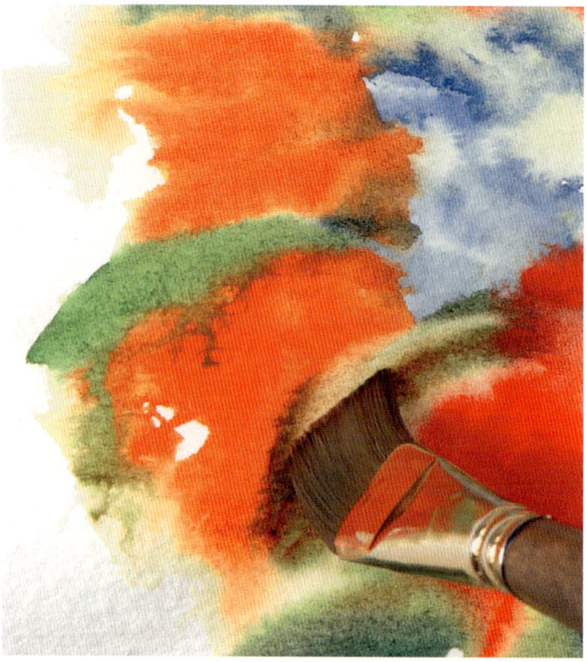

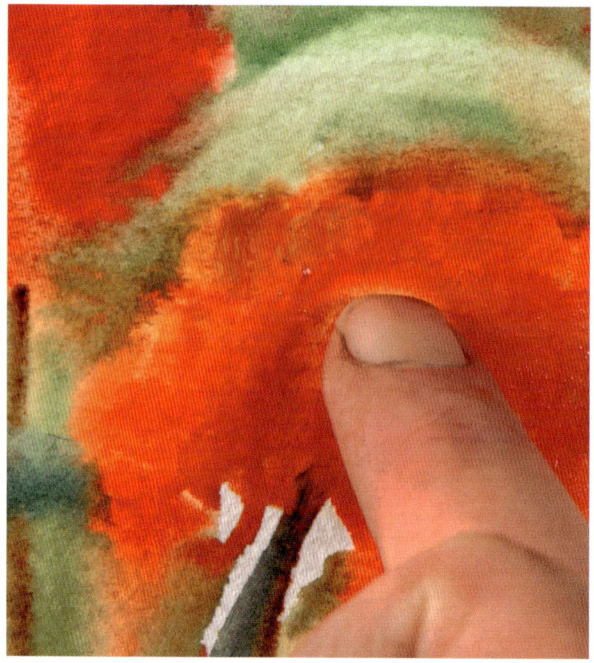

1. You can lift out pigment to create light areas even if the paint has dried – but it's a lot easier working on wet washes. Wash out the brush and squeeze the excess water from the bristles, then suck the paint off the paper to reveal the lightest areas, such as light reflecting off the tops of flowers and leaves. Make sure you don't overdo this effect.

2. To take off and lift out small areas of paint, such as in the middle of a bloom, without going all the way back to the white of the paper, use a dry finger – you have a surprising amount of control over the paint this way.

# EXERCISE: FINISHING TOUCHES

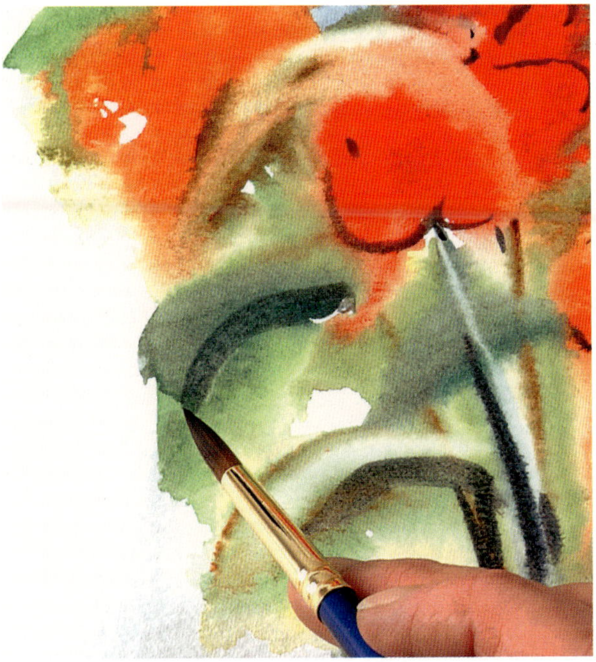

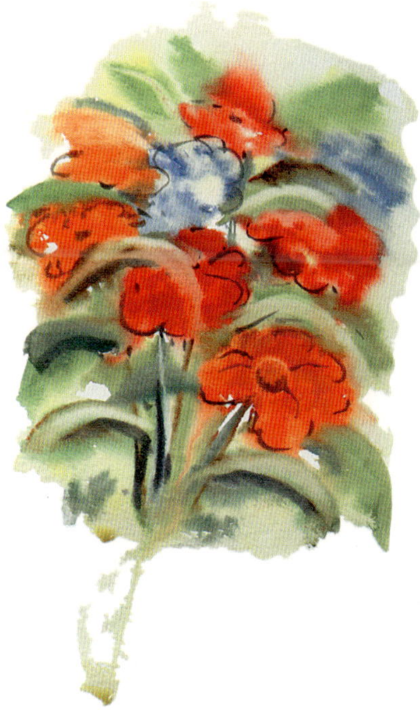

**1.** Details and finishing touches are best added with a No. 8 round brush. Use the tip to put in mixes of ultramarine and burnt sienna: watery washes for shadows under the leaves ...

**2.** ... and stronger washes for a very few defining outlines. You don't need any more than this.

### TRY IT YOURSELF

Drop a selection of colours on to your paper and let them mix. With a clean, damp brush, lift out paint and create shapes. Note how long you have to work in this way before the paint dries.

# Wildflower path

This is an outbuilding in the garden of John Ruskin's house in the English Lake District. I like the way the bright borders frame the path that leads to the building, with just a hint of trees and woodland in the distance. To get this effect you need quite a few colours – I used 11 – and the mixes can range from direct and vibrant to quite subtle and understated.

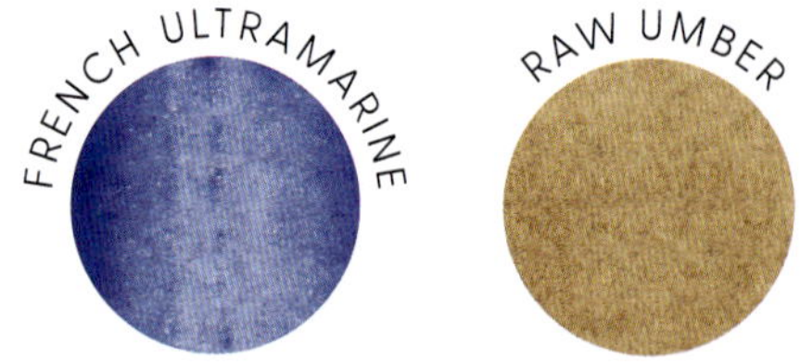


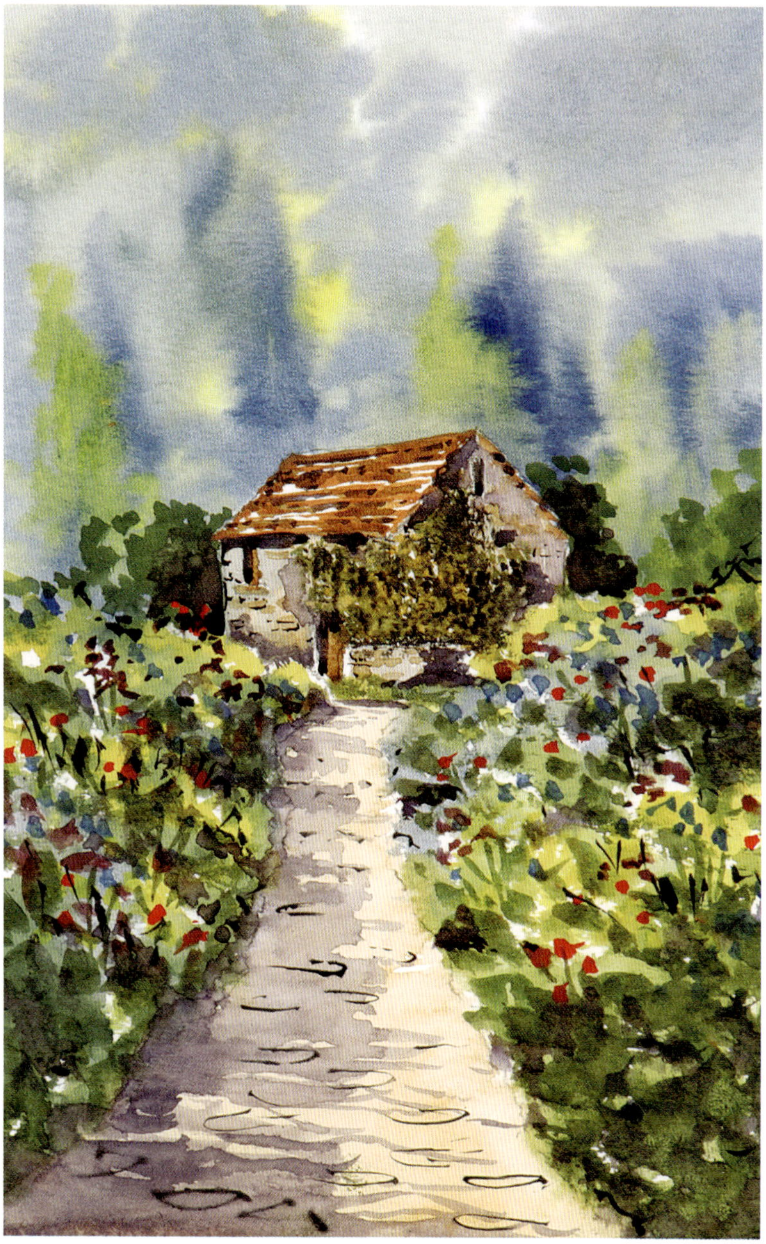

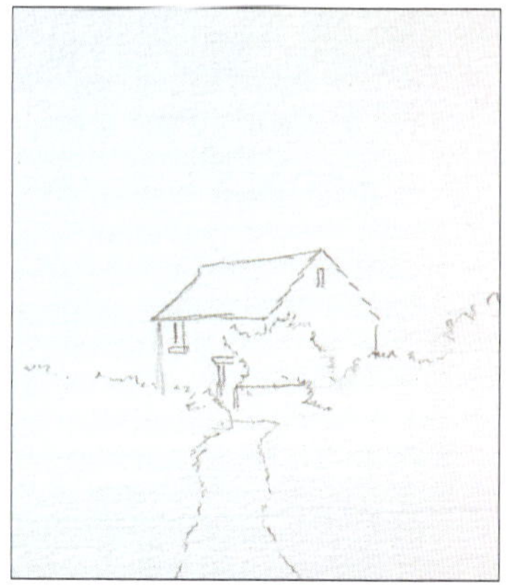

**PRELIMINARY DRAWING**
The outline here is intended to do nothing more than fix the position and proportions of the building, lane and borders – everything else will be done by the watercolours. Using the portrait format accentuates the feeling of height and leads the eye along the lane.

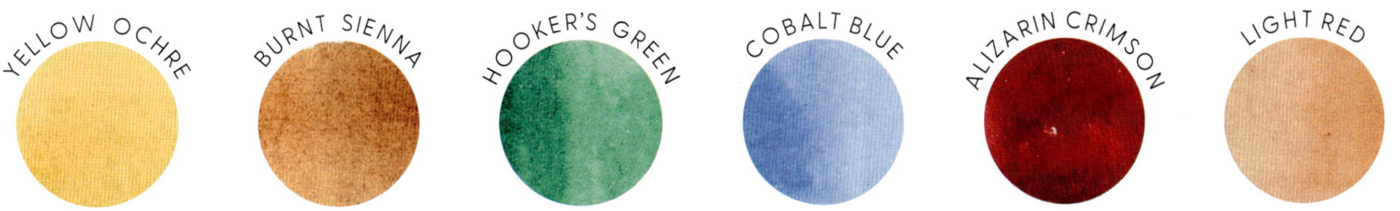


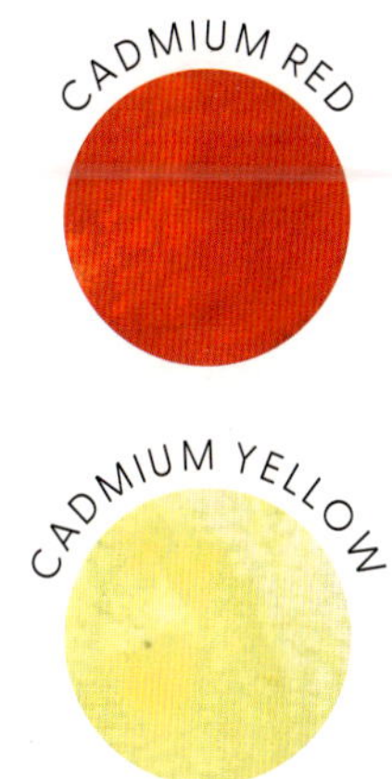


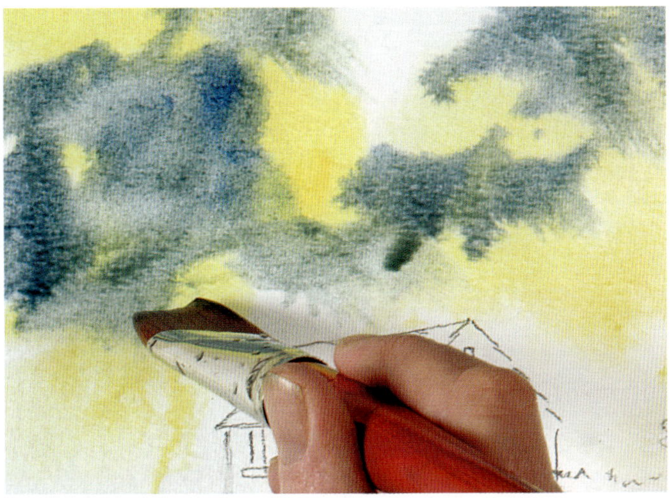

**STEP 1**

The top of the scene is not so much a sky wash as a background colour. Start by wetting the area with a lot of clean water, then drop in cadmium yellow with a 38mm (1½in) flat wash brush. While this is wet add ultramarine, working up to the building and borders; use a stronger ultramarine wash to suggest trees in the distance.

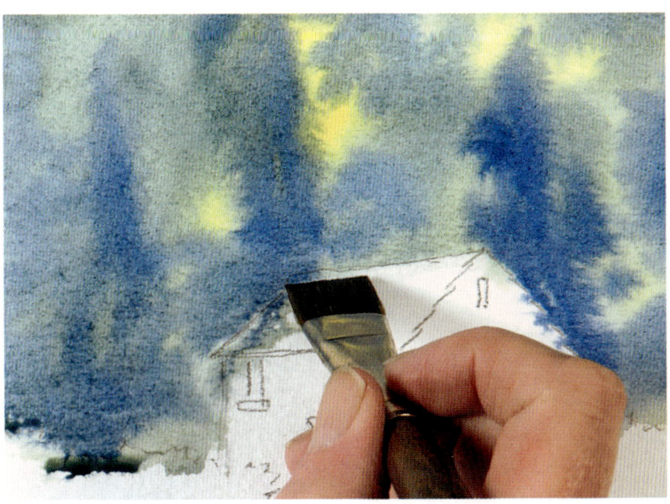

**STEP 2**

Wet and squeeze out a 19mm (¾in) wash brush, and lift out some of the washes to provide some variety. Continue to add the yellow and ultramarine washes, being careful not to overwork what should be a simple, quick background. Let everything dry completely.

**STEP 3**
With the same brush and a mix of yellow ochre and ultramarine with a tiny bit of raw umber, paint the building the unusual Lakeland stone colour. Block in the walls, working around the door, windows and ivy, and while this wash is wet drop in a few warm touches of burnt sienna from a No. 8 round brush, letting the colours soften as they run together.

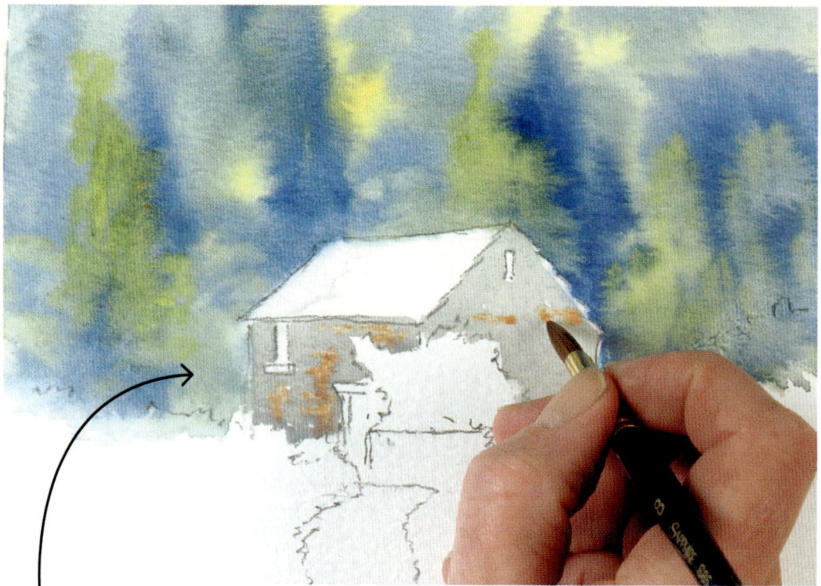

*All of the mushy background is still wet by the time it is finished. Give it plenty of time to dry before carrying on.*

*It's important not to put too many stones in. Otherwise, the building will look far too busy.*

**STEP 4**
Work along the direction of the roof with long strokes of burnt sienna; let some white paper remain to give the effect of light hitting the roof tiles. Fill in the windows and door with a mix of raw umber and burnt sienna, and use yellow ochre and raw umber for the sills, plus a bit more variety in the stonework and a little on the roof.

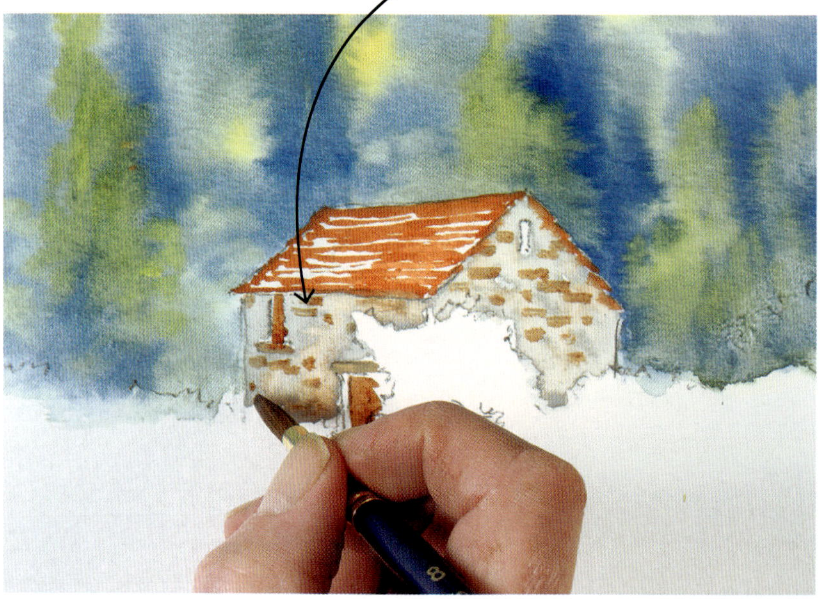

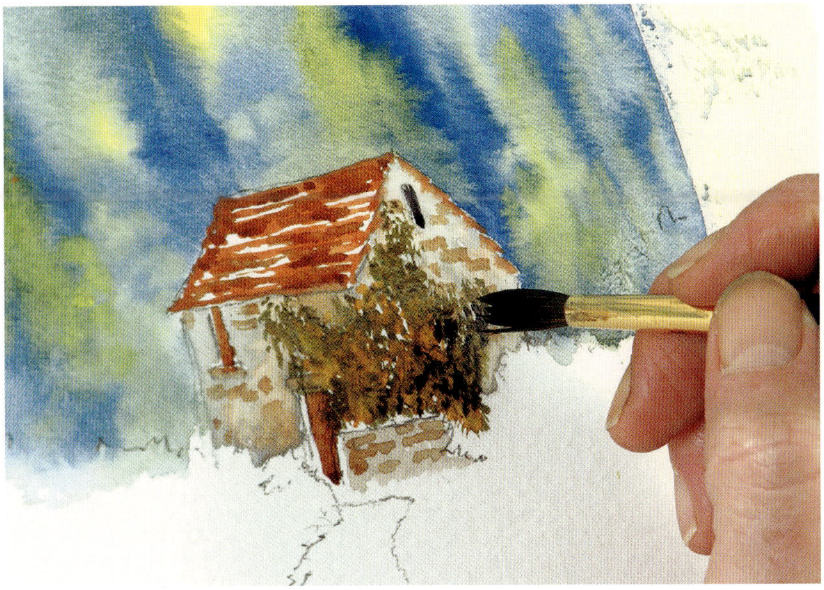

**STEP 5**

To start the ivy, 'split' the No. 8 brush (as described in Trees and foliage: Countryside Walk) and stipple on a watery wash of yellow ochre, followed by darker washes of Hooker's green and burnt sienna, and ultramarine and burnt sienna. Allow these to dry a little, then add the shadows, starting with a weak mix of ultramarine, alizarin crimson and a touch of burnt sienna on the right side. Strengthen the mix for the harder-edged shadows on the building and wall.

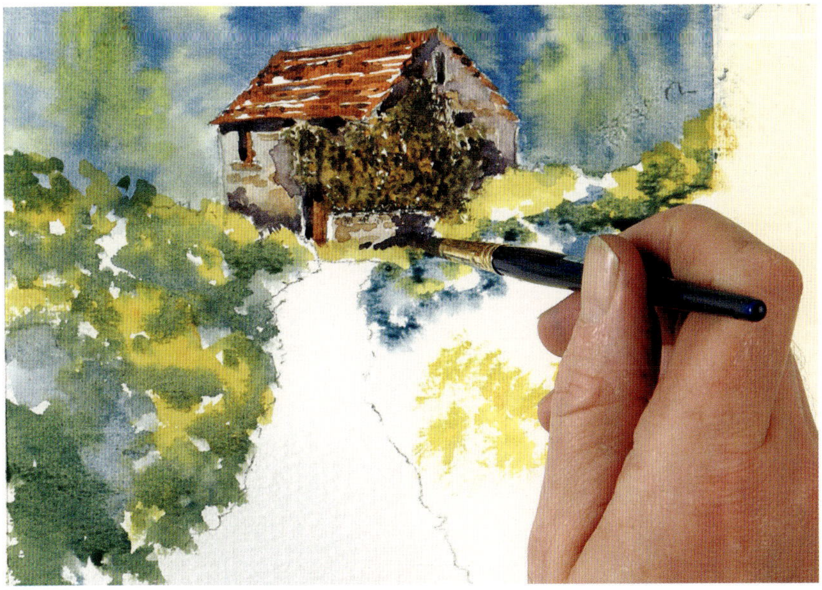

**STEP 6**

For the big splodgy areas in the borders drop in a few blobs of cadmium yellow, then a very watery ultramarine wash. Working quickly, follow this with a mix of Hooker's green and yellow ochre – just slap it on and make a mess – then do the same on the other border. Let everything dry a little.

**STEP 7**
The path should be bright and fairly flat, to contrast with the flowers in the borders: lightly stroke on a mix of yellow ochre and light red with the smaller wash brush. While this is wet add a few undulations in a stronger mix, this time using the edge of the brush.

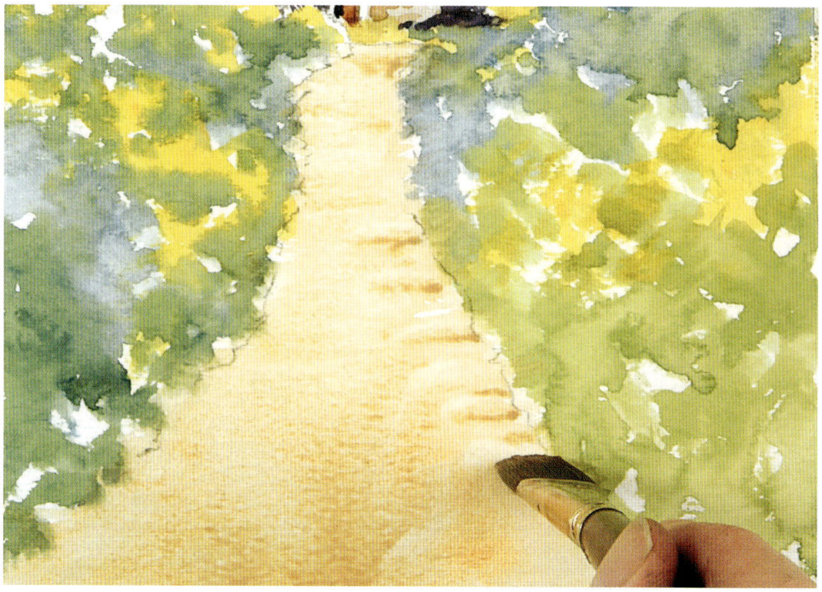

*Just a few blobs of different colours is enough to suggest flowers without painting petals.*

**STEP 8**
Now for the flowers. Using the No. 8 brush, stipple on a very strong wash of alizarin crimson – don't go mad and put too much in any one area, just a few dots here and there. Then do the same with cobalt blue.

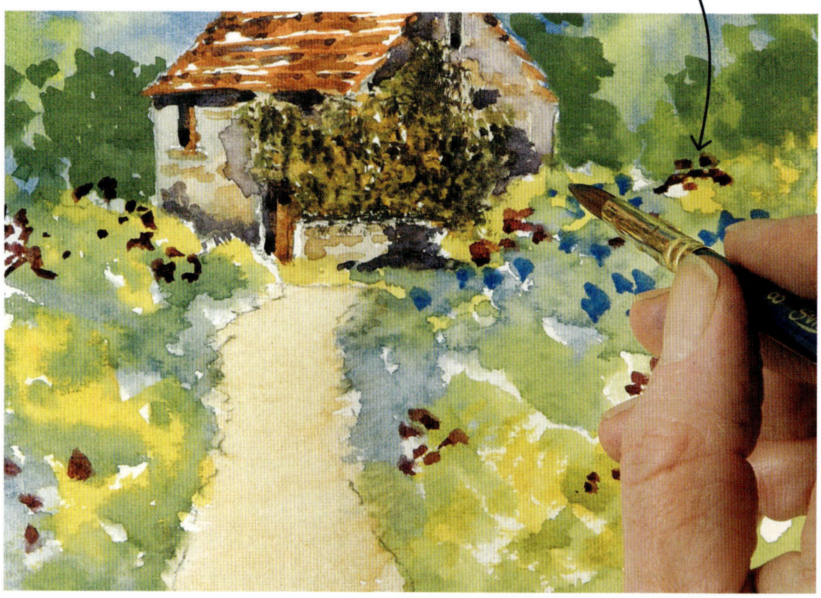

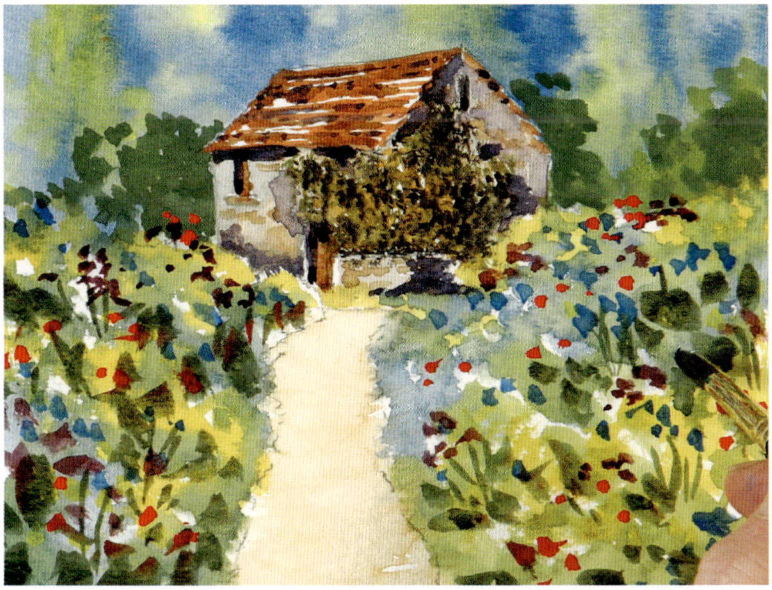

**STEP 9**

Next add strong cadmium yellow and a few touches of cadmium red – less is more here, remember, and it's better to have a few blooms standing out than a mass of indistinguishable ones. Use a mix of Hooker's green and burnt sienna to add a few simple blobs for leaves and lines for stems; make these a bit darker in the foreground. Let this dry a little.

*Don't make the shadows too strong.*

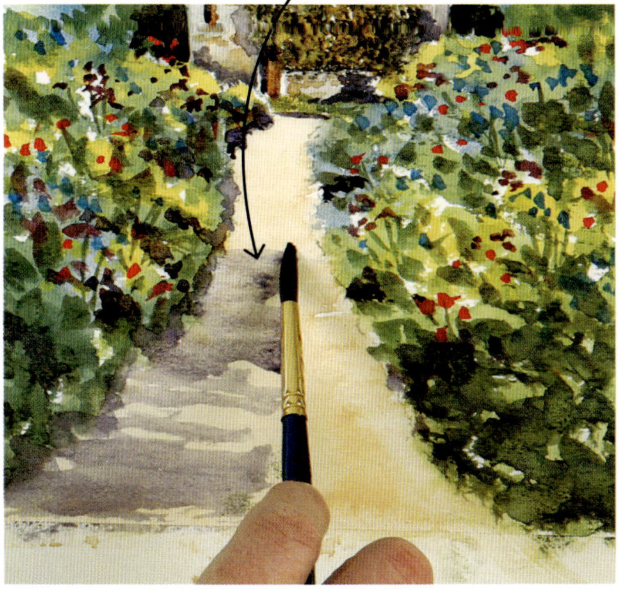

**STEP 10**

Mix ultramarine, alizarin crimson and a little burnt sienna for the shadow areas, and start by adding shadows to the bushes near the building – soften the edges to make the building stand out. Use the same mix for the border on the left, bringing the shadow at its foot across the path, and a lot less in the right border, which is in sunshine. Make a very dark mix of ultramarine and burnt sienna, and use a No. 4 rigger brush to add a few squiggly marks and lines to the path and borders to pull everything together. That's it – and you haven't painted a single flower in detail!

# Still life

The good thing about still lifes is that you don't have to go far to paint one – just set it up and enjoy it. However, while you do have total control over your subject, you also have to think hard about how to compose a picture and, particularly, how to get the lighting right: the step-by-step exercises for this project are designed to give you some guidelines.

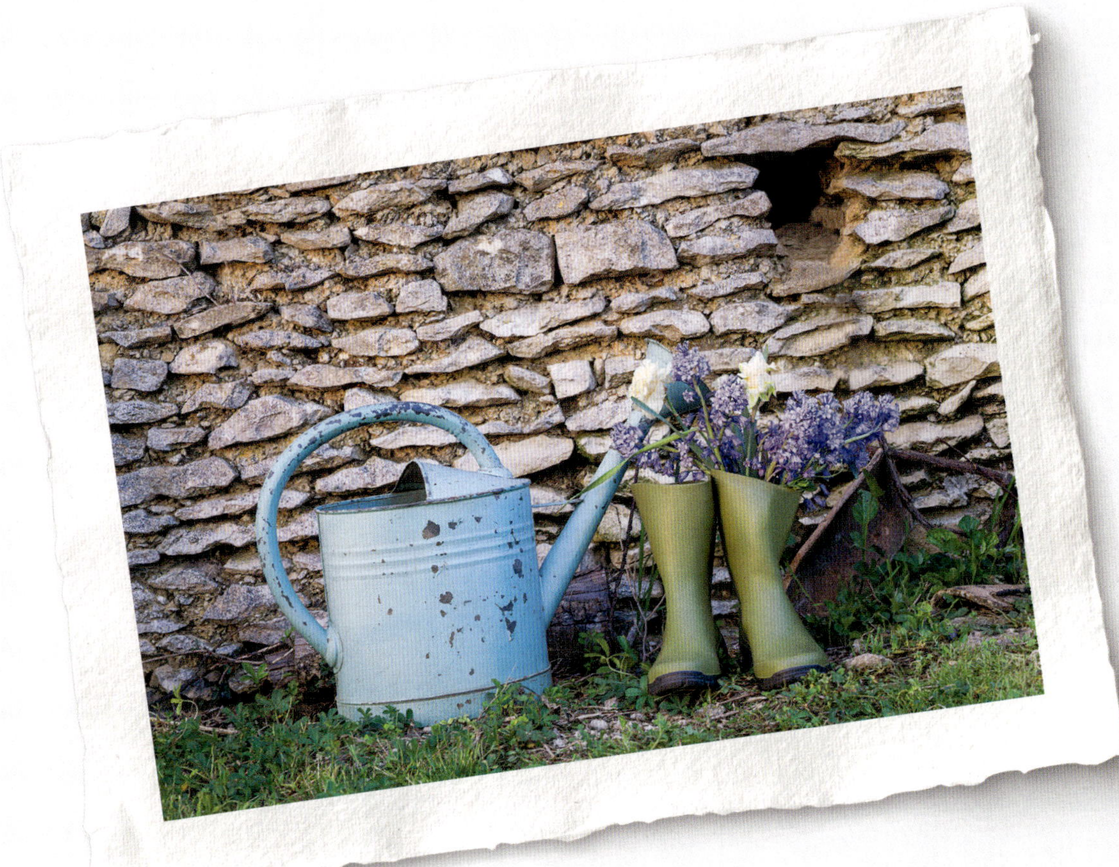

REFERENCE PHOTO
Working from a photograph allows you to work at your leisure in a studio rather than outside. It is useful for reminding you of the shape and size of your subject.

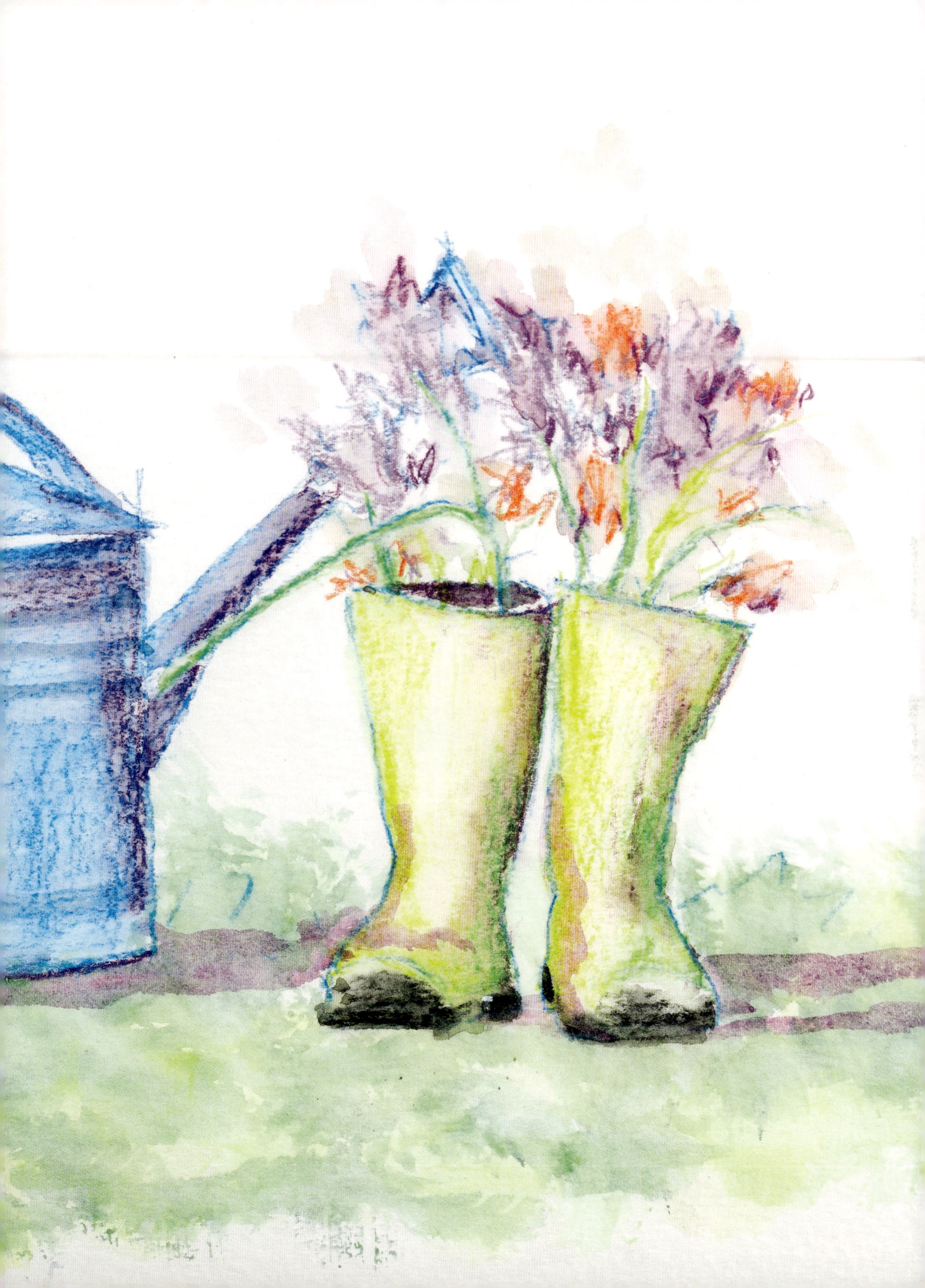

## EXERCISE: COMPOSITION

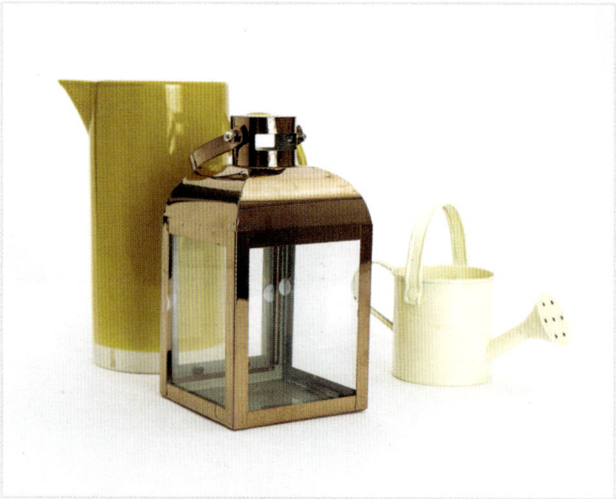

These three objects were the first that came to hand in my kitchen, but they turned out to be a good choice: the jug is tall and reflective, the lantern is shorter and transparent, and the watering can, although white, has plenty of tone on it. Before you even think of drawing or picking up a brush, you need to spend time trying out different positions and placings.

In the setting below, although you can see all three objects clearly, the overall effect is pretty boring – not least because the jug and watering can are facing the same way, with their handles on the left. There's no overlap between the three as there is in the setting above, where the lantern blocks out part of the other two objects.

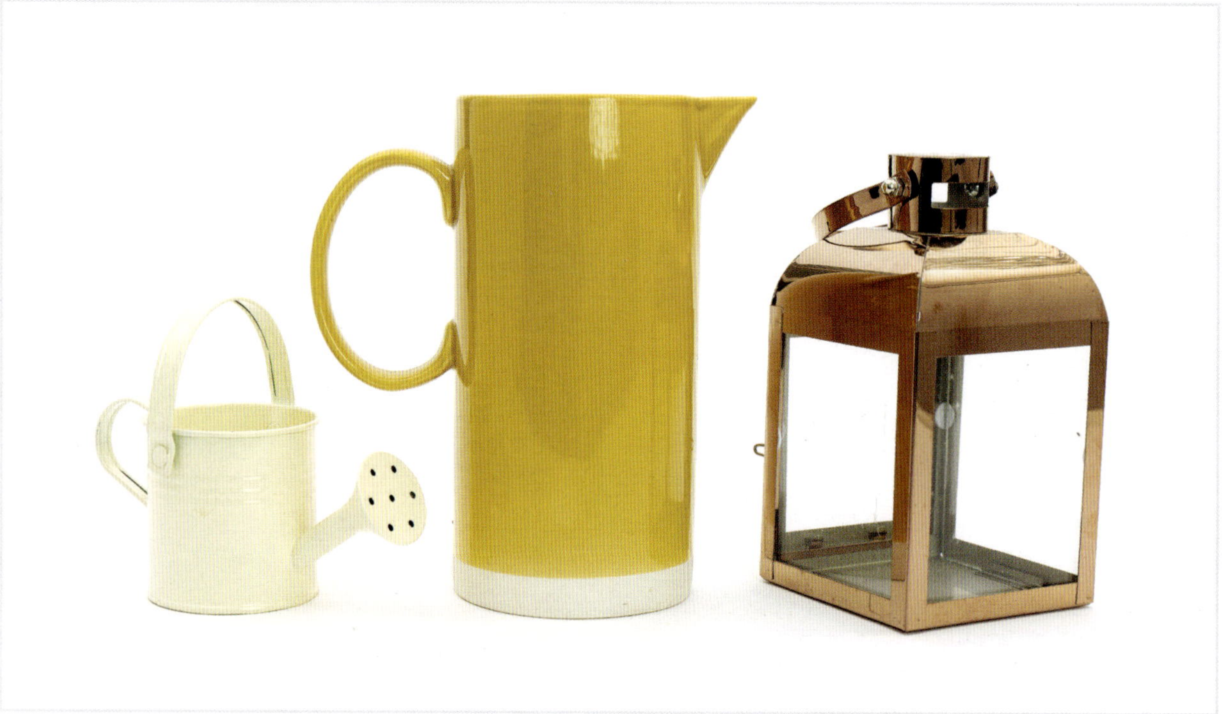

The arrangement on this page offers a more pleasing view, with the objects increasing in size from the front to the rear of the composition.

As you can see from these few examples, there is no one right way to compose a still life, but some settings do look more attractive than others. Make lots of drawings – just the rough outlines with no detail – to see how your subjects fit together in a composition, and experiment with the format you want to use: landscape (horizontal) or portrait (vertical) are the most used, but consider a square frame for your picture as well.

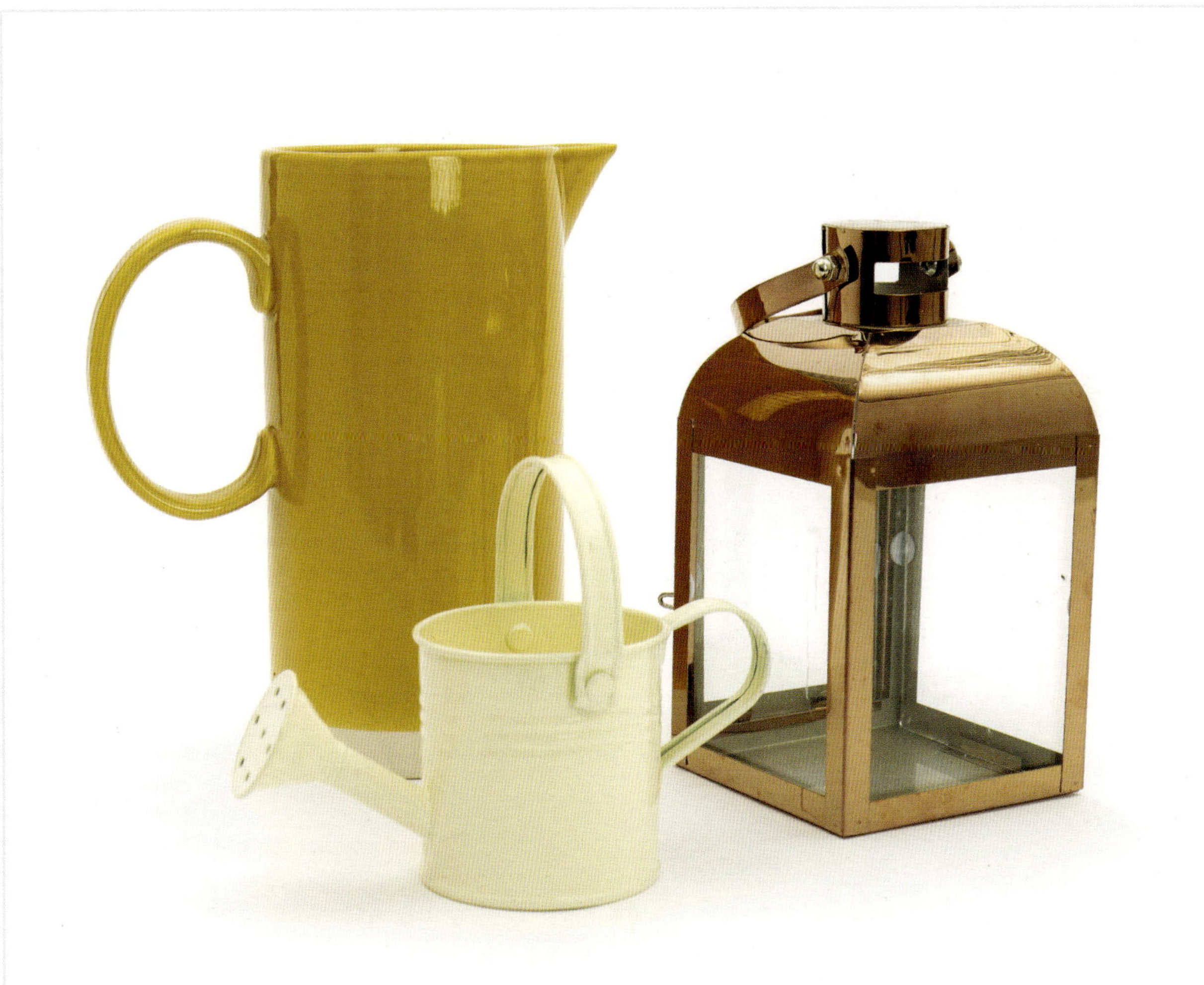

# EXERCISE: LIGHTING AND SHADOWS

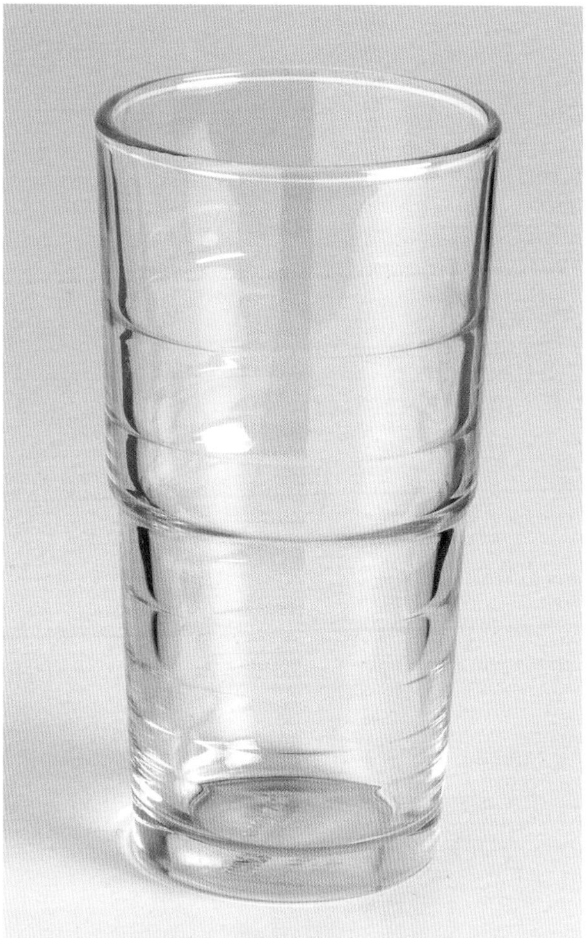

I used a glass for this section to show how a highly reflective surface is affected by light. In this photo the light is coming from the right but only faintly: there is only a little cast shadow from the glass, but quite a strong one inside it.

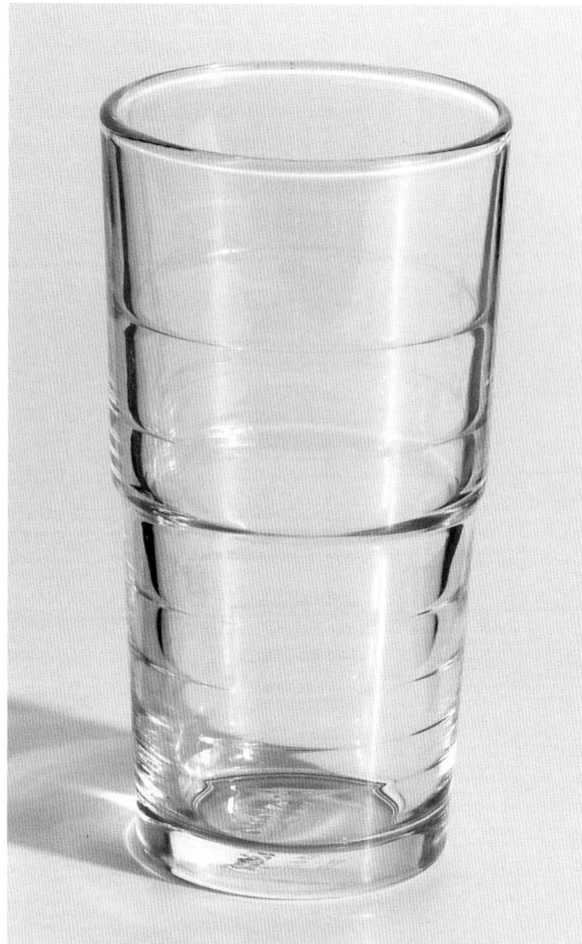

Here, the light from the right is very strong, producing a shadow that is darker than the glass itself. The single diffused reflection in the example on the left has been replaced by two sharp ones, and the indentations around the glass towards the base are more visible.

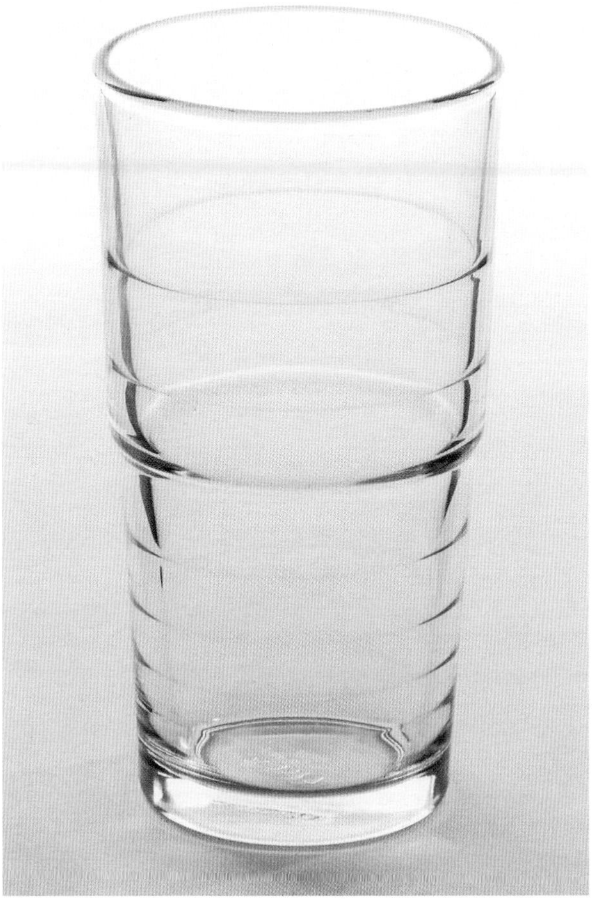

With no directional light, as above, the glass can be seen in more detail, but the reflections have been lost, except at the base. It looks more 'solid' like this.

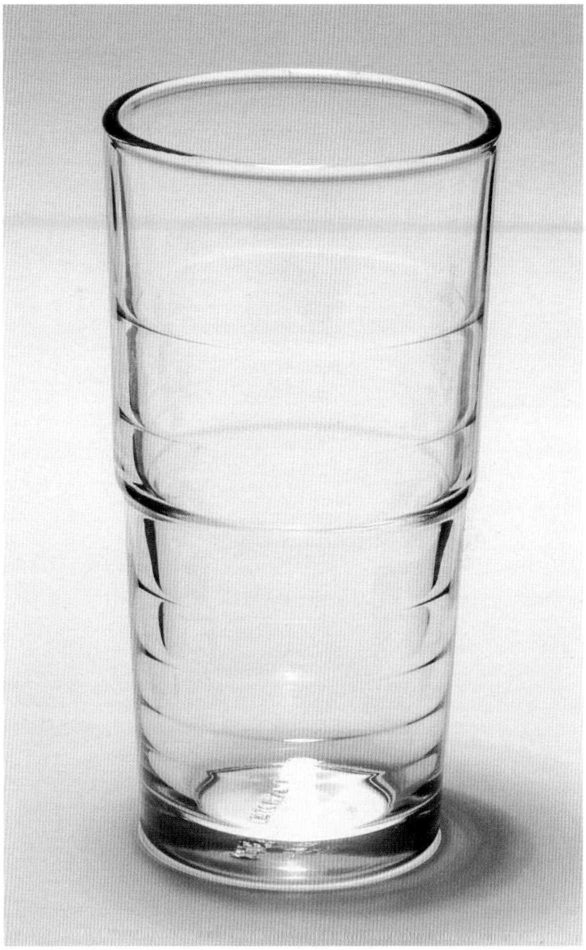

Here the light is coming from directly above the glass, and is reflected strongly back up from the base – the resulting oval is diffused by the front of the glass and thus distorted. To paint shadows in any of these lighting situations, you need to look at the cool colours of the blues first, mixing them to match the situation.

# In the garden

This is a very pleasing little garden sketch in watercolour pencils. Painted outside with natural light, it has a fresh and lively feel to it.

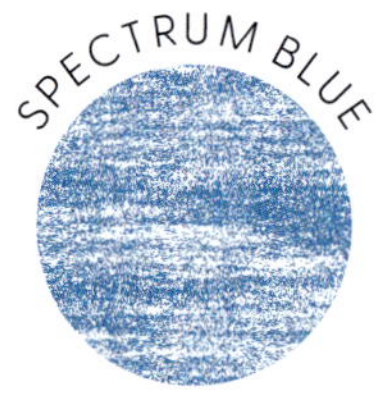


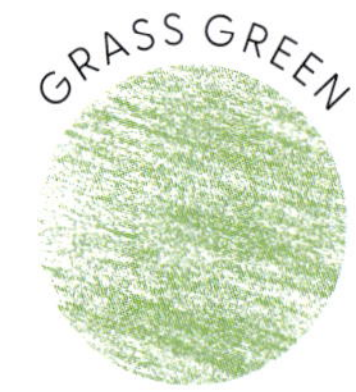


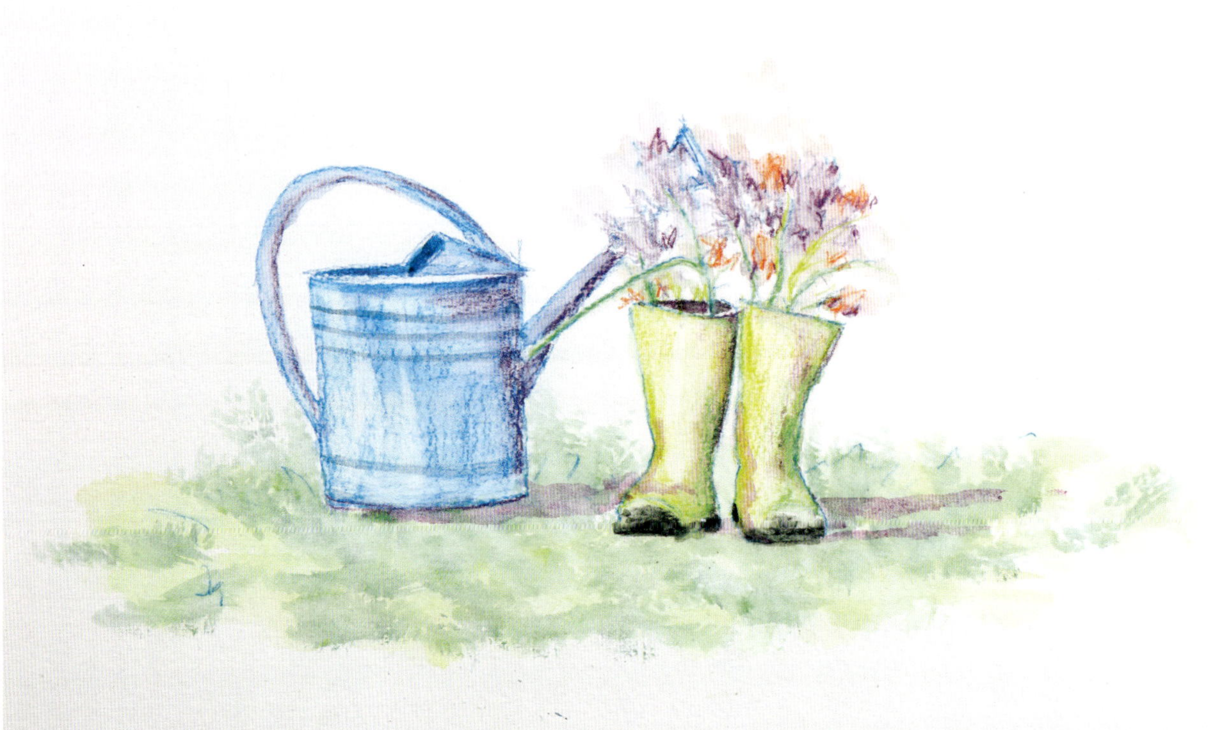

**PRELIMINARY DRAWING**
Aim to get a roundness to the top of the watering can and the top of the boots. Don't spend too long drawing the flowers as these will come to life when you add the colour. I used a Derwent spectrum blue watercolour pencil to create this initial drawing.

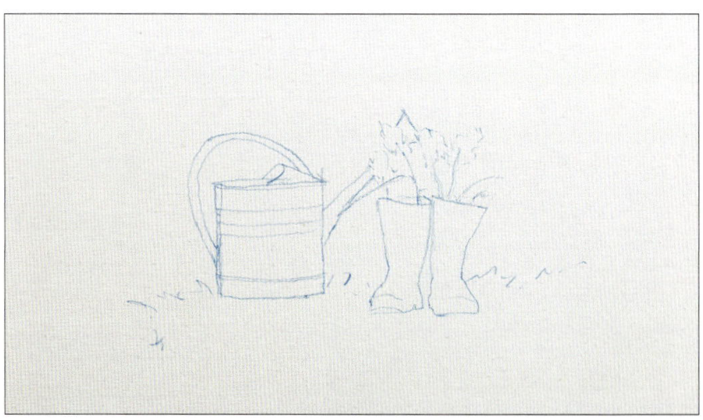

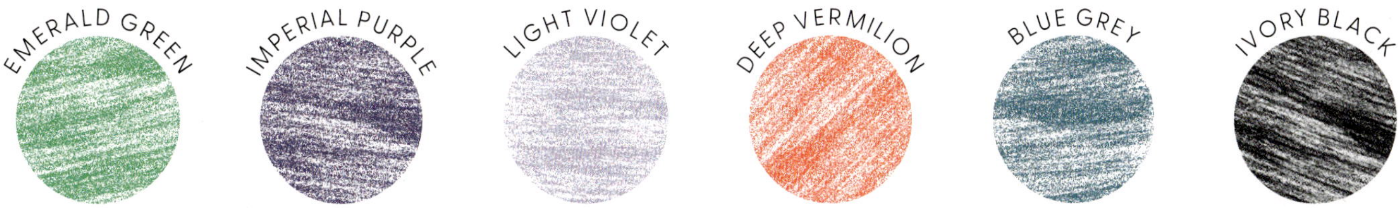


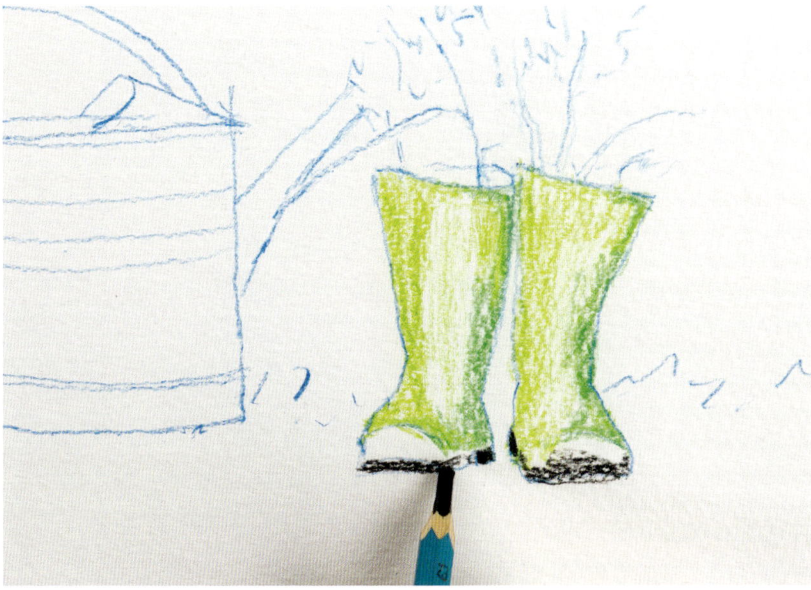

**STEP 1**

Shade one side of the wellies using grass green. Then use emerald green to colour the other side, so there are different shades of green making up the wellies. Colour the soles with ivory black. Leave little bits of white paper showing through here and there between the areas - these will merge when you add water, so leave spaces to merge the colours.

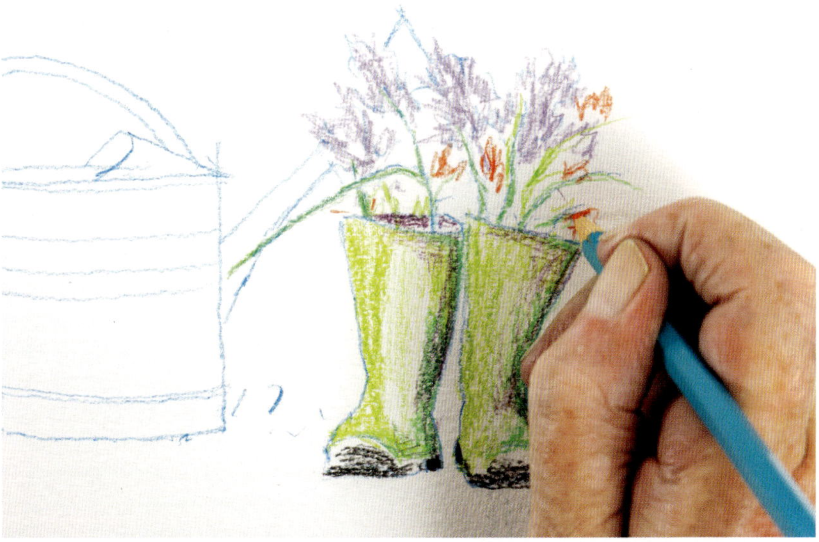

**STEP 2**

Use imperial purple for the shaded areas on the wellies, including inside, and the same green shades as the wellies for the stems. I added a few more colours into the flowers than are actually in the photograph just to give a bit more variation: light violet and deep vermilion, with some more imperial purple to add depth.

The stronger the colour you want, the harder you press with the watercolour pencil.

**STEP 3**
Fill in the outline of the watering can with spectrum blue. Use the same colour for the inside of the can, but pressing on a lot harder and leaving a little bit of the white paper showing on the top and between the base and the lid. Then use imperial purple to add the shadows on the right-hand edges of the watering can.

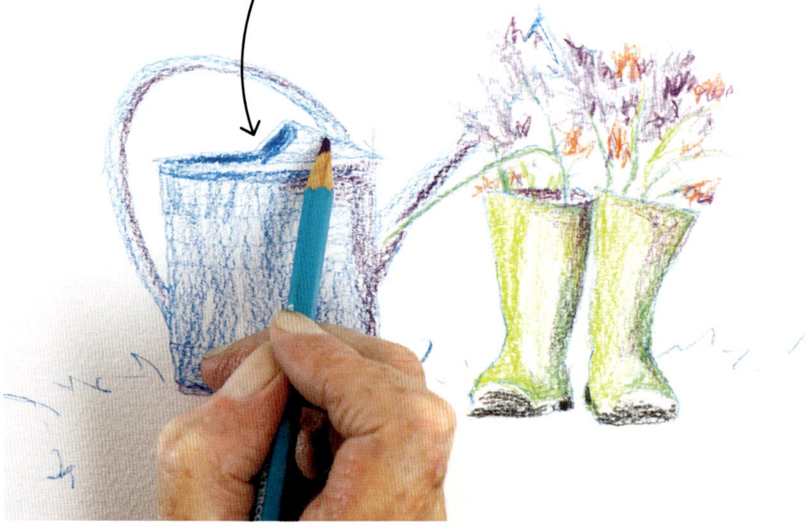

**STEP 4**
And now to add the water. With a clean, damp No. 8 round brush, pick up the paint and move it around one of the wellies, dabbing here and there to leave some lighter touches. Then with a 19mm (¾in) flat brush move the paint around and take light out.

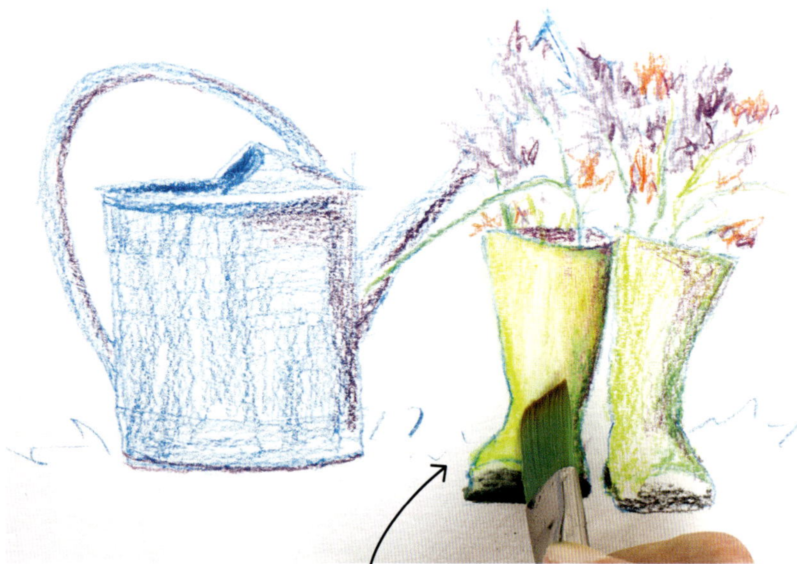

Remember that colour from watercolour pencils behaves just like paint once it's on the paper and wet.

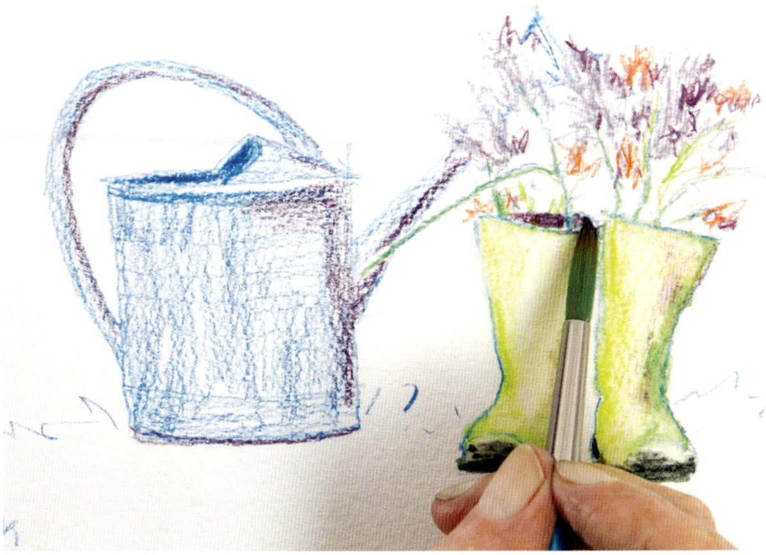

### STEP 5

Repeat on the other welly. Pick up some black from the soles with a No. 8 round brush and drop it inside the welly on to the shadow colour, leaving that little bit of white paper showing at the top.

*Even though the colour is already on the paper, don't be too precise with the flowers.*

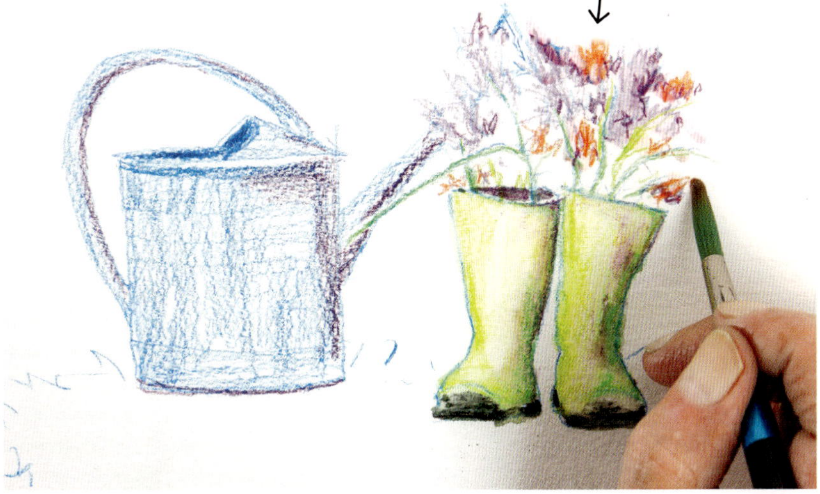

### STEP 6

For the flowers, simply stipple over the colour with a wet No. 8 round brush. Now stroke over the green stems with a clean, wet brush, letting the colour merge with the rest of the picture.

*Start with the top handle for the can, so you don't have to put your hand over the bottom bit to paint it later.*

### STEP 7

With a No. 8 round brush, wet the blue areas on the handle. Then pick up the purple on the inside of the handle and blend it into the rest. Moving into the spout, wet the blue bit first, then blend into the dark and dab on to spread upwards. Keep the colour nice and dark on the inside of the can.

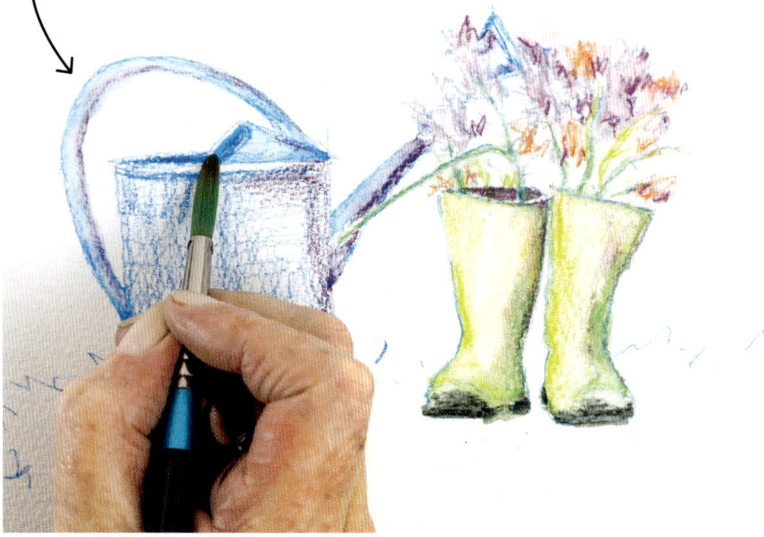

### STEP 8

Wet the colour on the base of the can, blending the shadow into the blue, still leaving that little bit of white paper showing through under the lip of the watering can. Then back to the 19mm (¾in) flat brush to take a little bit of light out down the side. While you let the bucket dry, move on to the grass underneath.

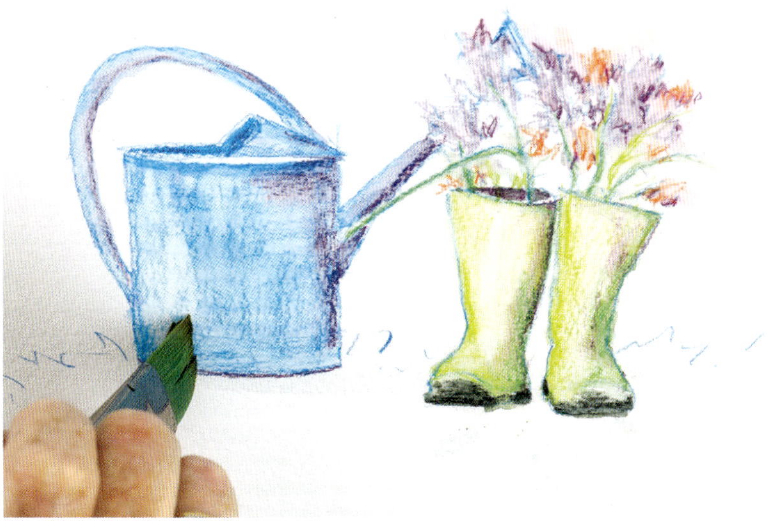

### STEP 9

Use a wet 19mm (¾in) flat brush to take the paint directly off the grass green pencil and stipple the colour on to the paper under the watering can and wellies. Then a little bit of blue grey mixed with the emerald green on to the same brush, and dab that on top for some depth.

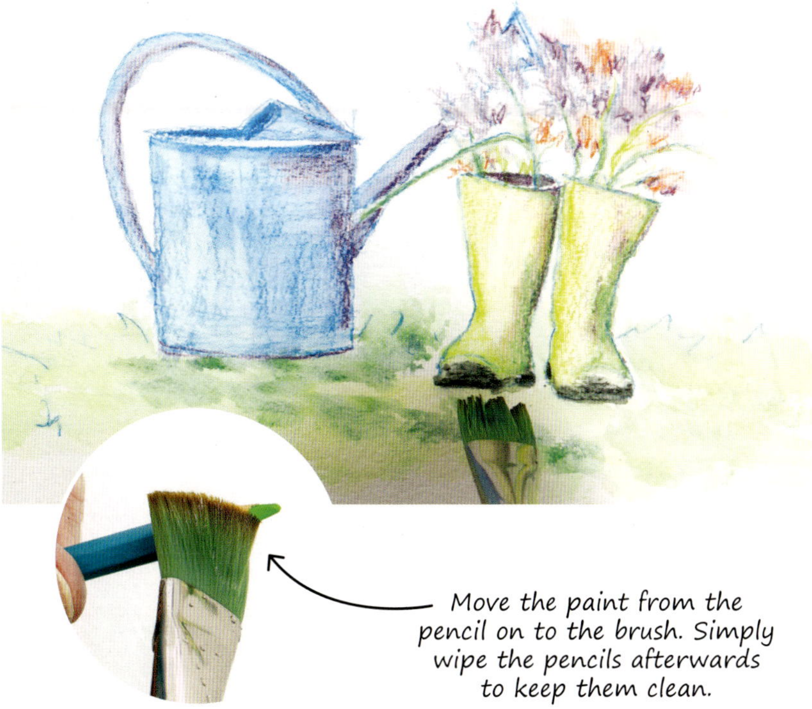

*Move the paint from the pencil on to the brush. Simply wipe the pencils afterwards to keep them clean.*

### STEP 10

Take some blue grey off the pencil on to a No. 8 round brush and paint a few curved lines on the can. Use more blue grey inside the watering can to darken it. Now use imperial purple to add the shadows with the same brush – first from the can casting across and up on to a welly, and then from one welly casting on to the other welly.

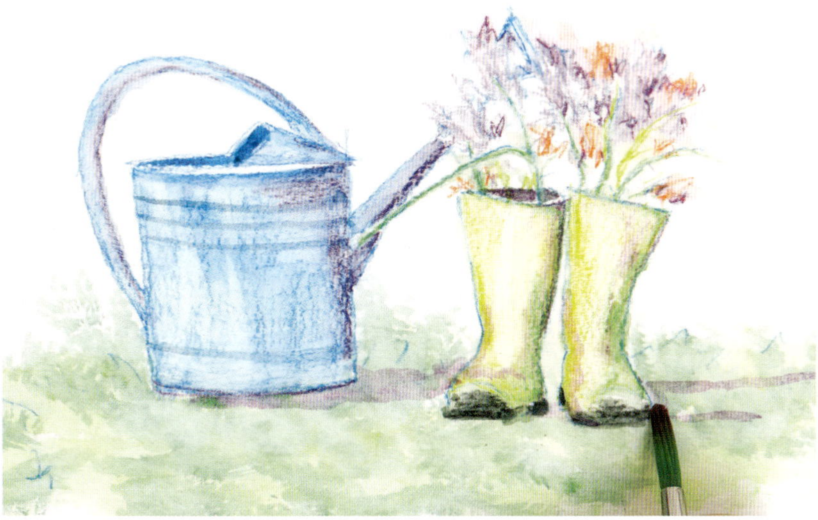

# Figures

How many landscapes do you see where either there are no figures to give a sense of scale and human interest, or they have been added as an afterthought and let everything down? Simple exercises that show how to paint figures, skin tones and clothing will give you the confidence to add them to your pictures.

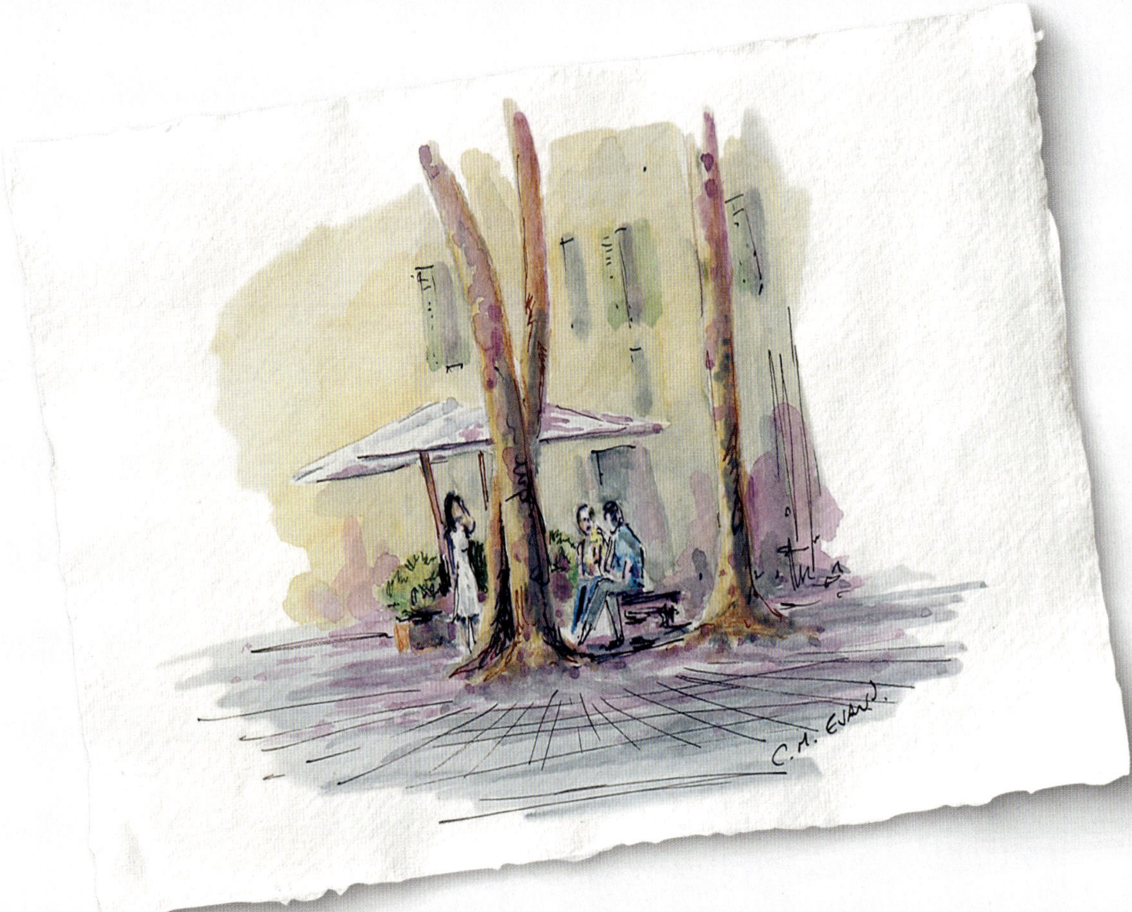


REFERENCE SKETCH

This quick sketch gave me enough information to work on for the placing of the trees, umbrellas and figures, and I added a little information about how the shadows fell. Note the pen lines in the foreground, which lead the eye into the point of focus.

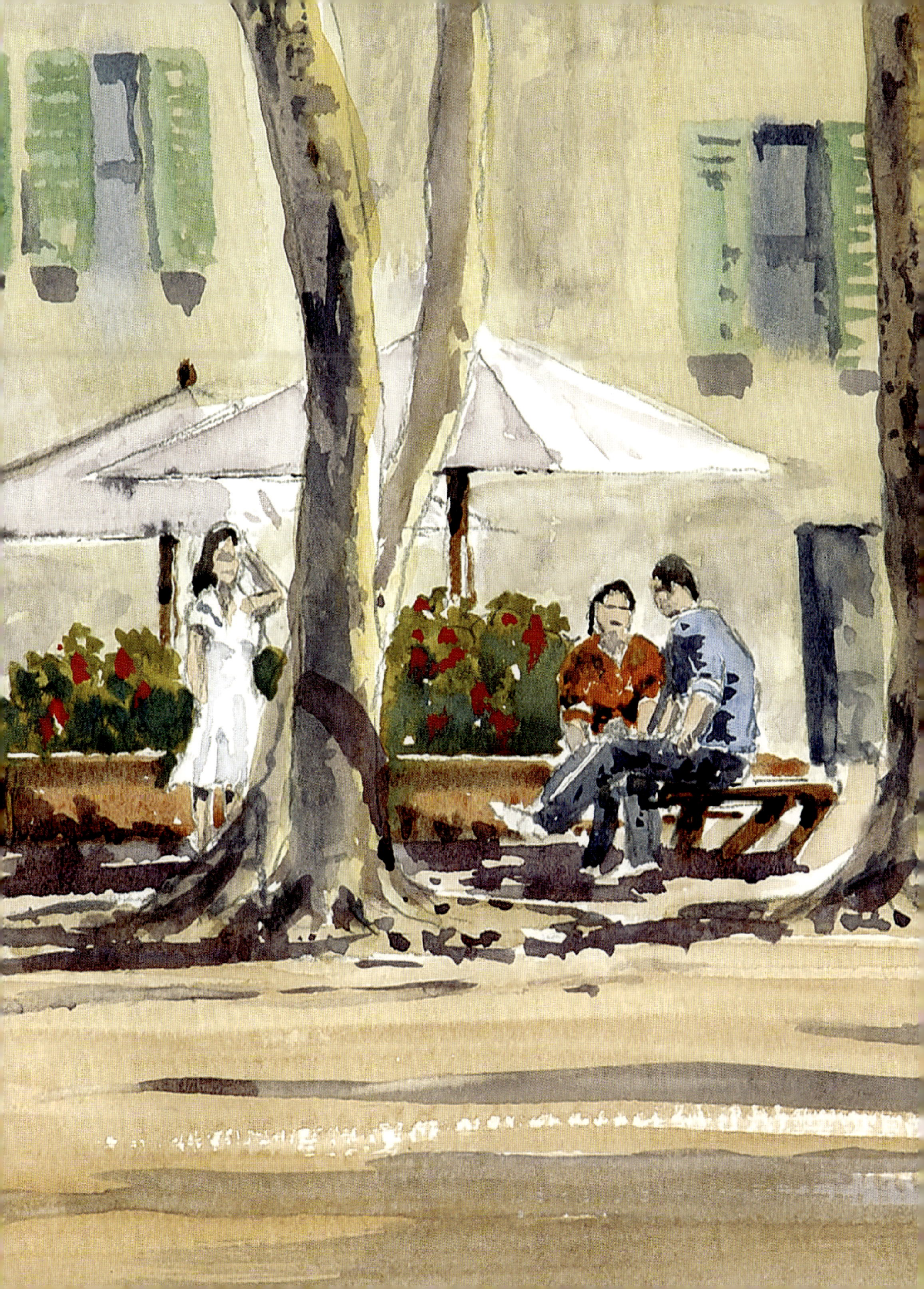

# EXERCISE: BASIC FIGURES

## SKIN TONES AND SHADING

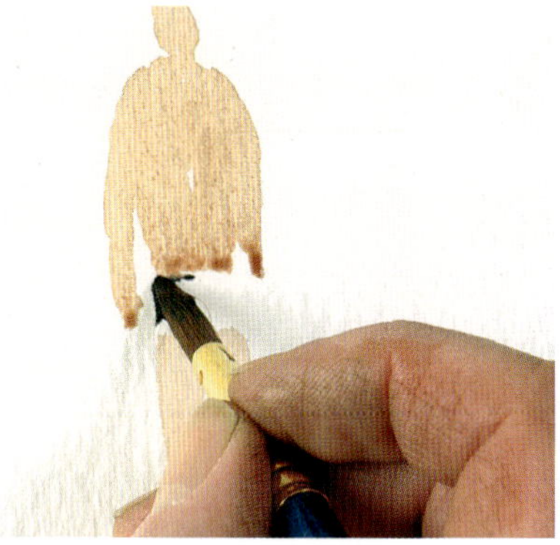

**1.** Make up a flesh tone from yellow ochre, alizarin crimson and a spot of ultramarine, then paint a blob for the head, a rectangle for the body and sticks for the arms.

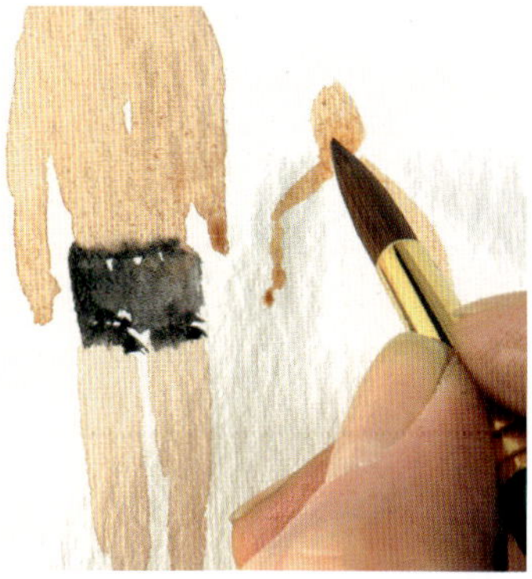

**2.** Use a mix of ultramarine and burnt sienna for the swimming trunks, then the flesh tone for the stick legs. Do the same for the smaller figure of the child.

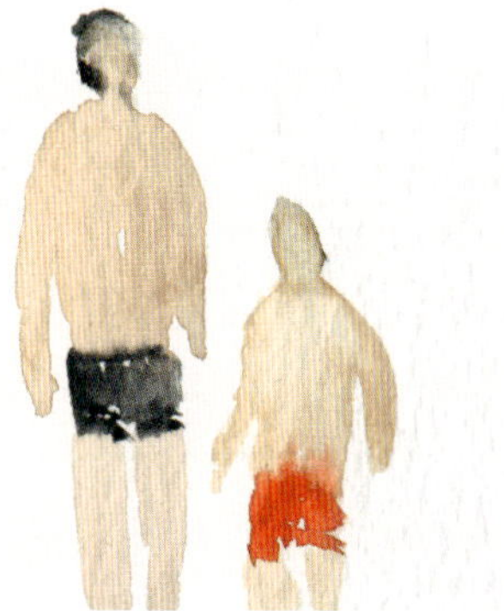

**3.** While everything is wet add some cadmium red for the child's trunks, and use a lighter mix of ultramarine and burnt sienna to drop in the man's hair.

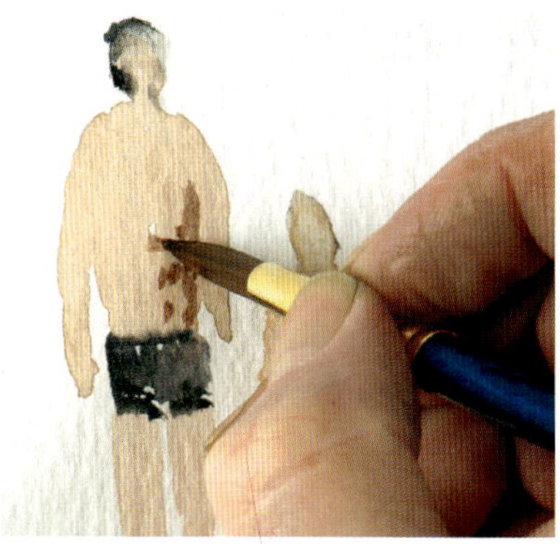

**4.** Let the washes dry, then put in some shadows – I added ultramarine to the flesh mix. The light is from the left, so the shadows go on the right.

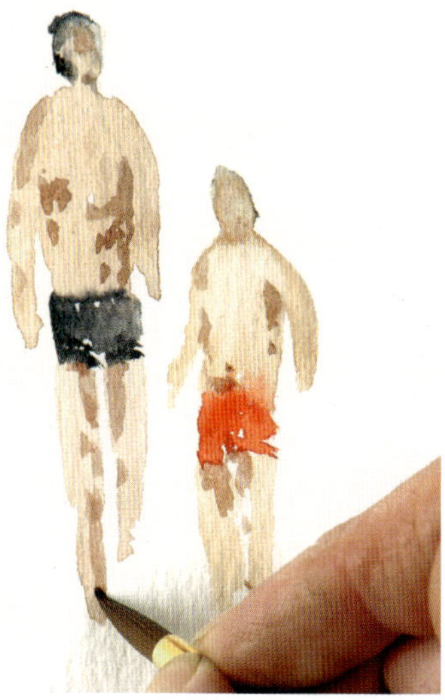

**5.** Use the shadows to add contours to the bodies, arms and legs – just a few darker tones here and there.

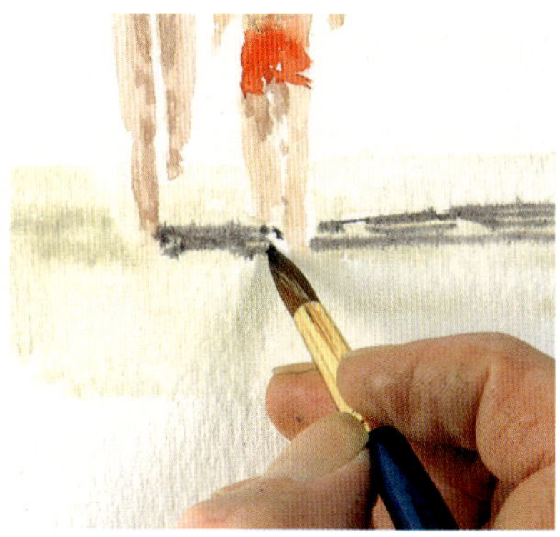

**6.** To ground the figures, paint some yellow ochre below and add cast shadows from the bodies, again remembering the direction of the light. If the sun is strong, as is likely since these figures are wearing swimming trunks on a beach, the shadows can be quite dark and hard-edged.

## DISTANT FIGURES

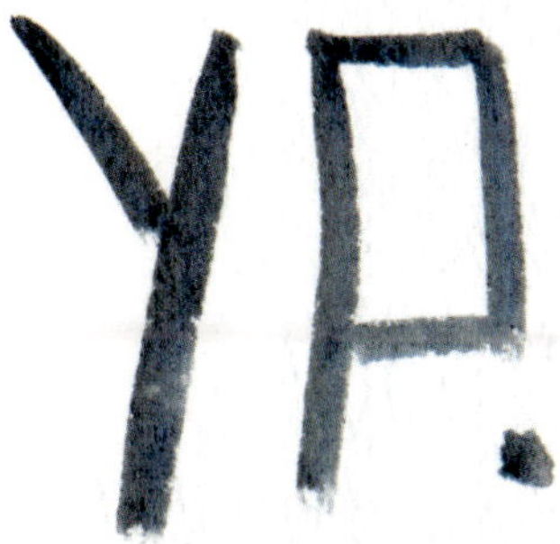


**1.** For distant figures, paint a ‘Y’ for the legs and a ‘P’ for the body. The head is a point.

**2.** Paint two points for the heads and block in two Ps for the bodies.

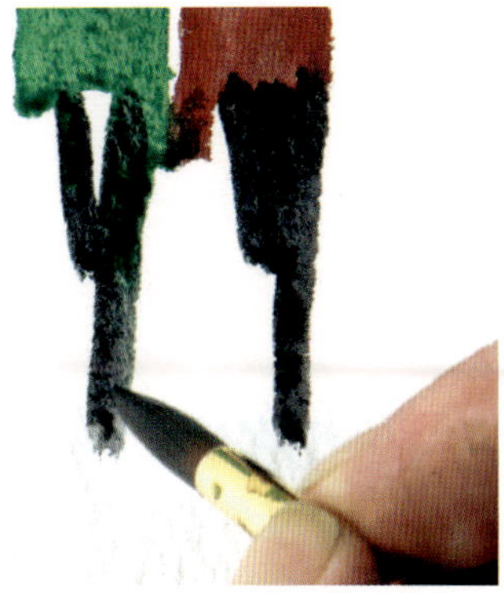

**3.** Now add the Ys for the legs and fill them in. A quick sweep of the brush gives you the ground.

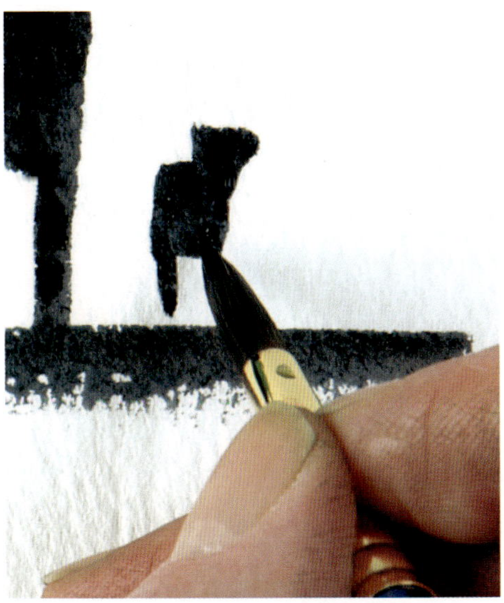

**4.** Paint a square for the dog’s body, a smaller one for the head and two sticks for the legs.

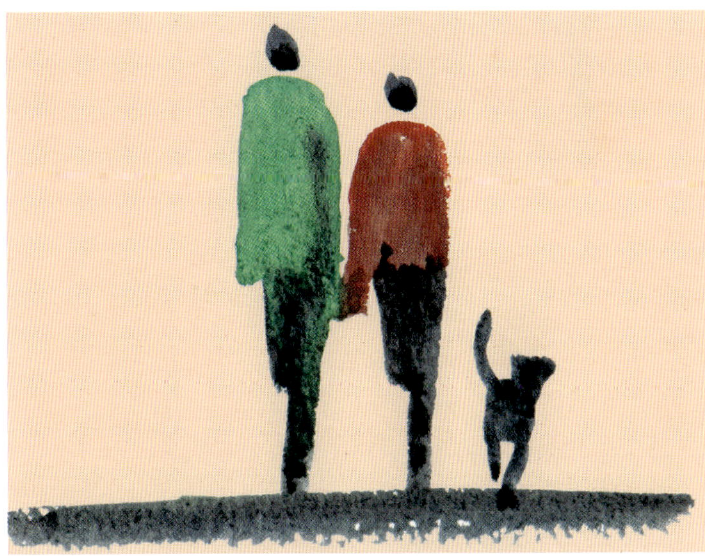

**5.** Add a curved line for the dog’s tail, and there you are – a couple and their dog out for a walk. Now that wasn’t hard, was it?

# EXERCISE: CLOTHED FIGURES

## FEMALE FIGURE

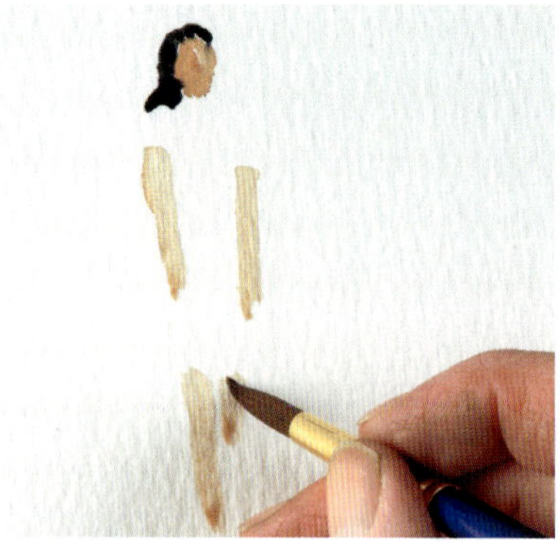

**1.** Use a No. 8 round brush to paint in a mix of ultramarine and burnt sienna for the hair, then quickly add the flesh tone from the previous pages for the head, arms and legs.

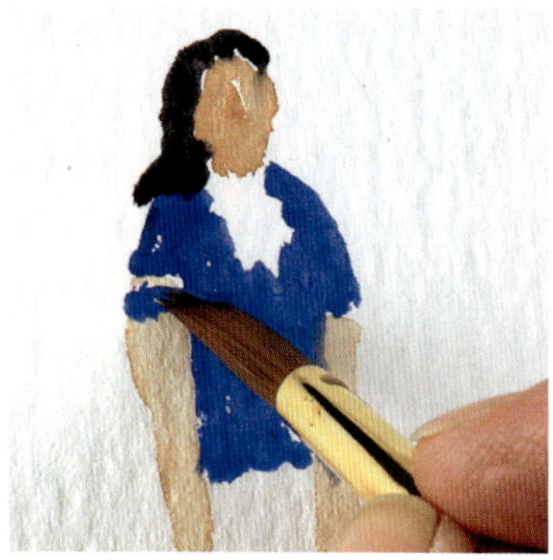

**2.** When thie washes have dried, use cobalt blue for the top, leaving white paper below the head for white fabric.

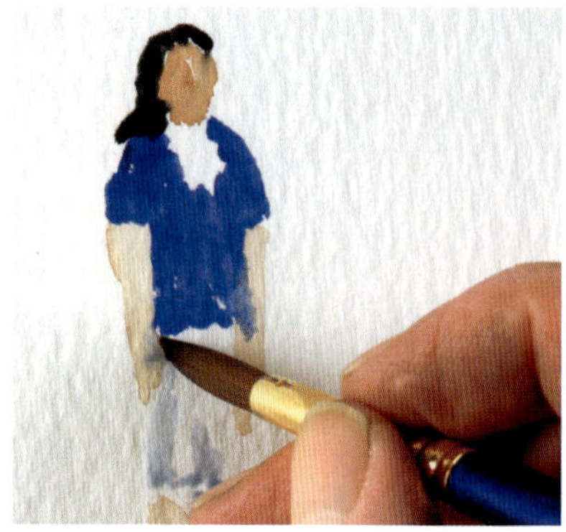

**3.** On a white skirt, all you'll see is the shadows. Use a diluted mix of cobalt blue and burnt sienna to add these.

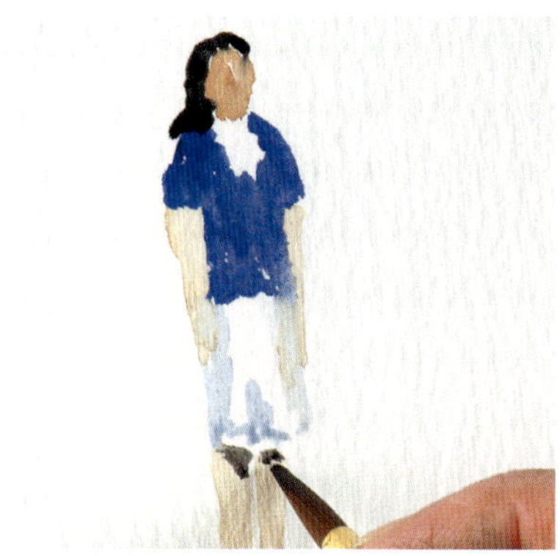

**4.** Make up a very watery version of the mix for the hair, and put in the shadows cast from the skirt on to the legs.

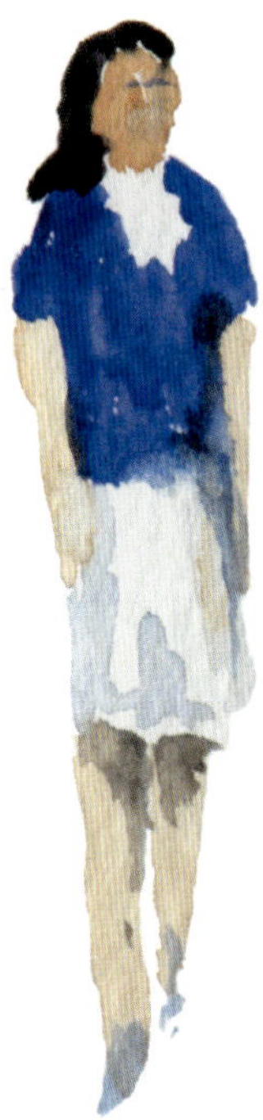

**5.** Add a couple of marks of the same mix for the features and other shadows, and the figure's done. This isn't a close-up, so a little suggestion is all you need.

### TRY IT YOURSELF

Experiment with people of different shapes and sizes. The colours can be any you choose. Put a few of these figures together in a line as though it's a group coming towards you.

## MALE FIGURE

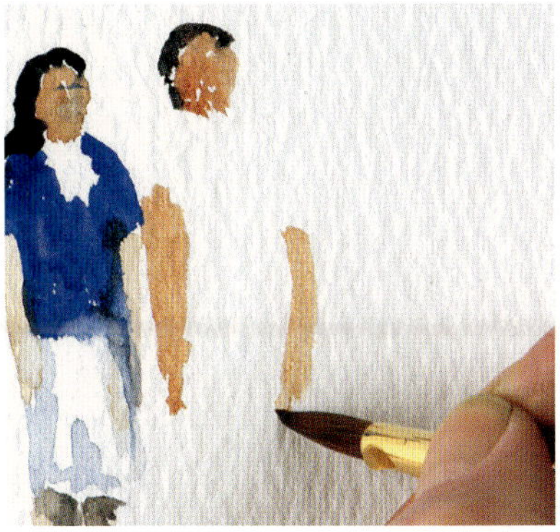

1. Start in the same way for the male figure – hair, head and arms at this stage.

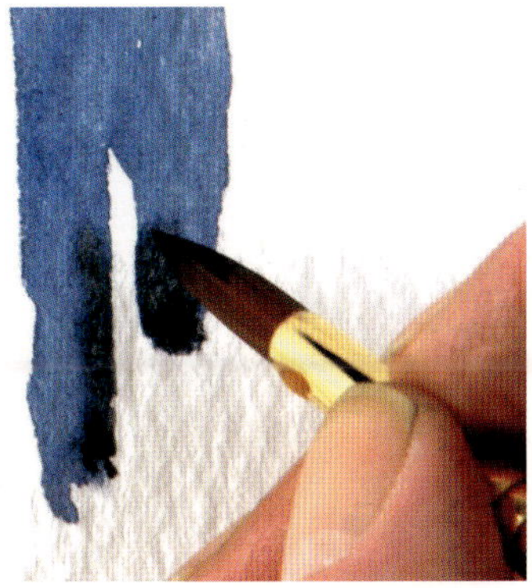

2. Add the jeans with a mid-strength mix of ultramarine and burnt sienna, suggesting the contours of the legs with a slightly stronger wash.

3. Most of the T-shirt can stay as white paper – use the same mix as for the skirt to add a few shadows.

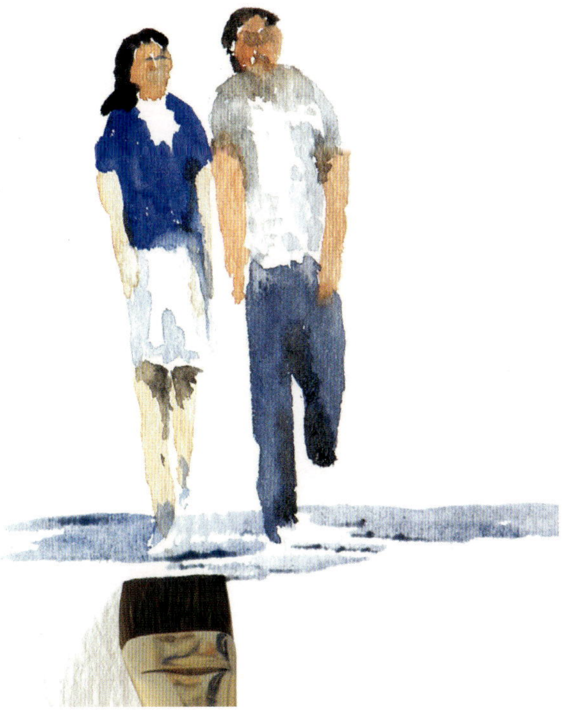

4. Make a few sweeping strokes at the bottom with a flat wash brush, and you've anchored your couple to the ground.

# Shaded street

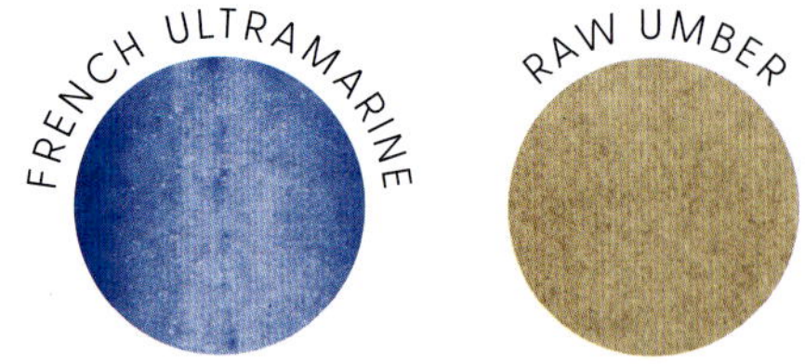


This group is enjoying a bit of shade in the square of a little market town in Tuscany – you'll find that in a grouping, an odd number of people makes a better composition than an even number (the same is true of birds in the sky), so I've painted three figures here, with the left-hand woman partly hidden by the trees.

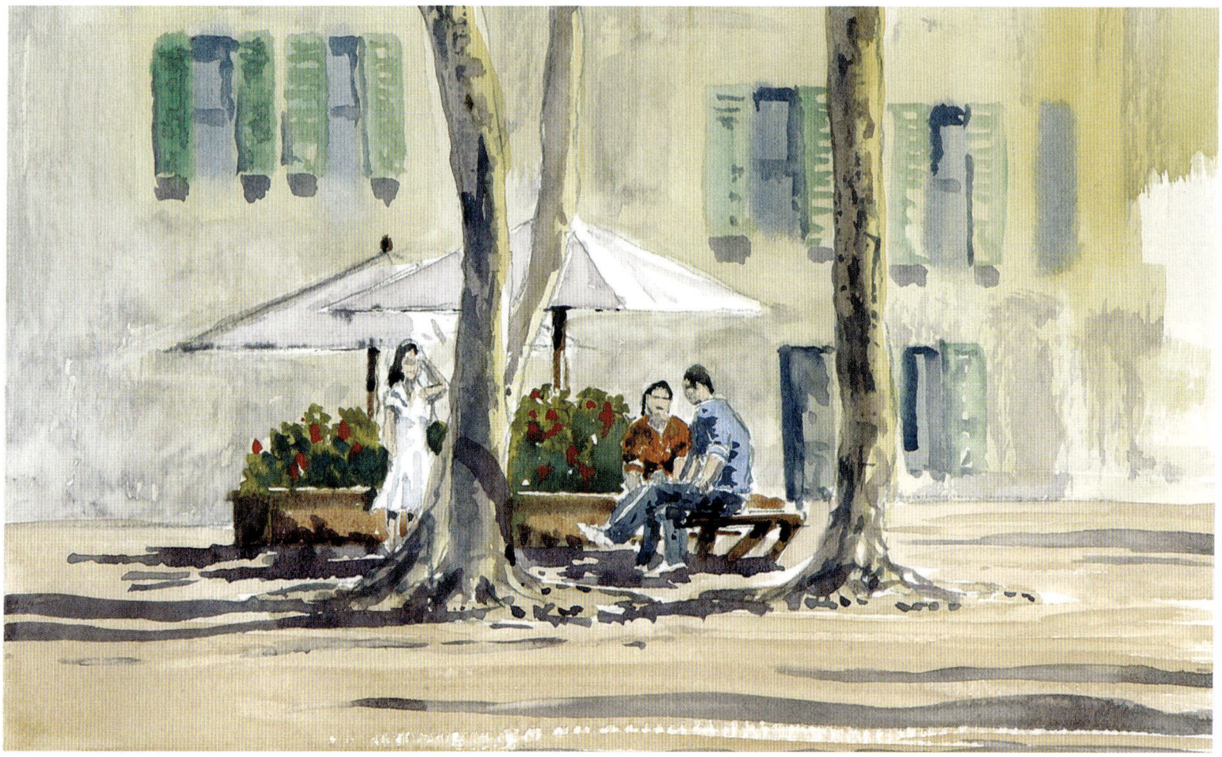

### PRELIMINARY DRAWING

Even in this last project I've kept the drawing to simple outlines. On the people you can see where the hair is and where the T-shirts and the skirt begin and end – but beyond that, the watercolours do the work for you.

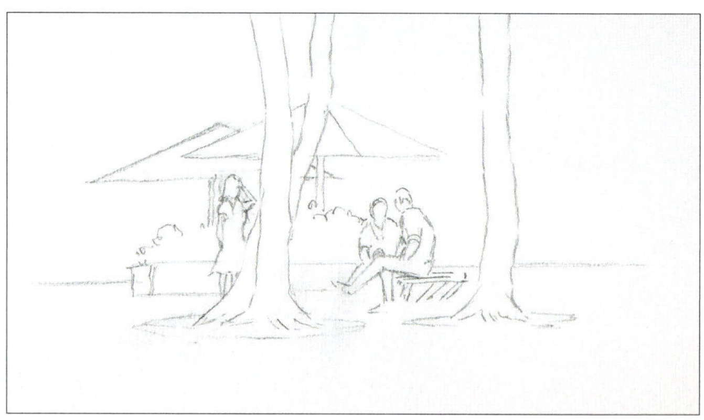

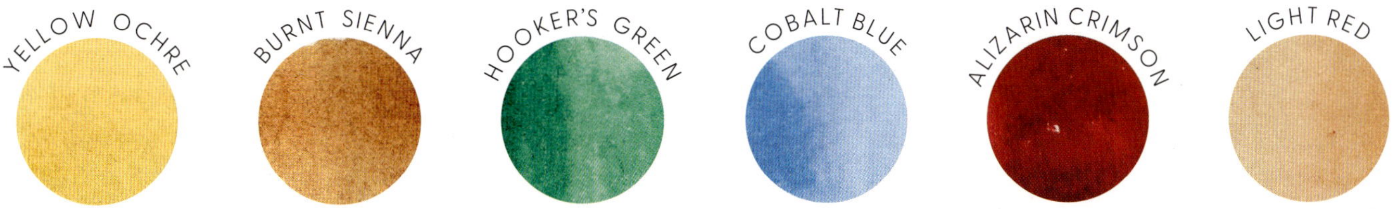


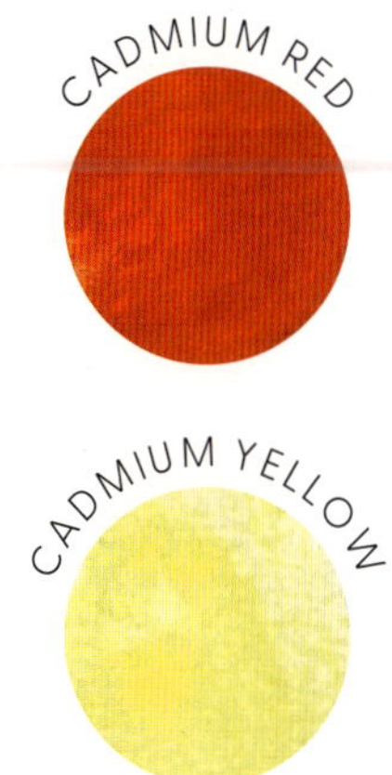


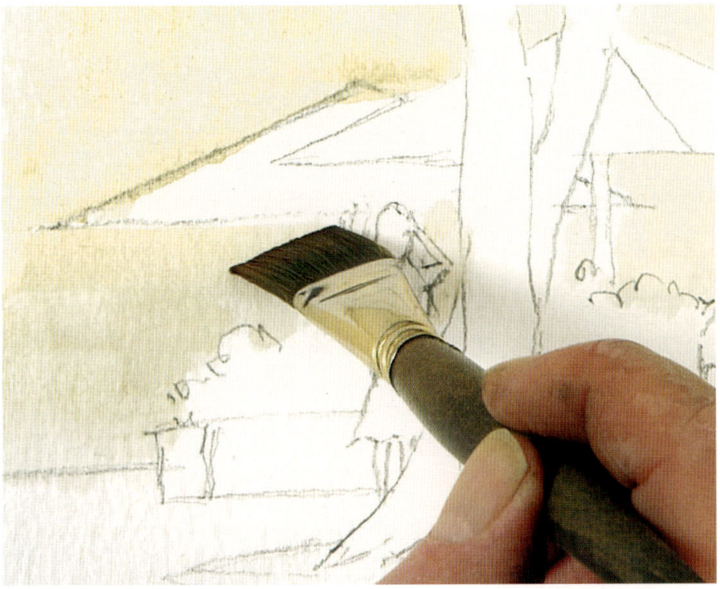

**STEP 1**

Use a 19mm (¾in) wash brush to lay on a flat wash of yellow ochre for the background walls. This wash is broken up by the trees and umbrella sunshades, so you don't have to work too quickly – don't dawdle, though.

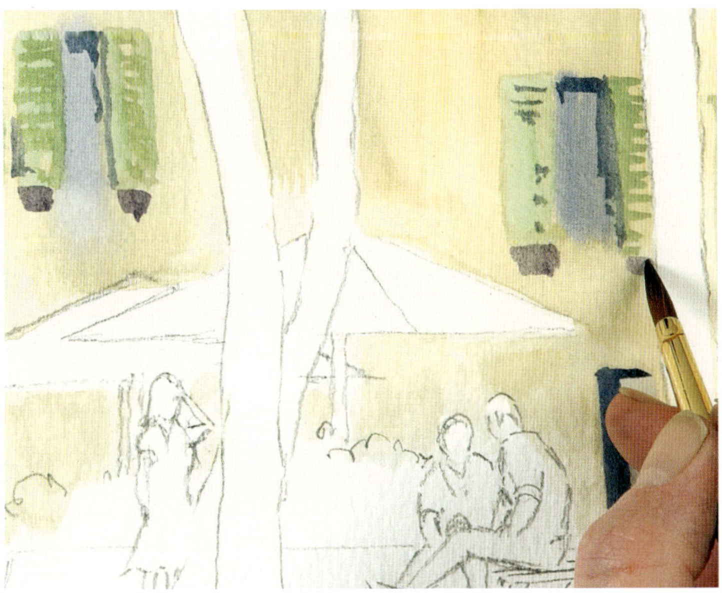

**STEP 2**

Let the wash dry, then put in a rough impression of the windows, using a mix of ultramarine and burnt sienna and a No. 8 round brush. The shutters are Hooker's green, and you need only add a few horizontal and vertical marks. When the windows have dried a little, add a darker mix for the recesses, and use alizarin crimson for the shadows cast by the shutters on the wall.

**STEP 3**
Start the trees with a strong wash of yellow ochre on the right side, where the sun hits the trunks. While this is wet add raw umber, letting it run into the ochre and blending for a soft, rounded edge. Quickly follow this with a mix of ultramarine and alizarin crimson for a warm shadow colour, and flick a few dots of this into the ochre to give texture.

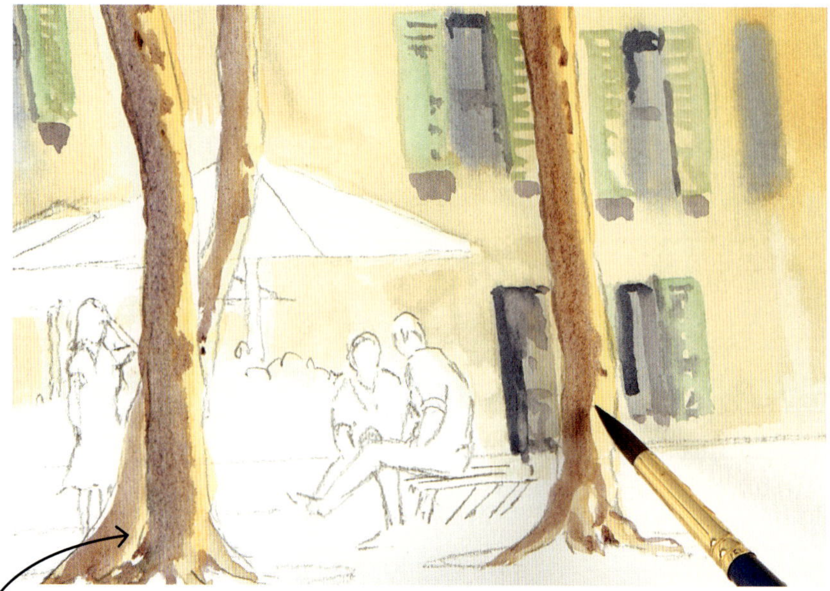

*Make sure all the colours in each tree go in while the paint is still wet.*

**STEP 4**
Use a lighter wash of ultramarine and alizarin crimson for the shadows on the white sunshades – lighter because they are white and further away than the trees. Paint the posts beneath with a mix of burnt sienna and raw umber, then add a strong shadow mix on the left of the posts – this may be a bit fiddly, but it's a detail that gives a lot of depth.

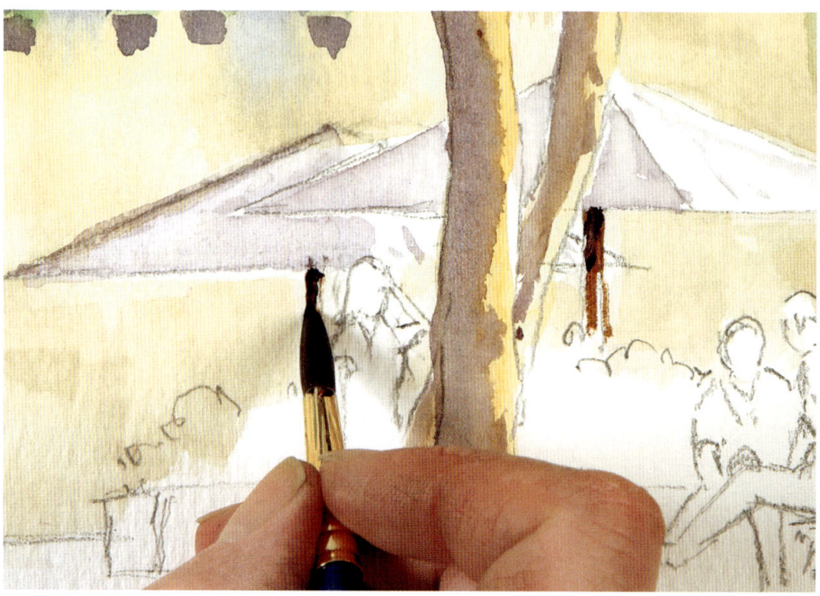

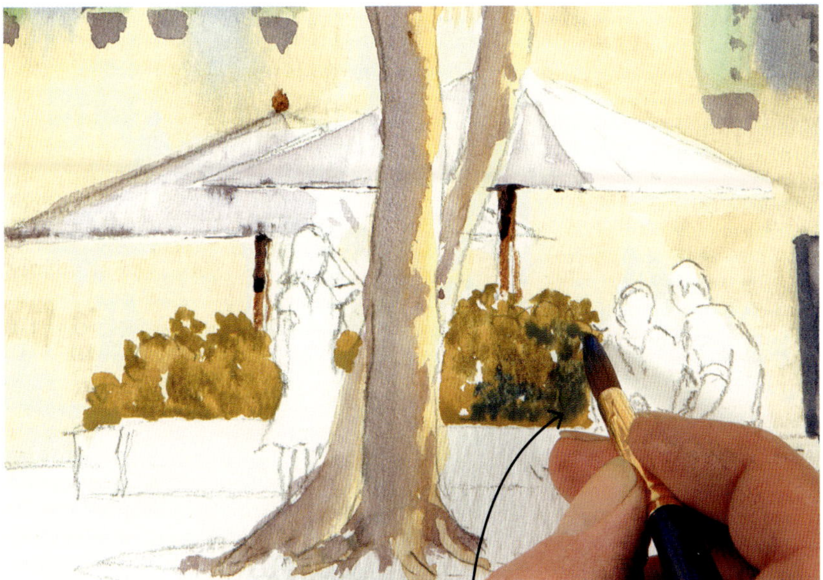

*The darkness to the right of the bushes helps push the figures further forward.*

### STEP 5

For the plants drop in a mix of yellow ochre and a little Hooker's green, leaving some white paper for highlights. Dab and dot a mix of Hooker's green and light red into this, followed by a little cobalt blue, allowing the first wash to remain visible in some parts.

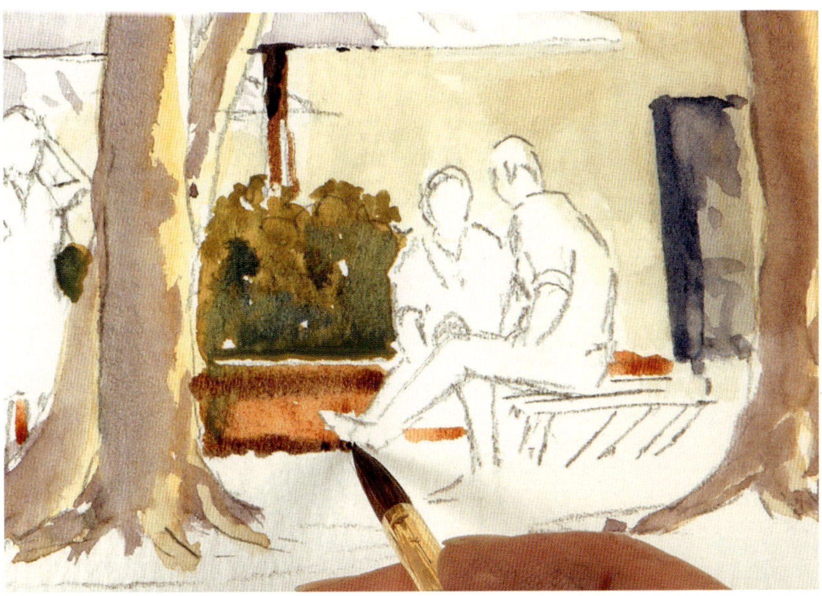

### STEP 6

Loosely dab on some light red for the terracotta plant holders, working around the people. Using the side of a No. 4 rigger brush, put a little more texture into the trees with a dark shadow mix. Then do the same up the sides of the buildings and at the base of the plant holders using the No. 8 brush and a watery mix of cobalt blue and alizarin crimson. Finish the flowers with a few blobs of cadmium red while these washes are drying.

**STEP 7**
As this is an Italian scene, I've given all the figures dark hair. Make up a very dark mix of ultramarine and burnt sienna and dab in the hair – use the No. 8 rather than the rigger, as you're just giving an impression.

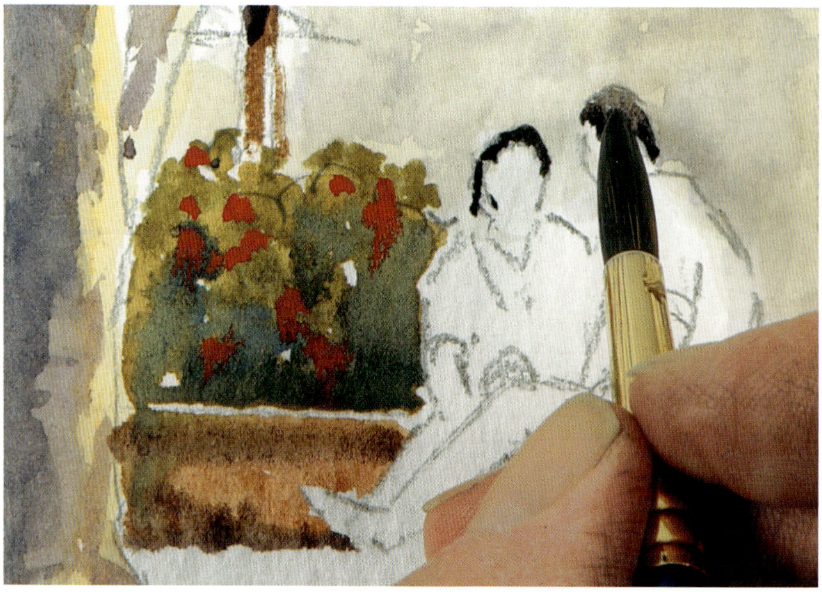

*Remember, the clothing needs shadows too. Think about the bend in the knee of the clothing or the person's bottom as it sits on the bench.*

**STEP 8**
The clothes are next – cobalt blue for the right-hand shirt, and a mix of cadmium red and cadmium yellow for the central one. Use darker and lighter mixes of ultramarine and burnt sienna for the trousers, and allow to dry.

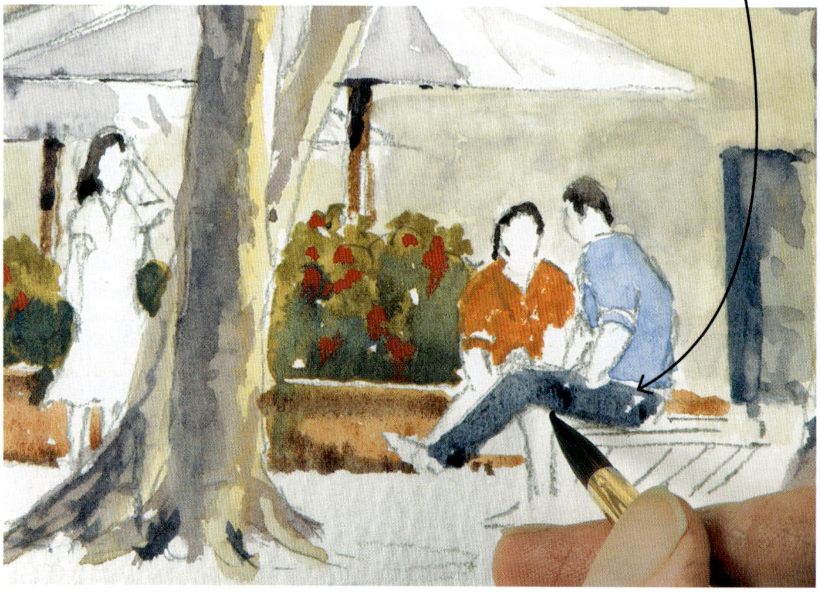

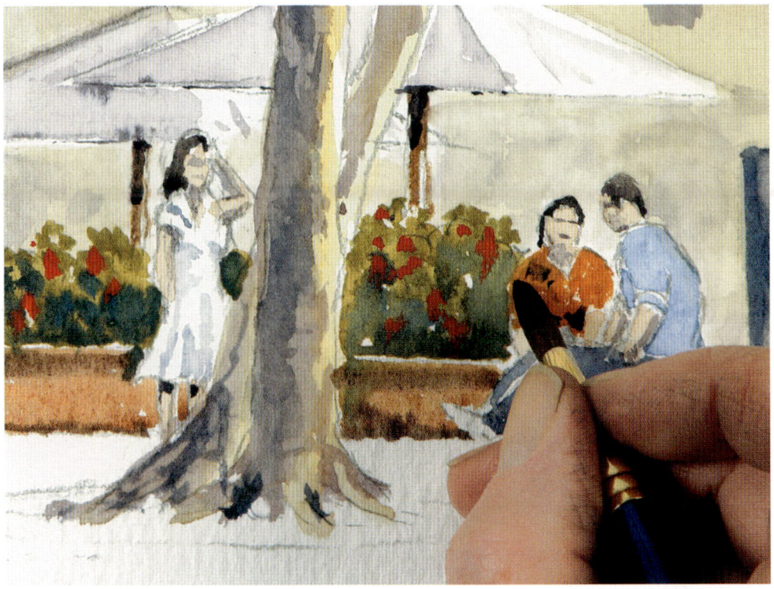

### STEP 9

Paint the faces with a mix of yellow ochre, alizarin crimson and a touch of ultramarine, then move on to the arms and the legs of the woman on the left. Let this dry completely, then drop in a few shadows for the features with a watery, light shadow mix – just a few spots here and there. Use the same colour for the shadows on the dress, going darker towards the bottom, and on the men's clothes. When dry, use raw umber and burnt sienna for the bench, and add some dark cast shadows beneath it and at the bases of the trees.

*Don't make the shadows cast by the figures or the bench too long, or they will not be grounded.*

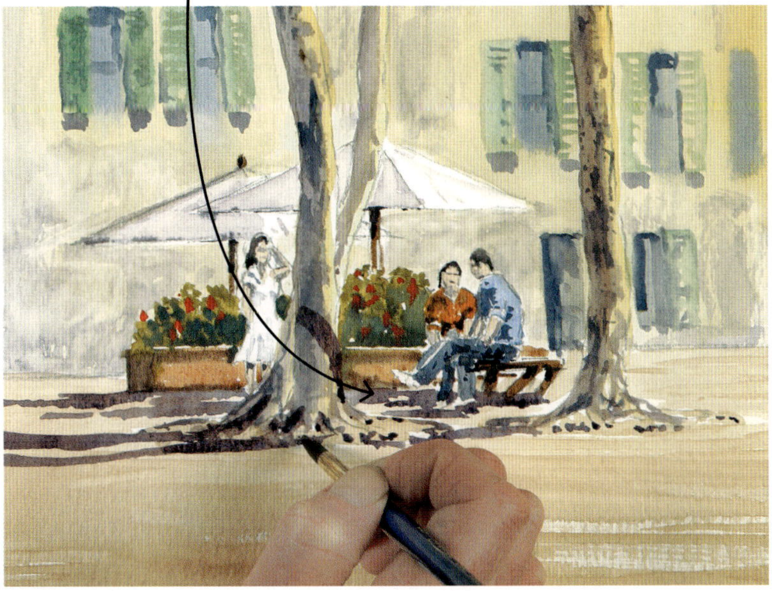

### STEP 10

To fill in the ground use the smaller wash brush with a watery mix of yellow ochre and light red; start at the base of the building and increase the mix strength as you come forward. Leave a little white paper showing through. Let this dry completely, then use the No. 8 brush to put in the shadows on the ground with a mix of cobalt blue, alizarin crimson and burnt sienna. Put a few blobs at the bases of the trees, then add the shadows themselves. Finally invent something out of view and bring its shadows across the foreground.

# Final thoughts

**You may think you have come to the end of the journey, but it's only the beginning for you.**

You should have at least gained enough confidence and knowledge to put to use the techniques you have learned in many different ways and scenarios. You should be able to go out into your environment and put your own thoughts and observations down on paper to produce an original painting rather than a photograph. Painting and drawing are both known to enhance your memory much more than just taking a photograph. They also give you a real sense of achievement once you have created a picture.

Overall, I hope this book has given you the confidence that you can actually do this, and your time has been used wisely! You can still use the book to refer back to and give yourself refreshers occasionally.

Remember, no-one takes a piano lesson and then expects to play the Royal Albert Hall the next weekend! It is the same with painting – don't take one workshop or book and then consider yourself a fully fledged artist. Painting, especially using watercolours, is a long-term process of constant learning. Just bear in mind that no-one starts painting to become a member of the Royal Academy. They start painting for enjoyment and pleasure. So don't get bogged down by all the difficulties you hear about watercolours. Keep it fun and practise, practise, practise. I've been painting for 100 years and I still love every minute!

C.M. Evans

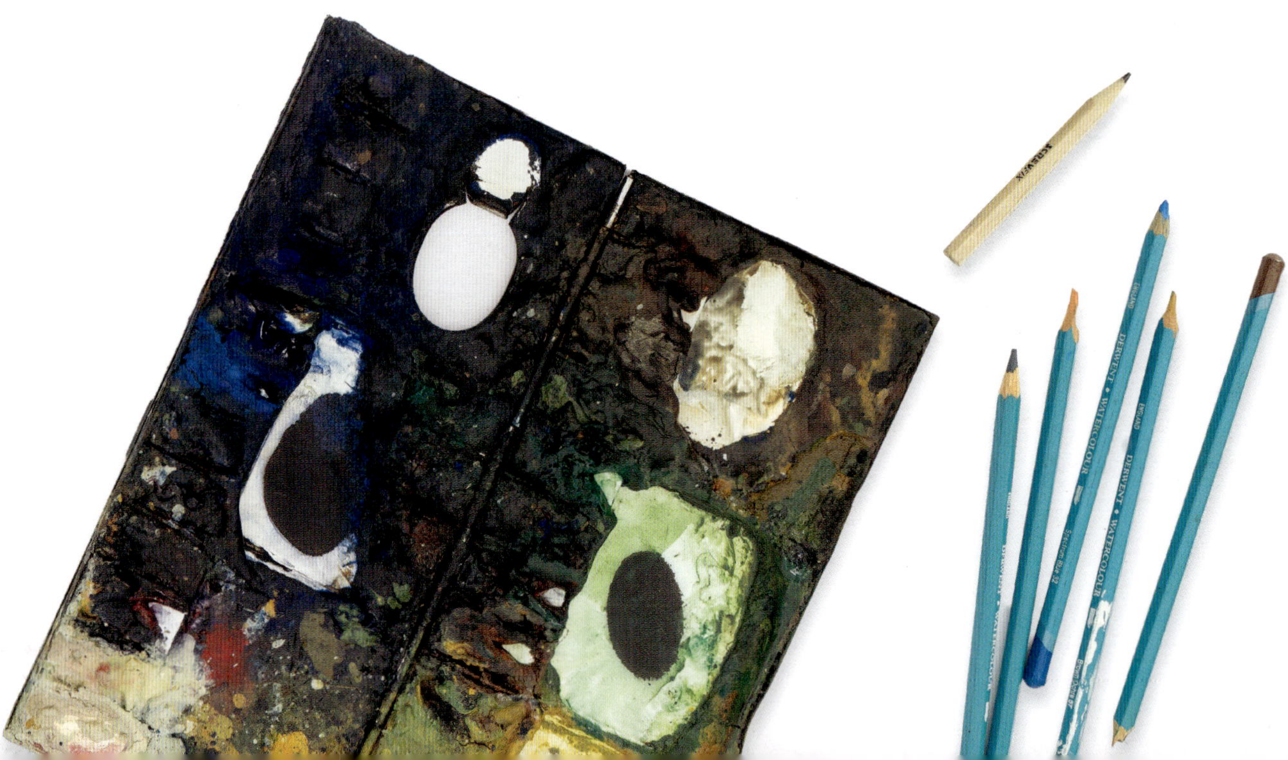

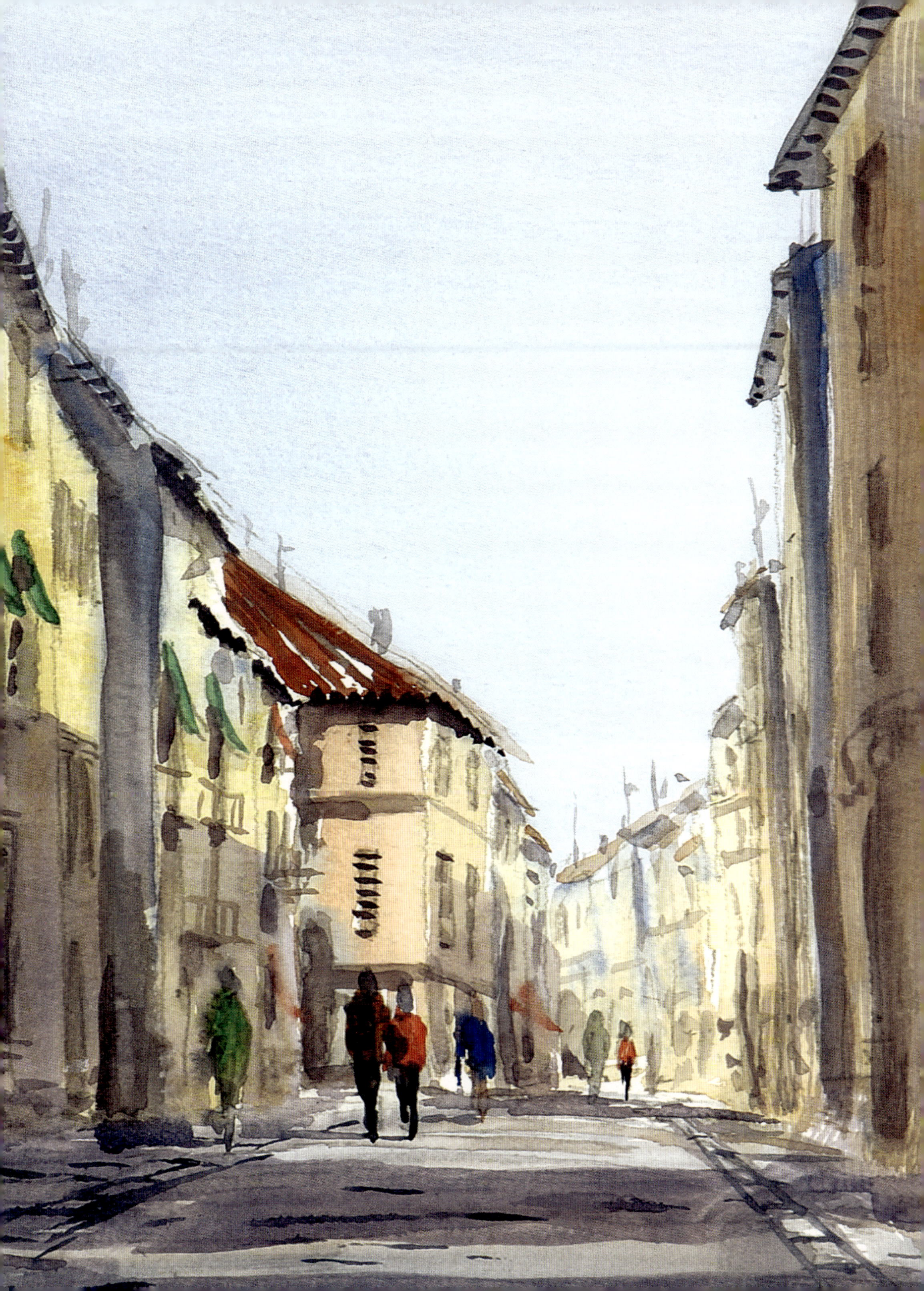

# Index

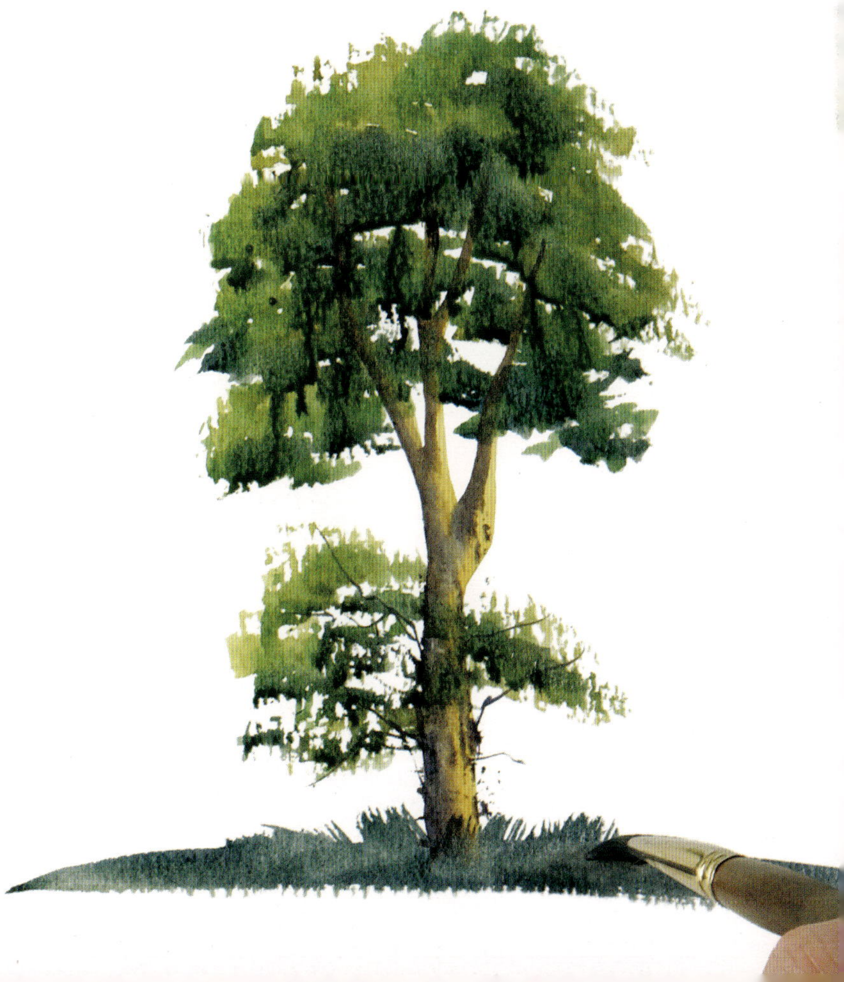

A DAVID AND CHARLES BOOK


David and Charles is an imprint of David and Charles, Ltd, Suite A, Tourism House, Pynes Hill, Exeter, EX2 5WS

EU GPSR Authorised Representative:
Logos Europe, 9 rue Nicolas Poussin,
17000, La Rochelle, France
Email: Contact@logoseurope.eu



Some content originally published as *Charles Evans' Watercolours in a Weekend* in 2007
This edition first published in the UK and USA in 2026



A catalogue record for this book is available from the British Library.

ISBN-13: 9781446316733 paperback
ISBN-13: 9781446316740 EPUB

This book has been printed on paper from approved suppliers and made from pulp from sustainable sources.

MIX
Paper | Supporting responsible forestry
FSC® C136333

Printed in China through Asia Pacific Offset for:
David and Charles, Ltd
Suite A, Tourism House, Pynes Hill, Exeter, EX2 5WS

10 9 8 7 6 5 4 3 2 1

Publishing Director: Ame Verso
Senior Commissioning Editor: Nigel Browning
Publishing Manager: Jeni Chown
Editorial Assistant: Jenna McGill
Project Editor: Anna Southgate
Design: Sam Staddon & Giulia Sandri
Pre-press Designer: Susan Reansbury
Photography: Jason Jenkins
Production Manager: Beverley Richardson

David and Charles publishes high-quality books on a wide range of subjects. For more information visit www.davidandcharles.com.

Share your art with us on social media using #dandcbooks and follow us on Facebook and Instagram by searching for @dandcbooks.

Layout of the digital edition of this book may vary depending on reader hardware and display settings.